45,—

W9-BXR-938

DAILY LIFE IN

MAYA CIVILIZATION

Recent Titles in
The Greenwood Press "Daily Life Through History" Series

Daily Life in Elizabethan England
Jeffrey L. Singman

Daily Life in Chaucer's England
Jeffrey L. Singman and Will McLean

Daily Life in the Inca Empire
Michael A. Malpass

DAILY LIFE IN

MAYA
CIVILIZATION

ROBERT J. SHARER

The Greenwood Press "Daily Life Through History" Series

GREENWOOD PRESS
Westport, Connecticut • London

Library of Congress Cataloging-in-Publication Data

Sharer, Robert J.
    Daily life in Maya civilization / Robert J. Sharer.
        p.   cm. — (The Greenwood Press "Daily life through history"
    series, ISSN 1080–4749)
    Includes bibliographical references and index.
    ISBN 0–313–29342–2 (alk. paper)
    1. Mayas—History.   2. Mayas—Social life and customs.   3. Mayas—
Antiquities.   4. Central America—Antiquities.   I. Title.
II. Series.
F1435.S54   1996
972.81'016—dc20   95–49672

British Library Cataloguing in Publication Data is available.

Copyright © 1996 by Robert J. Sharer

All rights reserved. No portion of this book may be
reproduced, by any process or technique, without the
express written consent of the publisher.

Library of Congress Catalog Card Number: 95–49672
ISBN: 0–313–29342–2
ISSN: 1080–4749

First published in 1996

Greenwood Press, 88 Post Road West, Westport, CT 06881
An imprint of Greenwood Publishing Group, Inc.

Printed in the United States of America

∞™

The paper used in this book complies with the
Permanent Paper Standard issued by the National
Information Standards Organization (Z39.48-1984).

10 9 8 7 6 5 4 3 2 1

Every reasonable effort has been made to trace the owners of
copyright materials in this book, but in some instances this has proven
impossible. The author and publisher will be glad to receive
information leading to more complete acknowledgments in
subsequent printings of the book and in the meantime extend their
apologies for any omissions.

For Dan, Michael, and Lisa

Contents

Preface

This book presents a reconstruction of a past society—the Maya, who created one of the most brilliant and successful of all ancient civilizations. As with any reconstruction of the past, a range of information is presented: established facts, informed hypotheses, and occasional speculations. Although the book presents as much as possible the latest thinking on the subject, new advances in the study of Maya civilization will certainly modify what is said here in the future.

The book draws on the author's personal experience of over 30 years of research in the Maya area, primarily directing archaeological excavations of Maya sites in El Salvador, Guatemala, and Honduras, but also including a study of traditional Maya people today in a Mam Mayan community in the highlands of Guatemala. It also draws on the investigations of hundreds of other researchers. In recent years there has been a veritable explosion of published works about Maya civilization. This huge body of literature represents many fields, including archaeology, ethnohistory, ethnography, linguistics, epigraphy, and art history.

During the preparation of this book, it became apparent that to do justice to the vast literature with citations in the text would be disruptive for most readers. So a less intrusive alternative has been used. At the end of each chapter is a listing of the principal sources of information relevant to that chapter. These source listings are a highly selective sample, chosen to represent published works that are accessible, current, and significant. The listings give the names of authors and year of publication; full citations can be found in the Bibliography at the end of the book.

This book could not have been written without the help of many individuals. Apart from drawing on the research and writings of scores of archaeologists and other Maya scholars, this book has benefited from many discussions with friends, colleagues, and students about the Maya past and present. Although it is impossible to acknowledge all of these people in this brief space, I want to specifically thank all of the researchers who have worked with me over the past decade at the beautiful Maya city of Copan, Honduras; most importantly, William Fash, Barbara Fash, Ricardo Agurcia, Oscar Cruz, Will Andrews, Rudy Larios, David Sedat, Julie Miller, Alfonso Morales, Christine Carrelli, Ellen Bell, Marcello Canuto, Christopher Powell, Charles Golden, and most especially, Loa Traxler, who in addition to her work at Copan has helped me in countless ways to write this book and prepare it for publication.

I would also like to thank all the people at Greenwood Publishing Group for their assistance, and especially Barbara Rader, Senior Editor, who helped me develop the content and scope of the book, and Desirée Bermani, who helped bring it into final shape. But above all, this book owes its greatest debt to the Maya people, past and present, whose brilliant achievements and perseverance are an inspiration for all of us in today's world.

Chronology of Maya Civilization
(Most dates are approximate)

EARLY AND MIDDLE PRECLASSIC (1500–400 B.C.): Earliest Chiefdoms (beginning of Early Maya Civilization)

LATE PRECLASSIC (400 B.C.–A.D. 250): Earliest States (Early Maya Civilization)

400–200 B.C.	Earliest carved monuments in southern Maya area
100 B.C.–A.D. 200	Apogee of Kaminaljuyu (highlands) and El Mirador (lowlands)
1–200	Earliest monuments with Long Count dates in southern Maya area
200–250	Ilopango eruption and decline of southern Maya; decline of El Mirador
219–238	Tikal royal founder (Yax Moch Xoc)

EARLY CLASSIC (A.D. 250–600): Expansion of Lowland States (beginning of Middle Maya Civilization)

292	Scroll Ahau Jaguar (Tikal king on earliest lowland dated stela)
320	Yaxchilan royal founder (Yat Balam)
376	Great Jaguar Paw (Tikal king)
378	Tikal takeover of Uaxactun (Smoking Frog)
411–456	Stormy Sky (11th Tikal king)
426	Copan royal founder (Yax Kuk Mo)
431	Palenque royal founder (Balam Kuk)

537–562	Double Bird (21st Tikal king); capture and sacrifice by Caracol-Calakmul alliance (562)
562–695	Hegemony of Calakmul alliance in lowlands
583–604	Lady Kanal Ikal (woman ruler of Palenque)

LATE CLASSIC (A.D. 600–800): Apogee of Lowland States (Middle Maya Civilization)

615–683	Pacal (Palenque king)
628–695	Smoke Imix (12th Copan king); reigned over Quirigua
647–698	Ruler 1 (Petexbatun); conquest state founded from Tikal
666–695	Jaguar Paw (Calakmul king)
671–742	Shield Jaguar II (Yaxchilan king)
679	Shield Skull (25th Tikal king) captured and sacrificed by Petexbatun
682–723	Ah Cacau (26th Tikal king); led revitalization of Tikal kingdom
684–702	Chan Balam (Palenque king)
695	Calakmul hegemony broken; Jaguar Paw captured and sacrificed by Tikal
695–738	18 Rabbit (13th Copan king)
702–711	Kan Xul (Palenque king)
711	Capture and sacrifice of Kan Xul by Tonina
725	Cauac Sky (Quirigua ruler) inaugurated as vassal of Copan
734–768	Yax Kin (27th Tikal king)
738	18 Rabbit captured and sacrificed by Cauac Sky; Quirigua gained independence from Copan
749–763	Smoke Shell (15th Copan king); Hieroglyphic Stairway dedicated
752–796	Bird Jaguar III (Yaxchilan king)
761	Fall of Petexbatun conquest state (capital at Dos Pilas sacked; Ruler 4 sacrificed)
763–820	Yax Pac (16th Copan king)
768–790	Chitam (29th Tikal king)
796–808	Shield Jaguar III (Yaxchilan king)

TERMINAL CLASSIC (A.D. 800–900): Decline of Southern Lowland States; Rise of Northern Lowland States (end of Middle Maya Civilization)

| 822 | U Cit Tok (failed Copan king) |
| 849 | Founding of Chichen Itza; hegemony in north began |

889	Last dated stela in former Tikal kingdom
909	Last dated stela at Tonina

EARLY POSTCLASSIC (A.D. 900–1200): Expansion of States in Northern Lowlands and Highlands (beginning of Late Maya Civilization)

LATE POSTCLASSIC (A.D. 1200–1524): Final States in Northern Lowlands and Highlands (end of Late Maya Civilization)

1221	Chichen Itza sacked; Mayapan became new capital in the north
1225–1250	Founding of Quiche Maya state in the highlands
1275–1475	Expansion of Quiche Maya state (capital at Utatlan)
1441	Mayapan sacked; rule by petty states in the north began
1475–1500	Founding of Cakchiquel Maya state in the highlands (capital at Iximche)
1500	First contacts with Spaniards

Spanish Conquest (A.D. 1524–1697)

1524–1527	Conquest of the Southern Maya led by Pedro de Alvarado
1527–1546	Conquest of the Northern Maya led by the Montejos (Elder and Younger)
1697	Conquest of the last independent Maya state (Tayasal) by Martin de Ursua

1

The Maya of Today and Yesterday

Today in southern Mexico, Guatemala, and Belize live the descendants of a great civilization. These people are the Maya. The great civilization of their ancestors flourished for over two thousand years, from about 400 B.C. until the Spanish began to conquer their lands in A.D. 1524. During that span a succession of independent kingdoms rose and fell across the varied landscape of the Maya homeland. The Maya population expanded into many millions of people supported by a rich array of crops and the bounty of forests, rivers, lakes, and seashores. Their settlements ranged from small villages to large cities. The largest cities were capitals of the many Maya kingdoms. In each of these cities were elaborate temples, palaces, carved monuments, roadways, plazas, markets, and the many houses of their inhabitants. In times of peace the cities prospered from a network of trade that linked the independent Maya kingdoms. In times of war famous Maya kings led their people in the conquest of neighboring kingdoms. Captured warriors were adopted by the families of the victors, but the most important captives were sacrificed in religious ceremonies that celebrated each victory.

The achievements of individual Maya kings were recorded on stone monuments and are being rediscovered as scholars decipher more and more of the complex Maya writing system. Although the kings and kingdoms are gone, the accomplishments of Maya civilization are still evident today—in domesticated plants such as maize (corn), chile peppers, and cacao (chocolate); causeways and reservoirs; great works of sculpture and painting; skillfully woven textiles; precious carved jades; sophisti-

cated systems of mathematics; complex calendars; and beautifully pro-
portioned buildings rendered in a variety of styles.

These achievements of Maya civilization are not well known to most
people. The history of our own culture is familiar to most students, with
its roots in the ancient civilizations of Egypt and Mesopotamia and in
the Classical civilizations of Greece and Rome. Most treatments of American history start with 1492 and the "discovery" of what Europeans
called the New World. Far less attention is paid to the peoples who had
occupied the Americas (both North and South America) for thousands
of years before the Europeans' arrival. So it is not surprising that most
students are far less familiar with the peoples of the Americas and the
history of their accomplishments, including those of Maya civilization,
all of which developed without any contacts with Europe or the rest of
the Old World.

DISCOVERY AND CONQUEST BY EUROPEANS

Imagine the surprise and wonder for the peoples of both the Old
World and the Americas to discover that there were entirely separate
and unknown peoples elsewhere in the world. For Europeans of five
hundred years ago, the realization that there was a New World across
the Atlantic Ocean, and that it was inhabited by a variety of societies,
came as a complete surprise. Even more unexpected was the discovery
that in at least two regions of the Americas—Mesoamerica (what is now
most of Mexico and upper Central America) and the Andean area of
South America—there were civilizations as sophisticated as those of the
Old World where thousands of people lived in cities as large as or larger
than those of Europe, with writing, metallurgy, stone architecture, painting, and sculpture.

These were the Inca of the Andes, and both the Aztec and Maya civilizations of Mesoamerica. Bernal Díaz del Castillo, a soldier in the con-
quering army of Hernán Cortés, recalled the awestruck reaction of the
first Europeans to see the great Aztec capital of Tenochtitlan from the
mountain pass overlooking the Valley of Mexico in 1519:

> when we saw so many cities and villages built in the water and
> other great towns on dry land and the straight and level causeway
> going towards Mexico, we were amazed and said that it was like
> the enchantments they tell of in the legend of Amadis, (with) the
> great towers . . . and buildings rising from the water . . . all built of
> masonry. And some of our soldiers even asked whether the things
> we saw were not a dream. . . . I do not know how to describe it

seeing things as we did that had never been heard of or seen before, not even dreamed about. (Díaz del Castillo 1956: 190–91; orig. 1632)

Both Cortés and Díaz del Castillo were from Spain, the European nation that sponsored the voyages of Columbus and led the discoveries of the great civilizations of the Inca, Aztec, and Maya. As a result Spain deserves much of the credit and much of the blame for what followed. We learn the history of the conquest and colonization of the New World from accounts written by the victors. Almost never do we learn of these events from the defeated peoples of the Americas. The victorious Europeans described their heroic struggles in the New World, colonizing a new land against all odds. Yet to the peoples already living in the Americas, this was an invasion of *their* lands. Seldom do we learn of the heroic struggles made by the peoples of the Americas to defend themselves against the strange people from the east who were interested only in the spoils of conquest and the exploitation of colonization.

For the great civilizations of Mesoamerica and the Andes, the end came relatively quickly. Within a few decades of the first European discoveries in the New World, civilizations that represented thousands of years of tradition were conquered and destroyed by plundering armies from Spain. In the Andes of South America, adventurers such as Pizzaro led the destruction of the Inca civilization. In Mesoamerica, Cortés led the destruction of the Aztec civilization of central Mexico. One of Cortés' lieutenants, Pedro de Alvarado, led the first conquest of the Maya civilization in the southern highlands; the Montejos, father and son, led the subjugation of the northern Maya civilization of the Yucatan peninsula. The toll from these and other conquests of New World societies is hard to imagine today, even when the methods of mass destruction are far more efficient than they were five centuries ago. But it is clear that the combination of European conquest and disease in Mesoamerica and the Andes caused the deaths of tens of millions of native peoples.

The Spanish were not the only Europeans who wanted to subjugate and colonize the New World. Portugal, England, and France competed with Spain to dominate the Americas. But Spain remained the primary power in what was to become Latin America. Because firearms and canons could kill and destroy far better than the spears and arrows used by the peoples of the Americas, the Europeans had a significant advantage in any conflict. In fact, the very concept of warfare was different in the Americas, where gaining prestige by humbling one's enemies and taking captives was more important than killing them. Warfare as practiced by the Spaniards and other Europeans meant killing as many enemies as possible and often destroying their cities and farms as well. Such total warfare was unknown in the Americas, and it gave the Europeans another advantage.

Equally unknown in the Americas were the epidemic diseases of the Old World. Without any natural immunities to measles, chicken pox, smallpox, and other illnesses, many more people in the Americas died from disease than by force of arms. Although they defended their homes, their cities, and their independence with great skill and valor, their resistance was undermined by a host of new diseases for which they had no defenses. One by one the weakened peoples of the Americas were defeated, subjugated, and in some cases exterminated by armies and colonists from Europe.

The conquest of the Americas by the Old World was far-ranging. Whole cities, such as the Aztec capital of Tenochtitlan, were demolished to make way for European settlements. Their achievements were belittled, and their religious rites were condemned as pagan and inhumane. The mass human sacrifices of the Aztecs were violent and cruel. But it is well to keep in mind that horrors such as human sacrifice were not limited to the peoples of the Americas. Indeed, Europeans of the sixteenth century themselves were burning people alive at the stake and using many methods of torture, even while they were condemning the "pagan" sacrifices of the Aztec and Maya.

Beyond the physical destruction, the ultimate means of attacking the peoples of the Americas was to proclaim that they were not able to develop civilization on their own. A myth was created to justify the European domination of "inferior" peoples. According to this myth, the "savages" of the Americas did not develop civilized practices such as writing, or the arts of painting and sculpture. Rather, it was claimed, all things that Europeans considered civilized had originated in the Old World. How did these civilized practices come to the Americas? Through long-lost voyagers from the Old World who came to the Americas before Columbus and taught the "savages" the ways of civilization. Thus the Aztec, Inca, and Maya civilizations were "explained" as offshoots from forgotten colonists from Egypt or Greece or Rome or (depending on who was making up the story) a host of other candidates such as Carthage, Phoenicia, Israel, Babylon, India, China, and Japan. Human sacrifice and other "pagan practices" were explained as "corruptions" that developed in the Americas after the seeds of civilization were planted from across the seas.

There is no evidence to support these claims. But, unfortunately, the core of this false belief can still be found in many popular books and articles. What actually happened, what the evidence clearly indicates, is that the evolution of civilization in the Americas was driven entirely by the peoples who had originally settled the Americas; it took place completely independently from the same process in the Old World.

The origins and growth of civilization in the Americas are being documented through archaeological research. In this book we will show that it is possible to learn about Maya civilization without resorting to fanciful Old World origins or prototypes. Maya civilization was shaped by their own efforts, along with what they learned from neighboring peoples of Mexico and Central America. It was not the result of a mythical Old World colonization. It was the result of growth processes that occur in all societies, including our own.

CONTINUITY AND CHANGE SINCE THE CONQUEST

Maya civilization may have ended with the Spanish Conquest, but the Maya people have survived to the present day. However, the Maya way of life has changed greatly over the past five hundred years. Many institutions that had governed Maya society were replaced by a Spanish colonial civil and religious administration. The old Maya elite class—rulers, nobles, priests, and military leaders—was all but destroyed, its few survivors stripped of their former wealth and power. Conversion to Christianity was used to justify the conquest and to help control the new subjects of the Spanish Crown. Many methods, including the cruel Spanish Inquisition, were used to crush any vestiges of old Maya ritual and belief. As a result, many of the arts—painting, sculpture, metallurgy, lapidary work, and featherwork—disappeared from Maya society.

Many intellectual achievements of Maya civilization were also lost. The Maya books (called "codices") were burned, and the use of Maya writing vanished. A great deal of knowledge has been lost as a result, including information about Maya history, religion (beliefs, deities, and rituals), medicine, and commerce.

The Maya economy was altered forever. New markets and methods of transport replaced much of the network of trade routes that had tied the Maya area together. New technologies, new products, and new demands replaced the old. Not all the changes were violent, of course. The Maya people readily accepted much of the new European technology, and iron and steel tools quickly replaced those of flint and obsidian. But all these changes, forced or voluntary, began a cycle of damage to the environment that continues to this day. The very landscape was ravaged for valuable minerals—especially gold and silver. The best agricultural lands were seized and plantations established by the wealthier Spanish colonists, who introduced new crops grown only for export such as bananas, coffee, and sugar cane. Moreover, the labor used to work the mines and fields was recruited, usually by force, from the conquered peoples of the Americas. Over the centuries, hundreds of thousands died from the abuses of a forced labor system that almost amounted to slavery. These abuses of native peoples began a cycle of exploitation that continues to this day.

Yet even after centuries of exploitation and change, important aspects of the Maya way of life have managed to survive. The traditions of the family and community have continued almost without change. The institutions of marriage and kinship that governed family life have sur-

vived because the Spanish administrators could not reach most of the
remote Maya agricultural villages. In these places, far from Spanish officials, the Maya kept their traditions alive from one generation to the
next. Realizing this, the Spaniards tried to forceably resettle Maya communities in areas where they could be more easily controlled, closer to
their towns and cities. But forceable resettlement was not applied everywhere and was seldom successful. In the face of threats from Spanish
authorities, some Maya families—even entire communities—"voted with
their feet" and resettled on their own terms farther away from the European settlements. In other cases, as long as the Maya paid the required
taxes and labor obligations to the Spanish Crown, they were allowed to
govern their own affairs.

Since the Conquest, the Maya family has continued to be essentially
self-sufficient. The introduction of steel tools and mechanical devices,
such as mills to grind maize (corn) have increased agricultural production somewhat. Traditional family-based crafts—weaving, basketry, pottery making—continue almost unchanged. A scaled-down version of
Maya-controlled trade has persisted. Locally produced food and crafts,
together with essentials that must be imported (salt, tools, etc.), are
bought and sold in village markets.

Several dozen related Mayan languages are spoken today. These languages, and the remnants of Maya religion, have been more resistant to
change than any other aspect of Maya civilization. This is because Mayan
language and religion reinforce the traditions of family and community
life. Even today, in the face of prolonged efforts by European mission-
aries to change the religion, many traditional beliefs and rituals concerned with the family and agriculture continue. Mayan languages
persist because they are often the first-learned or only language spoken
in the traditional Maya family. Some knowledge of Spanish is necessary
to interact with the non-Maya world, but even in today's world of instant
electronic communication at least four million people continue to speak
a Mayan language.

DESTRUCTION OF THE MAYA HERITAGE

The modern world has had profound effects on traditional Maya culture. Traditions that survived over some five hundred years of European
conquest, colonization, and exploitation are now changing or disappearing because of economic, political, and social changes originating far beyond the Maya world. But this is not the only heritage that is
disappearing.

The Maya past is disappearing even more rapidly. The ruins of hundreds of ancient Maya cities are being looted and destroyed in illegal
searches for jade, painted pottery, and sculpture that can be sold on the

View of a Maya market in the highlands of Guatemala.

View of a Maya woman weaving on the traditional Maya belt loom.

thriving antiquities market. Ruined cities that have lain undisturbed for a thousand years, including many never seen by the Spanish conquistadores, have been pillaged and destroyed for a few objects that have commercial value.

Most of the information in this book comes from the studies of Maya ruins by archaeologists, along with epigraphers (experts in reading ancient Maya writing), art historians, and other scholars. These ruins, and all other remains from the past ranging from the smallest bit of broken pottery to the largest temple or city, are sources of archaeological evidence. Like pieces of a jigsaw puzzle, that evidence reveals a picture only when its parts are found and put into place. The plundering of archaeological sites destroys many individual pieces; but just as important, it destroys the patterns and associations of those pieces so they can never be put back together again. A looted Maya site is like a jigsaw puzzle that has had most of its pieces destroyed and the shapes and colors on most of the remaining pieces erased. No one could reassemble such a damaged and altered puzzle. But Maya sites are not just jigsaw puzzles; each one is part of a *nonrenewable resource*—a unique representative of Maya civilization. As each site is destroyed by looting, the Maya of today lose another portion of their heritage, and the world loses another piece of evidence that could allow us to further understand Maya civilization. Once destroyed, this evidence is gone forever.

Can the wanton destruction be stopped? Contemporary countries in which Maya sites are located—Mexico, Guatemala, Belize, Honduras, and El Salvador—all have laws against looting of archaeological sites. It is illegal to import looted materials into the United States and many other countries. But no nation has the resources to police all its archaeological sites or prevent all antiquity smuggling. The only solution to looting is economic. Looting continues because some people are willing to pay huge sums for Maya objects, especially jade, painted pottery, and sculpture. The solution, therefore, is to decrease the demand for new objects—looting will be stopped only if collectors and dealers refuse to buy these objects.

Today the interest and progress being made in understanding Maya civilization is at an all-time high. It is tragically ironic that so much of traditional Maya culture is rapidly disappearing, and that the archaeological resources that give us our knowledge of this brilliant civilization are being utterly destroyed.

PRINCIPAL PUBLISHED SOURCES

Chiappelli 1976; Díaz del Castillo 1956; Farriss 1984; Jones 1989; Meyer 1977; Stephens 1962 [1841]; Sullivan 1989.

2

Understanding Maya Civilization

In this chapter we consider (1) basic concepts underlying the study of past civilizations such as the Maya; (2) how archaeologists find and use evidence from the past to reconstruct such civilizations; and (3) the environment of the Maya homeland and the chronology we will use to understand the development of Maya civilization.

THE GROWTH OF CIVILIZATIONS

First we must define certain basic concepts. *Civilization* is a term often used to refer to complex and sophisticated cultural developments. Civilization implies the development of cities as well as large-scale public architecture, writing, organized religion, far-flung trade, art, and other achievements. *Cities* are large and concentrated settlements of people who specialize in non-food producing activities. Although city dwellers may have gardens or may cultivate plots of land outside the city, at least some of them specialize in manufacturing or trade, religion, or politics. Cities and their populations exchange goods and services with an agricultural hinterland that produces food.

Civilizations are also associated with a particular kind of political and economic organization known as the *state*. The first states to develop in various parts of the world are called *preindustrial states*. These were characterized by full-time craft specializations, complex social stratification (i.e., society is divided into two or more classes, including an upper or elite class), and a centralized political authority (such as a king). The centralized authority may be supported and perpetuated by a series of institutions within the society, such as "official" religions, laws, courts, palace guards, and armies. But preindustrial states were very different from the *modern industrial states* that developed after the Industrial Revolution. Preindustrial states did not have machine-based mass production of goods, rapid communication, and efficient transport—all of which are typical of modern states. Preindustrial states relied on human and animal power rather than the far greater energy available from steam, electric, internal combustion, and nuclear power. Thus the size and economic output of preindustrial states was far less than that of industrial states such as our own.

In this book we use the terms *polity* or *kingdom* to refer to each independent preindustrial state. Throughout much of their development, Maya polities were small in scale; that is, each independent state controlled a relatively limited territory, measuring only several hundred square miles, with a population measured in tens of thousands of people. But as with preindustrial states elsewhere in the world, in time the Maya civilization experienced a trend toward increasingly larger polities—in both population and territory. At times, some of the most aggressive and successful Maya polities controlled large territories with populations of several hundreds of thousands of people.

Archaeologists can recognize the beginnings and development of preindustrial states from clues found in the ruins of ancient cities. Most preindustrial states developed from somewhat less complex societies known as *chiefdoms*. These are societies managed by an elite group under one ultimate authority, the chief. But unlike the rulers of states, chiefs have little coercive or political power. They rule by controlling religion and wealth; that is, their ability to control others comes from religious beliefs and the tribute they collect as a result of those beliefs. In such societies people believe that the chief has supernatural power and can use it to either help or harm his subjects. To ensure that the supernatural power is used for good purposes, people offer tribute to the chief—food, goods, even labor service. The chief in turn can dispense some tribute to others to show favor and, of course, maintain their loyalty to him.

ARCHAEOLOGY AND RECONSTRUCTING THE PAST

The study of past civilizations is a special concern of the field of archaeology (the science of past societies). Archaeologists have developed methods to recognize chiefdoms and preindustrial states from the remains these societies have left behind. These remains are known as the *archaeological record*. It ranges from *artifacts* (small portable items that can be moved or traded far and near) to permanent *features* (roads, buildings, fields, canals, temples, palaces, and settlements). Any concentration of artifacts and features defines an archaeological *site*; thus a site can range from a small hunting camp consisting of the remains of a cooking fire and a few hunting tools, to an entire city covering many square miles.

Artifacts and features are not the only remains used by archaeologists to reconstruct the past. Clues to ancient environmental conditions can help archaeologists determine the natural resources that were used and traded. Plant and animal remains tell them what foods were used to support an ancient society. For most preindustrial states, some of the best clues are found in recovered written records, because writing systems were often used to record the political and economic affairs of rulers and administrators. Later we will see examples of these "royal" records from Maya civilization.

But archaeologists reconstruct all kinds of societies—those without writing systems as well as those with written records. They do this not from individual artifacts or features but from the larger patterns evident in many such remains. For example, they study the patterns of archaeological sites distributed across the landscape, and the patterns of connections between sites (routes used for movement of trade goods, people, and ideas). By mapping sites and connections, archaeologists can detect hierarchies of sites based on size and location. These patterns, known as *settlement hierarchies*, allow archaeologists to reconstruct the size and complexity of ancient societies.

To better understand how this is done, we can use an example based on one part of our modern (industrial) nation-state. We will consider the organization of one of our states, which is fairly close in size to many individual preindustrial states. If we look at a map of one state, such as Indiana, we see that its largest city, Indianapolis, is near the center. Indianapolis is both the political and economic capital of the state, and the hub of road and other communication and transportation networks that radiate out to the rest of the state. In the territory surrounding this capital are a series of secondary political and economic centers—the county seats. Each of these counties contains even smaller political and economic units—townships—as well as cities, towns, and villages. Settlements at each level include clusters of dwellings and other buildings serving political, economic, religious, and similar functions, along with a scattering of dwellings dispersed throughout the countryside. The map of Indiana, therefore, reflects a hierarchy of settlements arranged on at least four levels: one capital, a number of second-level centers (county seats), even more third-level centers (townships), and far more fourth-level centers (villages, towns, and cities).

This is essentially what archaeologists reconstruct by mapping distributions of ancient settlements and their connections. The resulting patterns reflect the political and economic organization of the ancient society. In most cases, finding a settlement hierarchy with four or more levels indicates that the society had a state organization. A settlement hierarchy with three levels often indicates a chiefdom organization. A hierarchy of less than three levels may indicate an even smaller-scale organization than a chiefdom.

Thus the size and complexity of settlement hierarchies can be an important clue toward understanding how an ancient society was organized. But archaeologists do not like to rely on just one source of evidence to reconstruct the past. Whenever possible, they test their conclusions by excavating in at least one site from each level of the hierarchy to see if further clues can be found to support or change their conclusions.

As we have mentioned, a three-level hierarchy usually reflects a chiefdom and a four-level hierarchy usually defines a preindustrial state. Many preindustrial states increased in size through time, by natural population increase or by successful conquests of other states and territories. Such expansions caused changes in the states' political and economic organization to accommodate and control more people. In some cases the changes can be recognized in the archaeological record—for example, through the addition of new levels to the organizational hierarchy, or the expansion in territory controlled.

THE MAYA HOMELAND

The Maya homeland is part of Mesoamerica, a large area that spreads from northern Mexico well into Central America. During the pre-Columbian era (before roughly A.D. 1500 and the Spanish Conquest), the Maya and their Mesoamerican neighbors developed (1) agriculture, (2) permanently settled villages, and (3) eventually, far larger and more complex societies with cities, monumental architecture, calendrical systems, writing, and other characteristics of civilization.

The settlement hierarchies that constituted Maya civilization were dispersed over a rich and varied environment. Indeed, the homeland of past Maya civilization and of Maya people today shows great environmental diversity. The area covers about 125,000 square miles in southeastern Mexico (including the Yucatan peninsula) and northwestern Central America (Guatemala, Belize, and western Honduras and El Salvador).

The Maya area is divided into three environmental zones: the Pacific coastal plain to the south, the highlands in the center, and the lowlands to the north. Considerable variation exists in environmental conditions within each zone, so that each is further divided into subzones. But the boundaries of each major zone and its subdivisions are seldom precise, because they define subtle environmental changes or transitions.

The environment of the Maya area is marked by contrasts. The terrain

Map of the Maya area with locations of major archaeological sites.

varies from rugged mountains to level plains. Altitude differences create cool temperate climates in the highlands and hot tropical conditions in the Pacific coastal plain and lowlands. Rainfall variations produce other contrasts. In some areas of both the highlands and lowlands there are dry, desert-like environments as well as areas of heavy rainfall that produce dense rain forests. Surface water is readily available in places adjacent to rivers, lakes, and cenotes (sinkholes or natural wells); but in other areas the Maya had to make great efforts to gain and store water by constructing wells, reservoirs, and canals. Plentiful food harvests came from regions with rich volcanic or alluvial soils, but areas with poorer soils required great efforts to support agriculture.

Certain environmental conditions have changed over time. Some shifts have been gradual, such as a long-term trend of decreasing rainfall in certain lowland areas. Other changes have been sudden and violent, such as frequent earthquakes and volcanic eruptions in the highlands. But the most drastic environmental changes have been caused by humans. At times in the past the Maya were too successful in exploiting their environment. The result was unchecked population growth that led to over-use of agricultural lands and destruction of forests. In areas where the soil and forest resources had been exhausted, people had no choice but to look for new and relatively undamaged areas to settle. Over time we can see shifts in the major population concentrations that reflect this process of exploitation, growth, over-exploitation, and migration. Of course, the process is not unique to the past; the same thing is happening today in the Maya area and in many other parts of the world.

At this point, we will briefly describe the environmental conditions in each of the three major zones of the Maya area. Later, we will explain how each zone contributed to the development of Maya civilization.

The Pacific Coastal Plain A fertile plain stretches along the Pacific coast from southern Mexico, well into Central America (southern Guatemala and western El Salvador). It is cut by many southward-trending rivers that flow from the chain of volcanoes dividing the coastal plain from the highlands to the north. Several subzones along the plain blend into each other with increasing elevation from the Pacific coast to the volcano slopes to the north.

The Pacific coastal plain has a tropical climate with mean (average) annual temperatures between 77° and 95°F. Temperatures become cooler with increasing altitude toward the north. Here, as in most portions of the Maya area, there are two seasons each year: a dry period from January to April, and a rainy season from May to December. The Pacific coastal plain has some of the heaviest rainfall in the Maya area. The western portion averages over 120 inches of rain each year. The remainder receives over 80 inches each year. In some areas relic stands of rain forest can still be found, whereas at higher elevations the rain forest has gradually been replaced by mixed oak and pine forest more typical of the highlands.

The earliest permanent settlements in the Maya area are found among the mangrove swamps and lagoons near the coast. This fertile environment has long provided a great variety of food resources. Rich habitats for land animals, birds, and both salt- and freshwater creatures are found close together, making it possible for people to hunt and gather wild food without moving great distances. Because the availability of food sources does not vary greatly from year to year, small groups can settle and live permanently in one place. If there is good soil nearby, such as the rich silt deposits along rivers, this environment can support agriculture, which allows populations to thrive and grow. Products from the coast, such as dried fish and salt from evaporated sea water, were traded far and wide. Further inland, the coastal plain became a prime location for growing cacao (chocolate), a product traded throughout the Maya area. Today agribusiness dominates the plain, producing sugarcane, cotton, and cattle.

The greatest diversity of environmental conditions is found in the Maya highlands, and many environmental sub-divisions can be defined for this mountainous area. The most obvious is marked by an east-west rift that splits the zone **The Highlands** into the southern highlands, highly populated and dominated by recent volcanic activity, and the northern highlands, less populated and without volcanic activity. Both have elevations generally above 2,500 feet. The climate is temperate and spring-like all year, although cooler conditions can be found in the highest mountain regions at elevations between 7,500 and 10,000 feet. Temperatures may average below 60°F in the highest mountains but may approach tropical conditions in the lower highland margins. Most areas have a dry season from January to April, followed by a rainy season from May to December. Rainfall is generally less than in the wetter areas of the Pacific plain, averaging 80–120 inches each year. Far less rain falls in areas sheltered from the prevailing easterly trade winds, such as the central Motagua valley. The rainy season becomes more intense and lasts longer in the north. On the northern margins annual rainfall averages over 120 inches, enough to support highland rain forests.

The belt of recent volcanoes that stretches from Mexico, through Guatemala, and into Central America forms the boundary between the Pacific plain and the highlands. North of this line are the rugged volcanic highlands, surfaced by thick deposits of lava and ash. Deep valleys have been cut into the deposits by the rivers that rise in the highlands and flow outward. The largest valleys allow tropical conditions to penetrate well into the highlands. Most rivers in the southern highlands flow northward to become part of the Motagua River, which flows eastward into the Caribbean through the continental rift. To the west, drainage produces the Grijalva River, which flows into the Gulf of Mexico through the central depression of Chiapas in Mexico. The many interior valleys and basins of the highlands possess ideal climates and fertile soils, as well as many natural routes of communication. Some highland basins contain lakes, such as the famous Lake Atitlan in central Guatemala.

Just north of the rift that divides the southern from the northern highlands are the highest mountains in the Maya area. These often rise above 10,000 feet. In the west are the Chiapas highlands and the Cuchumatanes mountains of northwestern Guatemala. In the east the Sierra de las Minas extend almost to the Caribbean. These mountains are rich in mineral resources; the Maya mined jade and serpentine from them.

The rugged northern highland ranges blend into lower limestone formations further north. These form dramatic landscapes of karst (limestone) hills, where rivers disappear under porous mountainsides only to reappear miles away. There are numerous underground caverns, waterfalls, and sinkholes. The sources for the greatest river of the Maya lowlands, the Usumacinta, lie in the northern highlands. After leaving the highlands the Usumacinta flows northwestward to the Gulf of Mexico. Many of the interior valleys have fertile soils. These, combined with plentiful rainfall and cool temperatures, make the basins of the Alta Verapaz, in central Guatemala, a prime area for modern coffee cultivation.

People living in the southern highlands have always been plagued by earthquakes and volcanic eruptions. Although the Maya did not record these events, they are detectable from archaeological evidence. A massive volcanic eruption around A.D. 200 created a caldera (collapse basin) and Lake Ilopango, near San Salvador. This catastrophic eruption destroyed all life within 20–30 km of the eruption. The huge cloud of volcanic ash fell over a widespread area, rendering everything within about 100 km of the volcano uninhabitable for one or two centuries. Even far smaller volcanic eruptions disrupt people's lives. Archaeological excavations at Cerén, El Salvador, have revealed an entire village and its fields that were instantaneously buried by ash from a nearby volcanic vent around A.D. 650. During the five hundred years since the Spanish Conquest, a succession of major quakes have been recorded. Earthquakes destroyed the colonial capital of Antigua in the eighteenth century, and in 1918 another all but destroyed Guatemala City. More recently, a rupture of the Motagua fault took more than 24,000 lives in 1976.

Despite the danger of earthquakes and volcanic eruptions, large numbers of people have inhabited the highlands for thousands of years, cultivating the fertile volcanic soils. Most highland basins and valleys contain many remains of pre-Columbian Maya settlements. The largest and most important is the ancient city of Kaminaljuyu in the Valley of Guatemala, also the location of modern Guatemala City.

The highlands are rich in important resources that have been used and traded for thousands of years by the Maya. In the south are several sources for obsidian (volcanic glass), which was mined to make sharp cutting tools. The grinding stones (known as manos and metates) used to prepare maize were made from volcanic rocks found throughout the southern highlands. To the north, jade and other minerals were mined and traded throughout the Maya area.

Thousands of years of human activity have drastically changed the highland environment. The original highland forest was a mixture of evergreen and deciduous trees. In remote areas and at the highest elevations, relatively undisturbed stands of oak, laurel, sweetgum, dogwood, and pine can still be found. Lower valleys support a varied semitropical vegetation.

Although highway construction, logging operations, petroleum exploitation, and hydroelectric power plants have disturbed even remote areas, there is a variety of wildlife, especially in the less-populated northern highlands. Mountain forests are the home of howler and spider monkeys, kinkajous, coatimundis, weasels, foxes, peccaries, and armadillos. Birds—including hawks, macaws, and parrots—are plentiful. The largest of the eagles, the Harpy, can also be seen. In a few high and remote forests, the rare quetzal bird is still found. It was sacred to the Maya; kings adorned their headdresses with its long, brilliant-green tail feathers.

The transition between the highlands and lowlands is gradual. The rain forest of the karst region of the northern highlands continues northward into the lower elevations extending over northern Guatemala, Belize, and the Yucatan peninsula of Mexico. The lowlands lie below 2,500 feet in elevation and have a warm tropical climate. Although they are not as mountainous as the highlands, many lowland areas are hilly. Rainfall, drainage, soils, and seasonal cycles all create variations in the environment. Until recently most of the lowland area was covered by forest. The ancient Maya adapted the lowland environment and made it very productive. Extensive areas of good soils were cultivated to produce a host of useful crops. Wild plants and animals provided food, clothing, shelter, and medicine. The underlying limestone was easily quarried with stone tools (the Maya had no hard metals) and used as a durable building material. By burning limestone and mixing it with water and sand, the Maya made plaster to cover and protect their buildings. They also mined chert, or flint, which was chipped into a variety of cutting, chopping, and scraping tools. With such resources and others imported from the highlands, the lowlands became the productive heartland of Maya civilization.

The rainy season in the lowlands extends from May through January but tends to be longer in the south and shorter in the north. The region

The Lowlands

averages 80–120 inches of rain each year. In areas of highest rainfall, the dry season may be limited to only a month or two (usually between March and May), but some rain may fall even during these periods. To the north, rainfall averages less than 80 inches a year; but the driest areas in northwestern Yucatan average less than 20 inches of rain each year. Temperatures fall in the 77°–90°F range typical of hot tropical climates, with generally cooler days in the wet season and highs rising well above 100°F in the dry season.

The lowlands can be subdivided into southern and northern areas. The southern lowlands feature broken karst terrain and both surface and subsurface drainage (caverns). Many large rivers flow out of the highlands to the south; the largest is the Usumacinta, which flows northwestward to the Gulf of Mexico. North of the Usumacinta River the rainfall decreases, the landscape becomes less rugged, and there are more lakes and seasonal swamps (*bajos*). In the center of the southern lowlands of Guatemala is a shallow basin known as the Peten. It contains about 14 freshwater lakes. The largest, Lake Peten Itza, is some 20 miles long and 2 miles wide. These lakes and rivers gave the Maya steady sources of water and canoe transport. To the east, along the Belize-Guatemala border, is a rugged highland outcrop called the Maya Mountains, with peaks as high as 700 feet.

To the north there is a gradual environmental transition as the tropical forests of the Peten merge into the bushlands of the Yucatan peninsula. The transformation is due largely to decreasing rainfall. The northern lowlands form a low, flat landscape that spreads across the northern half of Yucatan. The soil is usually not more than a few inches deep, in contrast to the Peten soil, which may be up to 3 feet deep. There are extensive outcroppings of underlying limestone. The only major change in elevation occurs in the low Puuc hills in northwestern Yucatan, with ridges about 300 feet high.

The porous limestone of the northern lowlands allows very little surface drainage, so availability of water has long been the most critical factor in the location of settlements. There are only a few lakes, such as those near the site of Coba in northeastern Yucatan, and there are far fewer rivers and streams. The only inland water sources during the long dry season are sinkholes or cenotes (from the Yucatec Mayan word *dz'onot*). Cenotes are found throughout the area, especially in the extreme north. Their depth varies. Near the northern coast the subterranean water is only a few feet below ground; but as one goes southward, cenote depth increases to several hundred feet.

In undisturbed areas the tropical forest is the most obvious feature of the lowland landscape. In the drier areas of Yucatan the forest is stunted, but there is an extension of the southern high forest into the somewhat wetter northeastern corner of Yucatan. In the south, wetter areas support stands of rain forest. The tallest trees, the mahogany and ceiba (the sacred "tree of life" for the Maya), form an upper forest canopy 130–230 feet high. A variety of other trees form a second canopy 75–150 feet high. A lower layer may also be present, between 45 and 75 feet above the ground. Many trees support other plants such as bromeliads, orchids, strangler vines, and lianas. Ferns, young trees, and many large-leafed plants grow in the deep shade of the forest floor.

A variety of animals live in the lowland forest, including many species found elsewhere. But today the carnivores, ocelots, jaguarundis, and jaguars (the largest New World cat) have become rare because of overhunting. The jaguar was a symbol of the power of Maya kings. In the past the Maya hunted other animals for food: agoutis and pacas (large rodents), tapirs, deer, and rabbits. Both howler and spider monkeys abound. There are parrots, macaws, woodpeckers, toucans, and edible birds including curassows, chachalacas, doves, quail, and the ocellated turkey. Reptiles and amphibians are also abundant. The rivers and lakes of the southern region provide fish and edible snails. Along coastal margins of the lowlands there are shellfish, fish, sea birds, sea turtles, and manatees.

DEVELOPMENT THROUGH TIME

The varied environments of the Maya area provided the settings for many closely related cultural developments. Although groups of people lived in areas with distinctive local environments, each was in contact with its neighbors. Networks of trade and social interaction, even collections of tribute and open warfare, stimulated growth and prevented any one area from being isolated from others.

A rich variety of societies developed during the time from the earliest migrations of peoples into the Americas, to the arrival of European colonists in the sixteenth century. We will briefly define the major trends that led to Maya civilization, and its changes through time, before considering these developments in the next few chapters.

Between 20,000 and 40,000 years ago, during the last ice age, the earliest peoples gradually moved across the Bering land bridge from Asia into the Americas. During this period small bands of hunters and gatherers roamed over much of the Americas, relying on simple tools of wood and chipped stone for obtaining wild food. But

Hunters and Gatherers (ca. 40/20,000– 6000 B.C.)

over time changes began to occur. The bands of people invented new tools and new techniques for finding food and other resources. Populations slowly increased, causing a steady growth in competition among the groups of hunters and gatherers.

One response to increased population and competition was that bands in each area reduced the size of their territory and increased the amount of food harvested from that territory. Each band became more specialized in ways of hunting and gathering its food. Some groups became adept at following herds of animals, such as bison or caribou, during their yearly migrations. Other groups began to rely more on the seasonal growth cycles of a few very productive food plants. This kind of specialization was successful when, supplemented by hunting or fishing, the plants produced enough food to feed a group of people throughout the year (as long as it could be safely stored during the non-growing season). Some plants produced more food if they were nurtured—that is, allowed to grow in the best soils, weeded, and watered when no rainfall was available.

These were the first steps toward two fundamental changes that paved the way for civilization: (1) the change from a nomadic way of life to settlement in permanent villages, and (2) the domestication of certain food plant and animal species. The two changes happened almost at the same time, but completely independently, in both the Old World and the Americas.

Sedentary Life and Agriculture (ca. 6000–1500 B.C.) The gradual shift to the new ways of life began about 8,000 years ago in the Americas. The beginnings of sedentary life and agriculture define the Archaic period (ca. 6000–1500 B.C.). The earliest known permanent settlements in Mesoamerica appeared along the Pacific coast. In such environments year-round settled life could be supported by rich shore and lagoon food resources. At about the same time, the increased nurturing of productive food plants led to the gradual domestication of manioc, potatoes, and various other crops in South America, and maize, squash, beans, and other plant species in Mesoamerica. Permanent settlements and stable sources of food supported ever larger populations and became the twin foundations for all the civilizations of the Americas.

In the Maya area the coastal margins were exploited long before permanent settlements appeared. The availability of land animals, birds, and both salt- and freshwater creatures made it possible to hunt and gather wild food without moving great distances. In this setting small groups first began to live permanently in one place. The addition of agriculture, made possible by clearing and planting the fertile silts along rivers, gave this environment an early edge in producing food surpluses. This, in turn, allowed populations to prosper and grow. Along the Caribbean coastal lowlands the many rivers gave access to lowlands in the west; agricultural settlements apparently spread into the interior along these riverine avenues.

The early cultural development in the Maya highlands apparently lagged somewhat behind that of the coasts, although traces of early oc-cupation probably lie undiscovered beneath deep volcanic and alluvial deposits. In time, however, the abundance of natural resources allowed the occupants of the highlands to catch up, especially in the southern part of the area.

The rise of the first civilizations throughout Mesoam-erica took place during what is usually called the Preclas-sic period. These developed in several different regions: the Gulf Coast lowlands of Mexico, the highland basins of the Valley of Mexico and Valley of Oaxaca, and the Maya area. The earliest civilizations built the first large civic and ceremonial centers which served as the capitals of chiefdoms and—somewhat later—the first states. Many of these early capitals are char-acterized by large-scale architecture, carved stone monuments, imported goods from distant lands, and the beginnings of writing. Such develop-ments reflect societal changes including social stratification (distinctions between an upper-class elite and a lower-class nonelite) and the growth of complex religious, economic, and political institutions.

Early Maya Civilization (ca. 1500 B.C.–A.D. 250)

The first civilizations established a cultural pattern that was followed by the later civilizations of Mesoamerica. Although some early civiliza-tions declined, others became larger and more complex. By this time writing systems were becoming more common and were often used to proclaim the achievements of rulers in order to boost their power and authority. The capitals of new polities and the commerce they fostered grew beyond previous levels, and populations peaked in some areas. Overall, these developments laid the foundations for the even larger and more populous civilizations to come.

The highlands and adjacent Pacific plain supported some of the earliest development of Maya civilization. During much of the pre-Columbian era, major population centers were located in the largest and richest highland valleys. Adjacent regions were dominated by important, but less powerful, centers. Most grew prosperous from the production and trade of highland resources such as obsidian, jade, and other minerals. On the adjacent Pacific coastal plain a series of sites arose as centers of marketing, ceremonial, and political activity. These early centers pros-pered from the production and trade of goods produced locally (e.g., cacao and salt) and from the control of important trade routes passing along the Pacific coastal plain from Mexico to Central America.

Most interior portions of the lowlands to the north were colonized after about 1000 B.C. But development was rapid thereafter, culminating in the appearance of the first major capitals by about 400 B.C. and a subsequent explosion of growth that included the construction of the largest temples ever built by the Maya. Early Maya civilization in the lowlands laid the essential foundations for the greatest achievements of Middle Maya civilization that followed.

In many ways Maya civilization in the southern area peaked during the early period, from about 1000 B.C. to A.D. 200. Although it remained an important area for agricultural production and trade throughout the pre-Columbian era, by the second century A.D. both the Pacific plain and much of the highlands had become secondary to the major centers of Maya civilization in the lowlands to the north.

Middle Maya Civilization (ca. A.D. 250–900) Over a span of less than 700 years, from about A.D. 250 to A.D. 900, Maya civilization reached its peak in the southern lowlands. This corresponds to what is often called the Classic period in Mesoamerica, or Middle Maya civilization. During the Classic period more powerful and more complex polities developed, population increased, and new and larger capitals were built. The Classic polities competed with each other to control even larger territories and more resources. The most successful non-Maya polities during this period had their capitals at the cities of Teotihuacan in the Valley of Mexico and Monte Alban in the Valley of Oaxaca.

For convenience we can divide Middle Maya civilization into three periods: the Early Classic (ca. A.D. 250–600), the Late Classic (ca. A.D. 600–800), and the Terminal Classic (ca. A.D. 800–900). Over this span the core of Maya civilization shifted northward into the lowlands. There had been large and important centers of Early Maya civilization in the southern lowlands, but between ca. A.D. 250 and 900 the southern lowlands were the undisputed center of development for Maya civilization. Population levels reached an all-time high, as did competition between polities. The southern lowlands were long dominated by rivalry between the two largest and greatest Maya cities, Tikal and Calakmul, that involved many adjacent and allied centers. Other important cities arose throughout the lowlands, such as those along the Usumacinta River. At the same time there were large centers in the northern lowlands. Trade and other contacts with the highlands remained strong, and important highland polities continued to develop during this era.

But in a span of about a century, roughly between A.D. 800 and 900, most polities in the southern lowland area went into a severe decline from which they never recovered. The great populations that had sustained the many powerful lowland cities slowly but surely dwindled away, as people increasingly moved to new and more prosperous locales. The two areas that received most of the new populations, and benefited most from the changes, were the northern lowlands and the highlands.

The final centuries before European intervention, between A.D. 900 and 1500, brought the last great era of Maya civilization. This span, usually called the Postclassic period throughout Mesoamerica, is subdivided into the Early Postclassic (ca. 900–1200) and Late Postclassic (ca. 1200–1500; active Spanish intervention actually began in 1524 in the Maya area). The Postclassic is marked by declines in some areas of Mesoamerica. But in other areas population continued to grow, cities and commerce expanded, and competition and warfare increased. These areas experienced the development of the most complex and powerful states in the Americas prior to European colonization. The most well known are the Toltec in the Early Postclassic, and the Mexica, or Aztec, in the Late Postclassic.

Late Maya Civilization (ca. A.D. 900–1500)

During the Late Maya civilization, many polities flourished and even reached their peak. In several areas of northern Yucatan the changes of the Terminal Classic period brought renewed prosperity. In western Yucatan a series of cities dominated for a time. But the greatest and most powerful northern Maya city was in the heart of the peninsula, at Chichen Itza, which dominated the Terminal Classic and Early Postclassic of the north. It was succeeded by a new capital, Mayapan, which in turn was replaced by many small and squabbling states. In fact, Yucatan was a house divided against itself on the eve of the Spanish Conquest.

Late Maya civilization in the highlands saw population growth, invasions, and warfare that caused settlement to shift away from valley floors to more defensible settings, such as hilltops or plateaus. Eventually a major conquest state arose in the highlands, that of the Quiche Maya. The Quiche conquests were checked by their chief rivals, the Cakchiquel Maya. But the highlands were never unified. Like the Maya of Yucatan, the highland Maya presented a fragmented political landscape to the Spanish conquerors.

PRINCIPAL PUBLISHED SOURCES

Ashmore and Sharer 1996; Helms 1975; Sabloff 1994; Sharer 1994; Wolf 1959.

3

The Foundations of Maya Civilization

Maya civilization did not develop in isolation, for the Maya were part of the wider area of Mesoamerica. Over a span of several thousand years, both the Maya and the other civilizations of Mesoamerica developed together.

ORIGINS OF SETTLED LIFE AND AGRICULTURE
(ca. 6000–1500 B.C.)

Maya civilization originated in sedentary life and agriculture. Two broad traditions can be seen in Mesoamerica: one in the highlands, the other along the coastal lowlands.

The best evidence of the development of village life and agriculture comes from the Archaic period in several high- **Highland** land valleys in Mexico, west of the Maya area. These are the **Mexico** Valley of Mexico, the Tehuacan Valley, and the Valley of Oaxaca. Excavations in the Tehuacan Valley reveal a 10,000-year sequence of gradual change from hunting and gathering to agriculture based on maize, beans, squash, and other crops. The semi-arid conditions in the Tehuacan Valley were right for the gradual domestication of wild maize and other food plants, a process that extended throughout the Archaic.

In the Valley of Oaxaca, excavations have documented a similar transition from nomadic hunting and gathering to settled agricultural villages during the Archaic period. The earliest domesticated crop in Oaxaca appears to have been squash. Both studies show that the development of settled communities and agriculture was a long, slow process extending over several thousand years. In the highland areas it took a great deal of time to perfect the agricultural methods that could support a group of people year-round. In the Valley of Oaxaca, permanent villages did not emerge until late in the Archaic period, about 2000 B.C. The sequence is similar in the Valley of Mexico, where permanent settlements are found by the end of the Archaic period as well. In the more marginal Tehuacan Valley, permanent settlements appeared somewhat later, about 1500 B.C.

**The Maya
Archaic Period
(ca. 6000–1500 B.C.)**

There is scant evidence from the Archaic period in most other Mesoamerican areas, so we know far less about the origins of settled communities and agriculture in the Maya homeland. In many parts of the highlands and lowlands, Archaic sites are deeply buried under later volcanic or erosional deposits. In the Maya highlands, Archaic occupation has been detected by finding distinctive chipped-stone hunting tools. One cave site was occupied by hunters and gatherers until about 3500 B.C.

Archaic period occupation has also been detected on both the Pacific and Caribbean coasts. Along the Caribban coastal lowlands a long sequence of human exploitation has been reconstructed, mostly from stone tools. The earliest peoples on the Pacific and Caribbean coasts lived by hunting and by gathering the plentiful resources of the sea, lagoons, rivers, and swamps. The dates of this occupation are not well established but seemingly began by at least 4000 B.C.

In the Maya area there is little evidence of transition from nomadic hunting and gathering to settled village life and agriculture. Therefore we must use evidence from other Mesoamerican areas to reconstruct what happened during the Archaic period in the Maya area. We can assume that the earliest peoples in the Maya area underwent a long, slow process of development, adapting agricultural methods to a variety of local conditions. Because of the environmental diversity of the Maya area (see Chapter 2), it is probable that social groups took a long time to adapt successfully to the conditions in each region. On the coasts, settled villages developed by relying more on plentiful wild food resources than on agriculture. In the highlands, settled life took hold when agriculture became productive enough to support a group of people year-round in one place.

The earliest good evidence of settled villages from the Maya area dates to the end of the Archaic. This evidence comes from the Pacific coast, where people used a kind of pottery that dates to ca. 1700–1500 B.C. In fact, pottery is one of the best indicators of permanent village life, because people who move from place to place seldom make and use fragile clay containers. The Pacific coastal villages were supported by seashore

The finding of pottery by archaeologists is a good indication of permanent settlements.

and lagoon fishing and gathering. The year-round availability of plentiful fish, shellfish, turtles, sea birds, reptiles, and other species made it possible for the early villagers to live permanently in one place. They also did some farming of manioc and maize. (Manioc is a lowland root crop originally from South America; maize is a highland crop that had been adapted to lowland conditions by this time.)

Village life along the Pacific coast continued dur-
The Maya   ing the Early Preclassic era (ca. 1500–1000 B.C). The
Early Preclassic   next stage of occupation, dated to ca. 1500–1200 B.C.,
Period   is determined by the use of more elaborately deco-
(ca. 1500–1000 B.C.)   rated pottery. By this time settled populations were
                           growing and people were spreading further inland.
Although hunting and gathering continued as more of the Pacific plain
and highlands were settled, agriculture became more important to support the growing numbers of people. Maize was especially crucial because it is the most productive of all the domesticated crops developed
in the Americas.

Similar growth of village life based on seashore fishing and gathering,
supplemented by agriculture, took place on the Caribbean coast. Slowly
these people also expanded inland, up the rivers into the Maya lowlands.
In the interior lowlands, permanent village life developed somewhat
later than in other areas. Pottery, the evidence of permanent settlement,
first appeared in the Maya lowlands at end of the Early Preclassic, about
1000 B.C., as a result of colonization by village agriculturalists from the
surrounding coastal and highland areas. The newly established settlements soon spread maize agriculture throughout the lowlands.

Village agricultural life was established throughout the Maya area by
1000 B.C. Populations were low, compared to levels reached in later periods, and there were still many uncleared areas without settled occupation. But changes were taking place in the village societies. Trade brought
contact between villages and distant areas, and this allowed the exchange
of ideas as well as products. Most important, the combination of settled
villages and agriculture had the potential to support far more people
than had been possible with hunting and gathering. To accommodate
the increasing number of people, new kinds of authority developed in
the economic, political, and religious organizations of Maya society.
These became the seeds for the growth of Maya civilization.

EARLY NEIGHBORS OF THE MAYA

We can better understand this development by looking at some neighboring Mesoamerican societies in the Early and Middle Preclassic periods. As mentioned previously, the Maya were in contact with the rest
of Mesoamerica. The earliest permanent Maya settlements were related
to similar villages elsewhere in Mesoamerica, where the traditions of
settled life and agriculture formed the foundations for numerous civilizations. The most important, the Olmec and Oaxacan civilizations, provide important lessons for better understanding Maya civilization.

The Olmec occupied the humid lowlands of the Gulf coast of Mexico, adapting to a tropical lowland environment very much like that of the lowland Maya. The Olmec civilization rose and fell during the Early and Middle Preclassic periods. Civilization in the Valley of Oaxaca, located in southern Mexico, rose at the same time but continued to develop, like the Maya, well into the Classic period. Early Oaxacan civilization developed a writing system used for political purposes, very much like the Maya. Both the Olmec and Oaxacan had trade and other contacts with the early Maya and with each other.

There is evidence in both the Olmec and Oaxacan civilizations of a growing elite that controlled most aspects of society. In fact, the core of all early Mesoamerican civilizations, including the Maya, lies in the characteristics of their ruling elite.

Olmec civilization arose from an early village tradition similar to that of the Pacific and Caribbean coasts of the Maya area. Dating to the Early Preclassic period, the early village foundations have been found at two key Olmec sites: La Venta and San Lorenzo.

Olmec Civilization (ca. 1500–400 B.C.)

Both became major Olmec capitals during the Middle Preclassic period.

La Venta is located on a low hill or "island" surrounded by lowland swamp. Study of the ancient settlement shows the growth in complexity of Olmec society. Like the lowland Maya, Olmec agriculture was adapted to the wet, swampy environment so as to support large populations and complex social and political organizations.

Olmec farmers grew maize and other crops on the fertile river levees in the swampy terrain surrounding La Venta. Other foods came from fishing, gathering, and hunting. People lived on both the levees and the main island. Permanent occupation began at the end of the Archaic (ca. 2000–1500 B.C.) and continued through the Early and Middle Preclassic (ca. 1500–400 B.C.). Population size increased substantially during this time. By the Middle Preclassic there was a three-level site hierarchy, headed by the main center on La Venta Island. This indicates that La Venta was the capital of a large and powerful chiefdom with a variety of economic, social, political, and religious distinctions. Nevertheless, La Venta was smaller and less complex than most preindustrial states.

Although the Olmec most likely developed their own writing system, very few examples survive from the Early and Middle Preclassic periods. Thus there is no direct evidence of Olmec religious beliefs, but we can be fairly certain of the basis of power held by Olmec rulers (a term referring to the leaders of both chiefdoms and preindustrial states). Olmec rulers held religious power through the rituals they conducted, which people believed would guarantee success in agriculture and other essential activities. They gained economic power by managing agriculture, from which they received food tribute, and by controlling trade networks. These networks gave Olmec rulers a variety of rare and precious products, including jade (used for ornaments) and magnetite (used for mirrors), which were displayed as symbols of their special powers and authority. When a ruler died, these status symbols were buried with him along with other offerings and human sacrifices to better serve him in the next world.

The most famous objects from La Venta and other Olmec sites are great carved stone monuments, many of which weigh several tons each. Most were made from basalt, a hard volcanic rock that was moved many miles by water (on huge log rafts) and land (on log rollers pulled by gangs of men). These carved monuments appeared by the end of the Early Preclassic and continued throughout the Middle Preclassic. They display carved portraits of Olmec rulers adorned with status symbols and insignia of office, such as mirrors and scepters. The most unique Olmec monuments are colossal portrait heads of rulers, carved in the round. There are two other common types: upright stones with full standing portraits carved in relief on one side; and rectangular stones with seated portraits, usually carved on all four sides.

The latter two types of Olmec monuments parallel Maya sculpture, called "stelae" (upright stones) and "altars" (rectangular or round flat stones). Moreover, the motifs carved on Olmec monuments relate to themes seen on later Maya monuments—for example, a portrait of a ruler seated in a monster mouth, symbolizing a cave at the entrance to the underworld. Some Olmec rulers are identified by emblems that indicate either names or titles. We know that portraits of Maya rulers are identified by hieroglyphs of their names and titles. After a ruler's death, both the Olmec and Maya followed the custom of defacing or breaking that ruler's monuments, probably to cancel the supernatural power within the stone.

Oaxacan Civilization (ca. 1500–400 B.C.) One of the best examples of early Mesoamerican civilization comes from the Valley of Oaxaca in southern Mexico. In this highland valley the first clues of social and economic divisions, and of chiefdom organizations, appeared by the Early Preclassic. By the Middle Preclassic the valley apparently was divided between several rival chiefdoms, each with a capital. Here each ruler lived in a palace close to the temples, separated from the houses of the rest of the population. The temples were used to worship agricultural deities who were believed to control vital forces such as rain and lightning. Middle Preclassic Oaxaca pottery was decorated with designs of "fire serpents" and "were-jaguars," powerful religious symbols used throughout Mesoamerica as emblems for elite families.

Also appearing in Oaxaca during the Middle Preclassic were the first monuments, carved with simple glyphs that record calendrical dates and

Stela 2 from the Olmec site of La Venta, Mexico, with a carved portrait of an Olmec ruler holding a scepter.

Carved portrait of a war captive from the site of Monte Alban in the Valley of Oaxaca, Mexico. Note the glyphs next to the head.

personal names. The central scenes display captives and sacrifices. These carved themes are very different from those used by the Olmec. Whereas the Middle Preclassic Olmec monuments were used by rulers to display their personal portraits and relate themselves to supernatural powers of earth and sky that reinforced their power and authority, the Middle Preclassic Oaxaca monuments were used by rulers to display their successes in warfare and taking captives. Of course, this also reinforced their power and authority. Later, the Maya rulers reinforced their authority by using both themes in public displays of power.

TRADE AND THE DEVELOPMENT OF CIVILIZATION

By the end of the Middle Preclassic period the Olmec civilization declined through competition from other polities and problems within its own society. But Oaxacan civilization went on to develop into a powerful and unified state. In addition to the Olmec and Oaxaca, there were similar developments in other Mesoamerican areas at about the same time. The central Mexican highlands, as well as the Maya highlands and the Pacific coastal plain, supported chiefdoms that soon grew into more complex preindustrial states. Such growth was stimulated by contacts between all these regions, especially by trade in status goods used by rulers and everyday items such as knives made from obsidian (volcanic glass).

Residents of each polity made or acquired local products to exchange for products from other regions. Thus a region with valuable mineral resources not only marketed them in other regions but used its trade contacts to learn new agricultural practices, new forms of social organizations, or new religious customs. Some exchange of ideas was undoubtedly used by rulers who were anxious to find better ways to unify their own society, organize their economy, or adopt new and more powerful symbols to reinforce their authority. Indeed, the Mesoamerican trade network exposed everyone to new products and ideas. Knowledge of new crops or better farming methods increased the food supply and led to increased populations. New natural resources, crafts, and markets increased prosperity and created a variety of specialists to make goods and middlemen to trade them. As societies became larger and more complex, the rulers in each polity consolidated their economic, political, and religious power. These Middle Preclassic developments spurred further growth of civilization.

The Maya, located in a diverse and rich environment at a crossroads between southern Mesoamerica and Central America, were perfectly situated to prosper from their natural wealth and learn from their neighbors. By adapting new ideas to their own customs, the Maya developed a distinctive and brilliant civilization that would thrive for some two thousand years.

THE FABRIC OF MAYA CIVILIZATION

The development of Maya civilization can be understood by considering a series of underlying factors. The interplay of Maya ideology, ecology, economy, political organization, and warfare created the unique characteristics of Maya civilization.

The Maya believed that supernatural powers, spirits, gods, and invisible forces governed all aspects of life. The ever- **Religion** present powers of the supernatural affected the ways in which they adapted to their environment and organized their society, trade, warfare, and all other aspects of culture and daily life.

Every member of Maya society—rulers, the elite, the common people (farmers and a variety of occupational specialists)—believed they had to keep the world an ordered place. If a person failed his or her duties, he or she would be punished by accidents, illness, or death by the supernatural powers that governed the universe. These powers could be visible as celestial objects such as the sun, moon, and stars. Invisible power was inside all things: animals, mountains, and other places in the landscape such as caves (believed to be entries to the underworld). The Maya believed that knowledge of these things was revealed to religious specialists—shamans and priests—who held special powers to communicate with the supernatural.

Maya rulers were both political and religious leaders. As king and high priest of their polities, they were responsible for the prosperity, health, and security of their subjects. Rulers controlled the most important supernatural powers and enjoyed greater wealth, prestige, and power as a result. Rulers and their elite allies directed public activities such as tribute collection, temple construction, trade, warfare, and the spectacular public rituals believed to ensure supernatural favor. If a polity fell on hard times, the ruler could be blamed for failing to keep the supernatural powers happy. Chapter 10 presents a full discussion of Maya religion.

The term *ecology* refers to the relationships between society and the environment. As we have seen, environmental diver- **Ecology** sity was critical to the development of Maya civilization. The ways in which Maya society adapted to the environment determined how much food was produced and the size, growth, health, and nutritional status of the population. The earliest means for acquiring food— hunting and gathering—can only support a limited number of people, usually in a nonsettled lifestyle. Although hunting continued to provide animal protein for the Maya, the growth of their civilization depended on large, permanently settled populations supported by agriculture.

The earliest Maya farmers cultivated the rich and naturally replenished riverbank soils, an approach that can support fairly large numbers of people in a concentrated area. In forested areas the Maya used an approach known as swiddening, that is, clearing, burning, and planting a field for two to three years until its soil is exhausted. Swiddening cannot support large numbers of people, and it keeps them spread out over the landscape. But it is adaptable to many conditions and is the most common method used by Maya farmers today.

Ancient Maya farmers practiced other methods that produced more food and supported more people. Most important, these methods allowed larger settlements. For example, on small plots next to each house were household gardens that produced a variety of foods and were replenished by refuse from the household. Such gardens continue to be important in Maya communities today. Ancient agricultural terraces, evidence of another method of farming, have been found in both the Maya highlands, where they are sometimes still used, and in hilly portions of the lowlands, where they enabled sloping land to become highly productive fields. No longer used today except in experimental areas, another method called raised fields were man-made islands of fertile soil built up from swamps and drained by canals on all sides; the canals also provide rich muck that was scooped up to renew the fields. The remains of Maya raised fields have been studied in several southern lowland areas.

Each farming method had different potentials for supporting people. The most favored areas and most efficient methods produced the greatest amounts of food to support population growth. Population growth led to development of more productive farming methods, more efficient ways of organizing labor, and increased competition for land and other resources. See Chapter 7 for a full discussion.

Trade   The Maya economy fostered the production and distribution of goods through a network of trade routes that extended throughout Mesoamerica. One axis of the network connected the Maya with central Mexico to the northwest and with Central America to the southeast. This axis consisted of many routes: those in the south that ran along the Pacific coastal plain, those in the southern lowlands (river canoes were used for transport wherever possible), and those in the north that followed the Yucatan coast (also making use of canoes wherever possible). The other axes were overland routes that ran north-south, connecting Yucatan, the lowlands, the highlands, and the Pacific plain.

Goods and services were exchanged in centralized markets. The system enabled people in one village to specialize in one product (such as pottery) and to exchange it for other necessities made elsewhere. This created an economic interdependence that unified the entire Maya area.

The economic system was crucial to the development of Maya civilization. Although much of the system was maintained without elite control, they probably managed some of the most important trade networks and markets. It is usually assumed that the state was minimally involved in trade, such as maintaining routes and providing facilities for markets. Centers that controlled access to essential goods or to important trade routes, or that held important markets, had an advantage over other settlements. Of course, the elite who controlled the favored settlements enjoyed more wealth, prestige, and power as a result. Rulers and the elite class directly boosted their status and authority by controlling status goods, such as jade and feathers, that symbolized their special powers. See Chapter 7 for a full discussion of trade.

Political organization determines how power is wielded by elite individuals with status and authority. The Maya were always politically divided into many polities. The fortunes of each independent kingdom varied over time. **Political Organization** Some polities increased their power and prestige by forming alliances with other polities. Others expanded by conquest—although few such military expansions were long-lived. Many factors contributed to the success or failure of each polity: location, environment, access to trade, organizational efficiency, prestige, military success, and the abilities and life span of individual rulers. These last factors often proved critical, for the Maya believed that the success or failure of their ruler reflected supernatural favor or disfavor.

Although the Maya polities were never politically unified, they were dependent on each other. No kingdom could succeed without cooperating with other polities. Cooperation made possible the trade and distribution of goods. Alliances between polities allowed smaller kingdoms to resist aggression from more powerful states. This interdependence is reflected in the episodes of growth and decline throughout Maya history. In the southern lowlands we can identify three cycles of growth and decline for most of the polities in the area. See Chapter 9 for a discussion of Maya government.

Warfare, or violent confrontations between groups, was part of the fabric of Maya civilization. But Maya warfare had different rules and purposes from warfare in the modern world. **Warfare** Indeed, warfare played a role in the origins of Maya civilization itself. As populations grew and farmers colonized more of the landscape, competition for land and other resources increased. Competition could be lessened by more productive methods of food production or by attempts to control more people by attracting them to markets or spectacular religious ceremonies. The more people a ruler could control, the more power he could gain from their labor and the goods they produced. But competition also led to violence, as one polity sought to take over the resources of others.

By the Middle Preclassic period, Maya polities were raiding each other for tribute and captives who were used for labor and ritual sacrifices (as part of spectacular religious ceremonies). Tribute meant more wealth for the victorious ruler and his people. Captives meant more labor and advertised the dominance of one polity over another. The prestige of the victorious ruler was enhanced, and the defeated rival ruler was eliminated by sacrifice. By the Classic period warfare intensified, so that alliances and conflicts between polities not only brought tribute, captives, and prestige but also were used to control the land, resources, and entire populations of defeated polities.

Success in war depends on well-organized and well-trained warriors. By the Classic period, full-time specialized warriors were part of Maya society (along with other specialists). As the threat of warfare increased, the organization of power changed. Because the best way of directing an attacking or defending army is to place more authority in the hands of one person (the ruler), over time warfare stimulated the development of a more complex society and greater power for Maya rulers.

Polities with a larger and better-organized population, and better ways of making decisions, had a better chance to defeat and dominate polities with fewer people and poorer organization. But even successful conquerors eventually reach a limit to their resources and capabilities. The Maya political and military organizations were not capable of large-scale conquest, nor could they administer very large territories and populations in the wake of conquest.

The expansion of powerful polities by warfare was also influenced by alliances. Thus a strong and successful polity could use alliances to advance its influence but could also be checked by alliances of lesser powers that cooperated for this purpose. Alternatively, two powerful rivals could form alliances and confront each other to see which would dominate center stage. See Chapter 9 for a full discussion of warfare.

The following chapter explains how these factors contributed to the rapid growth of Maya civilization between about 600 B.C. and A.D. 250 (the later Middle Preclassic and the Late Preclassic periods).

PRINCIPAL PUBLISHED SOURCES

Drennen and Uribe 1987; Flannery 1976; Grove 1984; Sanders and Price 1968; Sharer and Grove 1989; Turner and Harrison 1983.

4

Early Maya Civilization

The first blooming of Maya civilization took place within two areas: the Pacific coast and highlands in the south, and the lowlands in the north. These developments date to the Middle Preclassic period (ca. 1000–400 B.C.), and the Late Preclassic period (ca. 400 B.C.–A.D. 250).

CHIEFDOMS OF THE MIDDLE PRECLASSIC (ca. 1000–400 B.C.)

In the Middle Preclassic a series of chiefdom societies linked by trading relationships existed in many regions of Mesoamerica. Because the most important route between Mexico and Central America was on the Pacific coastal plain, the Maya living there were especially important in keeping it open and prosperous.

Middle Preclassic chiefdoms of the Maya area define the beginnings of Early Maya civilization. By this time there were growing populations, an increase in the size and number of settlements, and expansion into new areas. Much of the interior of the southern Maya lowlands was colonized during the Middle Preclassic. As the numbers of people grew, constructions began to appear in larger settlements that were far bigger than normal house platforms. These were platforms of stone or adobe (sun-baked earth) that supported temples and elite houses. In parts of the highlands and Pacific plain, some larger settlements began to erect carved stone monuments as well. These constructions and monuments in the Maya area mark the appearance of chiefdom societies managed by a small but powerful elite class.

Carved monuments of the Middle Preclassic display portraits of local rulers whose power and wealth derived from their religious powers and their control over local resources and trade. These rulers (and their elite kin) lived in residences far larger than those of the rest of society, conducted rituals in temples elevated on platforms higher than any other building, and were buried with symbols of authority in special tombs that were often located beneath temples. These buildings, tombs, and monuments are clues to the origins of later political institutions.

Middle Preclassic rulers reinforced their authority by using political and religious symbols found throughout Mesoamerica. Some motifs were carved on monuments and resemble those used by the Gulf coast Olmec. For example, a Middle Preclassic carved boulder at Chalchuapa, El Salvador, has four figures. The two largest represent local rulers who were portrayed with these powerful symbols, including costumes, headdresses, and scepters very similar to those found on Olmec monuments. At Chalchuapa is a very large Middle Preclassic earthen temple platform, some 65 feet high, that remained in use for many centuries.

The same pattern can be seen elsewhere but was not always related to Olmec motifs. In the Valley of Guatemala the major center of Kaminaljuyu became a dominant power, the largest Preclassic site in the entire southern area. Some of the best evidence for the growth of Middle Preclassic society comes from the Salama Valley, located north of Kaminaljuyu. The fertile Salama Valley is at a crossroads of routes serving both the southern highlands and the lowlands to the north. There was steady population growth throughout the Preclassic, with a decline at the end of the period. But although connections existed with other Mesoamerican areas at Kaminaljuyu and in the Salama Valley, neither has much evidence of Olmec-style motifs.

Between ca. 800 and 500 B.C. large adobe temple platforms, distinct and elaborate elite residences, and tombs appear in the Salama Valley. The tombs of several rulers were excavated from beneath a single platform. The largest is a stone-lined crypt containing the bones of an adult male buried on his back. He was accompanied by status goods of jade and shell, a carved stone scepter, and three trophy heads. The best indication of his power were the remains of at least 12 human sacrifices found around the crypt, some bound, others dismembered, and all buried face down, presumably to serve the dead ruler in the Maya underworld.

Around 500 B.C. there was a shift in the settlement of the Salama Valley. A small settlement in the center of the valley, known as El Porton, was transformed into the political and religious capital of the entire valley. Large adobe platforms were constructed that supported temples and palaces. A sequence of paired stelae and altars was placed in front of one platform, perhaps the house or shrine of the ruling family. The ear-

Boulder sculpture from Chalchuapa, El Salvador, depicting a local ruler with scepter dressed in Olmec-style costume (carved lines outlined by chalk).

liest and largest stela, carved with a now-eroded scene and a column of glyphs (symbols) and numerals, may commemorate the ruler who founded this local capital. It dates to about 400 B.C. Its glyphs are an early form of later Maya writing—the earliest example of Maya writing yet discovered.

Further north, rapid population growth and the first indications of civilization appeared a few centuries after the colonization of the central lowlands by farming peoples (ca. 1000–800 B.C.). These migrants came from the margins of the lowlands, from the coastal areas to the east and west, and from the highlands to the south. The earliest lowland communities were situated near rivers and lakes that provided fertile soil for farming, water, and canoe transport. One such farming village has been excavated at Cuello in northern Belize. The settlers here built low house platforms coated with lime plaster that supported pole-and-thatch houses (indicated by the pattern of postholes left in the platforms). There are remains of hearths, human burials, maize and other foods, pottery, and stone tools, including manos and metates for grinding corn.

During the later Middle Preclassic, as lowland populations grew, the number of villages increased and settlements expanded from the river and lake locations into interior forested regions. Expansion into this less fertile environment was made possible by (1) swidden agriculture (slash-and-burn), which allowed people to farm the heavily forested inland areas, and (2) the digging of underground cisterns (*chultunes*) to trap and hold water during the rainy season.

The first monumental buildings appeared in the lowlands during the later Middle Preclassic (ca. 600–400 B.C.). The most dramatic examples have been recently discovered at Nakbe in northernmost Guatemala. Nakbe has the largest-known examples of Middle Preclassic architecture in the Maya lowlands. The two tallest platforms are 90 and 135 feet high. A carved monument has been found that depicts two facing figures, perhaps a ruler and his successor; but unlike monuments in the highlands, it bears no hieroglyphic text. The growth of Nakbe was rapid, for it occurred within a few centuries of the first settling of the central lowlands.

The Middle Preclassic saw new settlements in many other areas of the lowlands. The northern lowlands of Yucatan were settled by ca. 700–650 B.C. as part of the same expansion of Maya farmers who colonized the rest of the lowlands. These initial Yucatecan populations made and used pottery very similar to that found to the south, and they constructed masonry platforms for their earliest public buildings. What is known of these developments has been learned from archaeological work at Preclassic sites such as Komchen, located in northeastern Yucatan.

Eroded glyphs from a stela at El Porton in the Salama Valley, Guatemala, dating to ca. 400 B.C.

ORIGINS OF STATES IN THE LATE PRECLASSIC
(ca. 400 B.C.–A.D. 250)

During the Late Preclassic era the first states arose throughout the Maya area, marking the full bloom of Early Maya civilization. The best signs of this development are the growth of cities that held large numbers of people, a society stratified into elite and nonelite classes, elaborate tombs, monumental buildings, complex rituals, a sophisticated art style, and the full development of Maya hieroglyphic writing. The uniquely Maya style of writing and its use for political purposes most clearly distinguish the peaking of Early Maya civilization from its forerunners of the Middle Preclassic.

Writing in Mesoamerica originated during the Middle Preclassic period. One example of Maya writing dating to ca. 400 B.C. has been found on the stela at El Porton; but there are more examples of Middle Preclassic writing in other parts of Mesoamerica, especially in Oaxaca. It is not yet clear whether the knowledge of writing was brought to the Maya from outside. The earliest examples are carved on stone and are fully developed. This implies that the origins of Maya writing occurred further back in time, perhaps using perishable wood and bark paper during the early stages rather than being carved on durable stone.

Whatever its origin, the knowledge of writing was quickly adapted for political purposes by Maya rulers—especially the emerging Late Preclassic polities in the southern Maya area—and is the hallmark of Early Maya civilization. A few glyphs and concepts were borrowed from other writing systems, but the rest was developed by the Maya themselves to create the most complex writing system in the pre-Columbian New World. It was used to record the genealogies and achievements of Maya kings, a tradition of political history that endured until the Spanish Conquest.

An important aspect of Maya writing is a calendrical system that provided dates for events. The most complex calendrical record used a fixed zero date, which is called the "Long Count" (this and other systems are discussed further in Chapter 11). The Long Count recorded the time elapsed from a fixed point in the past (the year 3114 B.C. in our calendar), using five time units. The Maya had symbols for both numbers and time units, but we now write these dates using numbers in descending order (separated by periods). For example, the Long Count date written as 8.4.6.0.3 refers to 8 *baktuns* (8 units of 144,000 days), 4 *katuns* (4 units of 7,200 days), 6 *tuns* (6 units of 360 days), 0 *winals* (0 units of 20 days), and 3 *kins* (3 units of 1 day). The most common Maya symbols for numbers were dots (for the number one) and bars (for the number five).

The Long Count was first used by Early Maya kings to record important events in their reigns and their lives. Dates and other information about events such as inaugurations, conquests, and deaths were most commonly carved on stone monuments, along with portraits of the rulers. These portraits often illustrated the events recorded by the hieroglyphic text, showing the kings impressively costumed with symbols of supernatural power. The monuments promoted the rulers' political and religious authority. Texts are also found on buildings and on portable items such as pottery, jewelry, and utensils.

There were two courses of development of Early Maya civilization during the Late Preclassic. In the highlands and on the coastal plain, civilization reached its apex during the Late Preclassic and then declined. In the lowlands, civilization went on to even greater developments after the Late Preclassic.

Early Maya Civilization in the Southern Area

Late Preclassic political capitals of the Pacific plain and highlands often have carved stone monuments, some with Long Count dates. The earliest monuments with Maya Long Count dates appear in the first century B.C. and continue in these regions for several hundred years before disappearing. This span of about 300 years defines the greatest period of development for the southern Maya area. The largest and most powerful center was Kaminaljuyu in the southern highlands. Like many other sites, it was the capital of a prosperous polity and a center for ceremonial, political, and economic activities.

As hosts of lavish ceremonies, the rulers of polity capitals invested in the construction of large temple platforms and adjacent plazas where large numbers of people could assemble. The most important political centers had areas for displaying carved monuments with portraits of the rulers and shrines that protected their lavish tombs. They were also market centers for trading cacao, foodstuffs, pottery, highland minerals, and other products from as far away as Mexico and Central America. The prosperity generated by this trade was enhanced by alliances between the rulers of neighboring polities.

The site of Kaminaljuyu ("place of the ancient ones") is located in the Valley of Guatemala. Although it has now been largely destroyed by modern Guatemala City, the site once covered about 3 square miles and contained over 200 earthen platforms that supported buildings of wood, plaster, and thatch. The site is laid out around a modified shallow lagoon used as a reservoir. A network of canals constructed during the Late Preclassic era supplied water to several areas of the site. More than half the platforms at Kaminaljuyu were Preclassic, including many of the largest temple structures.

Kaminaljuyu was founded during the Early Preclassic and grew into a polity capital during the Middle Preclassic. Its power and prosperity peaked during the Late Preclassic. Its many carved monuments depict rulers with trappings of power; several have hieroglyphic texts. Control

Stela 5 from Abaj Takalik, Guatemala: a) view of Stela 5 (left) and its
companion "throne stone" excavated from the base of a temple stairway.
(Courtesy of John Graham, Abaj Takalik Project)

of one of the most important obsidian quarries, El Chayal (located 12
miles to the northeast), made Kaminaljuyu the center of trade in essential
cutting tools exported throughout the Maya area. The power and wealth
of the Late Preclassic kings of Kaminaljuyu is best seen in two spectacular royal tombs. Both were found within a large earthen platform that
originally supported ancestral shrines built over the tombs. The rulers'
remains were found in the center of both tombs, adorned with jade and
other status goods and surrounded by hundreds of pots for food and
other offerings. Both tombs included sacrificed companions; in one were
two children and a young adult placed face down in the chamber.

Smaller sites with similar architecture, tombs, and monuments are
found throughout the highland and coastal regions. These southern monuments are the first in the Maya area to combine written and visual
records of royal events. Not all southern monuments have Long Count
dates, but their portraits are carved in an early Maya style that fore-
shadows the later Classic style of the Maya lowlands.

These carved portraits proclaim the ceremonial and political authority

b) two eroded long count dates using bar and dot numerals, flanked on each side by portraits of a ruler and his successor. The date on the left reads 8.4.5.17.11, corresponding to A.D. 126. (Courtesy of John Graham, Abaj Takalik Project)

Stela 11 from Kaminaljuyu, Guatemala,
showing a Preclassic ruler with an elaborate
god mask and headdress holding an axe
("decapitator").

of the Late Preclassic rulers. The scenes relate either to warfare or to succession of rulership. Warfare themes show weapons or human heads, taken as trophies in battle. Succession of rulership is depicted by two standing figures facing each other. The same motif is found on what may be the earliest lowland Maya monument discovered thus far, Nakbe Stela 1.

The carved motifs link the southern area and the lowlands to the north. In addition, there are other connections in common political and religious institutions. Late Preclassic sites in both areas have monumental funerary shrines associated with tombs of rulers. Not all temples had tombs, however. Unfortunately, many Late Preclassic Maya tombs have been illegally plundered, but when excavated by archaeologists they furnish vivid evidence of the prestige and exalted status of the early Maya kings.

In the Maya lowlands similar polities that were larger and more complex developed during the Late Preclassic, and sites founded during the Middle Preclassic increased greatly in size. In addition, many more new sites were founded. The distinctions between commoner and elite became more pronounced. The tombs of kings contain a varied inventory of imported luxury goods: jadeite, seashells, pottery, and stingray spines used for ritual bloodletting by the ruling class. Besides reflecting differences in class and status, these goods indicate increased occupational specialization and trade contact with other regions.

Early Maya Civilization in the Lowlands

Late Preclassic architecture also reflects these trends. At the site of Tikal (to be discussed in Chapter 5) a monumental temple was constructed, the Lost World Pyramid. In addition, the North Acropolis was begun, destined to be the place of burial for Tikal's rulers. The walls of one Late Preclassic shrine buried beneath later buildings were decorated with paintings closely related to the highland Maya style of Kaminaljuyu.

The largest individual buildings ever constructed by the Maya date from the Late Preclassic. The very largest are found at El Mirador, the grandest of all known Late Preclassic Maya capitals. The huge scale of architecture at El Mirador—so much larger than other Late Preclassic lowland sites—indicates that it must have been much more powerful than its neighbors, at least during the peak of Early Maya civilization.

El Mirador is located north of Tikal on the edge of a large seasonal lake. Radiating outward from its center is a network of causeways, including one that connects El Mirador to Nakbe some 7 miles to the southeast. The causeways moved people and goods and gave El Mirador political and economic control over its outlying and subordinate centers. Archaeological excavations show that El Mirador was founded during the Middle Preclassic, but most of its buildings date to the Late Preclassic. After its abandonment at the end of the Preclassic, parts of the site were re-occupied during the Late Classic era.

El Mirador's civic and ceremonial core covers almost a mile from east to west. A distinctive Late Preclassic building found here is the triadic temple. This is a tall, terraced platform that supports three summit temples—the largest in the center, flanked by two smaller temples on each side. The platform is decorated with huge masks modeled in plaster and painted in several colors. Triadic temples are found at several other lowland sites, but there are more at El Mirador than anywhere else. El Mirador's largest triadic temple, El Tigre, covers a surface area six times greater than Tikal's largest Classic-period building.

Extensive plazas flanked El Mirador's massive temples, so that large

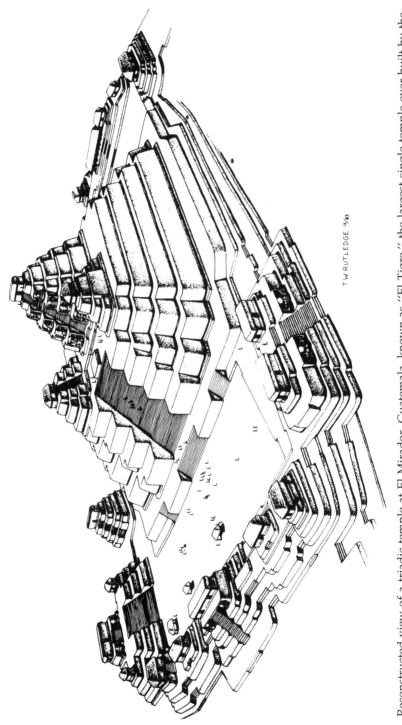

T.W.RUTLEDGE '¹²/₈₃

Reconstructed view of a triadic temple at El Mirador, Guatemala, known as "El Tigre," the largest single temple ever built by the Maya. (Courtesy of Richard Hansen, Northern Peten Regional Archaeological Project)

crowds could assemble for public ceremonies. One contains the eroded fragments of several stelae, carved in the distinctive Late Preclassic style seen in the highlands and on the Pacific coast far to the south.

Evidence indicates that a series of small state-level polities developed across the Maya area during the **Political Power** Late Preclassic period. Each polity was headed by a **in Early** capital with similar architecture, artifacts, sculpture, **Maya Civilization** and writing. The same attributes are found during Middle Maya civilization that blossomed in the lowlands during the next era.

Early Maya civilization was characterized by regional differences in the ways political power was proclaimed to the public. In the Late Pre-classic lowlands, symbols of political and religious power were com-bined and presented on huge temples. Of course, temple size also expresses power; but it is significant that the lowland temples were dec-orated with huge painted plaster masks of the Maya gods, not the Maya kings.

In contrast, in the highlands and on the Pacific coast the symbols of political power were carved stelae with portraits of rulers and historical texts bearing Long Count dates. These written and visual records pro-claimed the ruler as a successful warrior, a sacrificer of captives, or a transmitter of power to his successor. Monumental temples also repre-sented the power of the state and its ruler; but unlike the lowlands, the symbols of political power in the southern Maya area were divided be-tween carved stelae and public architecture.

In time these distinctions began to fade. The southern custom of dis-playing stelae combining texts and images spread to the lowlands, where during Middle Maya civilization it was adopted by kings at site after site. The lowland rulers continued to build great sacred temples, where they performed impressive rituals that ensured the blessings of the gods. But in addition they could now present beautifully carved records of their achievements in both writing and visual images.

THE DECLINE OF EARLY MAYA CIVILIZATION

Early Maya civilization experienced a severe decline between A.D. 200 and 250. The setback was more widespread in the south than in the lowlands to the north. Some sites in the lowlands seem to have survived the upheavals of this period, but the most powerful Late Preclassic pol-ity, El Mirador, declined dramatically. Certain other sites were com-pletely abandoned.

In the southern area almost every site of consequence underwent changes at the close of the Preclassic period. Many sites declined or were abandoned. The most profound change is seen in the disappearance of the custom of erecting carved stelae with hieroglyphic texts. Although many sites such as Kaminaljuyu recovered and experienced further glories in later times, this custom was never revived in the south.

The decline of Early Maya civilization in the south may have been caused by a natural disaster and economic disruptions. The trigger was a major eruption of Ilopango volcano, located in central El Salvador, that occurred around A.D. 250. It was followed by disruptions in both agriculture and human populations. Huge amounts of volcanic ash buried a vast portion of the southeastern Maya area, making the growing of crops impossible. This caused population decline, as people were forced to flee the disaster area. For example, the Late Preclassic center of Chalchuapa, on the edge of the heaviest ash fall zone, was almost completely abandoned for a century or more.

This caused a severe economic disruption that radiated throughout the Maya area like ripples on a pond. In the southeast, not only were crops lost but the population decline stopped the movement of goods. This severed the important coastal trade routes that connected Central America with Mexico. The loss of trade connections produced a far broader economic disaster, affecting people well beyond the volcanic eruption area. Kaminaljuyu, for example, was outside the ash fall zone but declined for a time, probably due to the loss of commerce.

The decline in southern trade and prosperity led to an increase in commerce further north, along the trans-lowland routes. Some lowland powers also suffered setbacks, especially those closely allied to Kaminaljuyu and other southern polities. Thus El Mirador, which may have maintained the closest ties to the south, was probably also weakened by the economic changes that followed the Ilopango eruption. In contrast, the fortunes of lowland polities able to take advantage of changing trade patterns were given a boost. Newly developing polities rapidly expanded at the expense of the weakened former powers and took center stage during Middle Maya civilization in the following Classic era.

OVERVIEW OF EARLY MAYA CIVILIZATION

The first flowering of Maya civilization occurred during the Middle Preclassic period. The southern Maya area was especially important because it was located along trade routes between Mexico and Central America. It was also a prime area for agriculture, producing local food crops and export crops such as cacao. At the same time Maya groups had successfully colonized the lowlands to the north, following the rivers inland to establish new centers in the northern tropical forests. Trade expanded as well. From the beginning, exchange networks linked the lowlands and highlands, promoting population growth and increased wealth and power. Everywhere, population growth and access to trade goods led to increasing wealth and power for a privileged segment of society, the elite class. Thereafter, Maya society would be divided between this small but powerful elite group and a more numerous but nearly powerless nonelite.

But the Maya area is diverse in resources and potential for human exploitation. Areas with good soil and rainfall, or locations that controlled valuable resources, or places that were believed to possess sacred powers, attracted and supported more people than less-favored locations. Favored areas grew more rapidly, leading to the first chiefdoms, and further emphasized the distinctions between elite and nonelite segments of society. The chief and his elite allies relied on the nonelite, who (1) farmed the land or extracted the resources destined for trade, and (2) provided tribute in labor or food. In their roles as rulers, the chiefs of each polity provided physical and psychological security to the populace. As leaders in war, they protected their subjects from enemies. As religious leaders, they held special powers over supernatural forces and sacred ancestors.

The places where chiefs and their elite allies lived became the settings for ceremonies, craft manufacturing, markets, and other activities. Markets furnished a variety of food, goods, services, and an outlet for the products of each household. By promoting economic exchange and the people who made crafts and carried out long-distance trade, the elite class gained new sources of wealth and power. Certain goods, such as jade, were believed to possess special powers, so they were reserved for elite use and thereby reinforced their prestige and authority. Thus the power held by rulers and the elite class was reinforced by the economic system.

The rapid growth of major population centers, characterized by monumental temple and funerary constructions as well as palaces for the elite, led to competition and conflict as each polity attempted to gain control over more land, people, and trade routes. Sometimes the advantage went to polities that controlled scarce but vital raw materials. By controlling highland products such as obsidian and jade, Kaminaljuyu became the dominant Early Maya capital of the southern area. Locations along major routes gave other polities control over the transport, exchange, and redistribution of products. Several lowland sites were situated to control the portages between river routes across the base of the Yucatan peninsula. Nakbe may have been the first major polity to control this strategic zone during the Middle Preclassic. By the Late Preclassic, El Mirador had taken over this role. But success was not simply due to location and economic control. Social, political, and religious activities were also crucial to the development of Preclassic polities.

The full flowering of Early Maya civilization is defined by the first Maya states that emerged in the southern area and the lowlands to the north during the Late Preclassic. The early states were marked by increases in the size of polities and the public proclamation of political power on both monuments and architecture. The rulers of each state used warfare and ceremonial displays, including passing their authority on to a successor, to advertise their power. Although these polities were linked by trade and other contacts, there were distinct features in both areas. Southern rulers used text and image on sculptured stone monuments to commemorate their achievements. Northern lowland rulers commemorated their power in massive architecture—the settings for elaborate ritual, decorated with symbols of the supernatural order. This difference may reflect a different political order in the lowlands during Early Maya civilization: perhaps less power concentrated in the hands of a single ruler. Nevertheless, the two traditions merged with the rise of the great states of Middle Maya civilization across the lowlands.

Early Maya civilization began a trend that would always dominate the Maya political landscape: the rise of one or more major polities that would seek, and often for a time succeed, to dominate the entire stage. Kaminaljuyu was one such polity in the highlands. In the lowlands, Nakbe may have been the first to try but was soon followed by El Mirador, which dominated the lowland political landscape during the later half of the Early Maya era.

Early Maya civilization ended with a decline that saw disturbances and changes in the economic and political landscape. An important factor in these changes was the eruption of Ilopango volcano in the southeastern Maya area, causing sudden changes in populations and trade routes. Not only did most southern polities fail, abandoning the tradition of carved royal stelae, but there were repercussions in the lowlands as well. Loss of commerce in the south led to increased trade in the north, which ushered in the era of Middle Maya civilization.

PRINCIPAL PUBLISHED SOURCES

Adams 1977; Bove 1989; Drennen and Uribe 1987; Sabloff 1994; Sharer 1994.

5

Middle Maya Civilization

Early Maya civilization emerged during the later portions of the Pre-classic period. At the close of the period, major changes in the economic and political landscape were followed in the southern lowlands by the apex of Maya growth and prosperity. This was the Middle Maya civilization, which dates to the Classic period (ca. A.D. 250–900).

The chronological divisions include (1) the Early Classic (ca. 250–600), when state-level polities expanded in the Maya area, especially in the southern lowlands; (2) the Late Classic (ca. 600–800), which saw the rise of important new polities and the peaking of population and cultural development in the southern lowlands; and (3) the Terminal Classic (ca. 800–900), which witnessed the decline of the southern lowlands and the rise of new polities in the northern lowlands of Yucatan and in the highlands.

LOWLAND STATES IN THE EARLY CLASSIC (ca. A.D. 250–600)

Middle Maya civilization developed in the Early Classic period with the rapid rise and dominance of two major lowland states: Calakmul and Tikal. Information about the rise of the Classic lowland polities comes from archaeology and the reading of Maya inscriptions. The origins of many capitals of these kingdoms, including both Tikal and Calakmul, lie in the Late Preclassic. Tikal, Calakmul, and other nearby lowland centers may have been dominated by El Mirador at this time. But when El Mirador declined at the end of the Preclassic, the stage was set for the expansion of these and other Classic period states.

View of Tikal, Guatemala; to the left is Temple I, the funerary shrine of Ah Cacau, Tikal's 26th king, and in the center is the royal palace complex where most of Tikal's rulers lived.

Inscriptions from the Classic period give many details about rulers and their activities but do not mention the common people. Two great centers of Middle Maya civilization, Tikal and Copan, have the most surviving inscriptions and the most archaeological evidence, so we know more about their history. We know less about the history of Tikal's great rival, Calakmul, because it has fewer surviving texts and has seen less archaeological work.

Tikal and Its Kings   Tikal's rise is marked by a historically recorded royal dynasty—beginning with a ruler recognized by his successors as the founder who established the right to rule. This founding ruler was named Yax Moch Xoc. There were earlier rulers at Tikal, but Yax Moch Xoc was given the title of dynastic founder by later rulers, perhaps because he was an outstanding war leader or the first to proclaim Tikal's political independence. Because no monuments from his reign have survived, the only records of his rule are those made by his successors. The best estimate places his reign at about A.D. 219–238.

Tikal had emerged as an independent state by this time. A succeeding ruler, Scroll Ahau Jaguar, dedicated a monument (known as Stela 29) on which is found the earliest known lowland date in the Maya Long Count system. It is deciphered as 8.12.14.8.15 (A.D. 292; from now on we will use only Gregorian dates—Maya calendars are explained in Chapter 11). On the front is the portrait of the king in royal regalia and holding a double-headed serpent bar, one of the most important symbols of Maya rulers. Above him is the head of an ancestor, possibly the dynastic founder. Scroll Ahau Jaguar's name is on a trophy head carried in his hand. Another trophy head is on his belt. Both it and the front head of the serpent bar are crowned with the Tikal emblem glyph. This emblem endured for some six hundred years as a symbol of Tikal and the power of its kings.

The next identified Tikal ruler has been named Moon Zero Bird. He is known from an incised jade celt (small plaque) bearing his portrait and the date of his "seating" as king in A.D. 320. This celt, known as the Leyden Plaque, shows the king in royal costume holding the double-headed serpent bar, standing over the prone figure of a captive about to be sacrificed to sanctify his inauguration.

The ninth successor of Yax Moch Xoc, named Great Jaguar Paw, is the first Tikal ruler to be identified by his place in the dynastic sequence. The lower portion of one of his monuments, Stela 39, was discovered in one of the oldest parts of Tikal. Stela 39 marks the ceremonies held in A.D. 376, marking the end the seventeenth *katun* (a cycle of 20 360-day years) in the Maya calendar. It shows Great Jaguar Paw standing over a bound captive while holding a sacrificial ax decorated with jaguar markings. Great Jaguar Paw's palace has been identified from a pottery vessel excavated under its west staircase. The text on this vessel says it was used in the dedication rituals for the *k'ul na* (sacred house) of Great Jaguar Paw.

By this time other lowland polities, great and small, were also expanding and carving monuments with portraits of their rulers. The site of Uaxactun, only a day's walk north of Tikal, commemorated its early political history with a series of six monuments between A.D. 328 and 416. More distant from Tikal, the city of Calakmul grew rapidly into a major Classic kingdom that was destined to be Tikal's greatest rival. To the southeast, protected by the Maya Mountains of Belize, the city of Caracol was also becoming a major power. To the southwest, Yaxchilan, on the Usumacinta River, became the dominant city in its region. Furthest to the southeast, Copan developed into the major power on the Central American frontier.

These and most other Early Classic lowland cities were evenly spread across the southern lowlands, suggesting that each was the capital of a small polity that was politically independent from its neighbors. But be-

Drawing of the Leyden Plaque
showing Tikal ruler Moon Zero Bird
standing on a captive; note the human
trophy head hanging from the back
belt (A.D. 320). (Courtesy of Tikal
Project, University of Pennsylvania
Museum)

fore long, some cities began to grow at the expense of adjacent ones. One
by one Tikal's nearest neighbors stopped carving monuments, a sure sign
that Tikal had taken them over by warfare or alliance. In war, the defeated ruler was sacrificed and a puppet ruler took his place. In alliance,
the local ruler acknowledged the supremacy of the Tikal king, an event
usually commemorated by the exchange of royal brides from the ruling
families of each city. Tikal's takeover of Uaxactun illustrates how political expansion worked.

The city of Uaxactun lost its independence to Tikal in A.D. 378 during
the last years of Great Jaguar Paw's reign. This date refers to the takeover

of Uaxactun by a member of the Tikal royal family named Smoking Frog, probably a son or nephew of Great Jaguar Paw. It is not known how Smoking Frog took control of Uaxactun, whether by royal marriage or by conquest. But certain warfare motifs at Uaxactun and a later reference on the famous Tikal Stela 31 claiming that Smoking Frog "threw down the buildings of Uaxactun" suggest that he led armed forces from Tikal to conquer it.

After the takeover, Smoking Frog ruled Uaxactun under Great Jaguar Paw. But the old Tikal king died shortly thereafter, and a new Tikal ruler, Curl Nose, came to power in A.D. 379. A passage on Tikal Stela 31 mentions that Curl Nose "displayed the royal scepter under the power of Smoking Frog." This means that after Great Jaguar Paw's death, the Uaxactun ruler Smoking Frog had seniority in the combined kingdom and that Curl Nose took power at Tikal as his subordinate.

Evidence from several texts at the site of Rio Azul, located in the northeastern corner of Guatemala, suggests that Tikal consolidated its power over this center during the reign of Curl Nose. Painted texts from the walls of several tombs at Rio Azul mention two Tikal kings—Curl Nose and his son and successor, Stormy Sky—along with a local lord named Six Sky. Apparently this ruler of Rio Azul was a grandson of Curl Nose and a son of Stormy Sky who ruled over the subordinate polity on behalf of Tikal.

The 10th Tikal ruler, Curl Nose died around A.D. 425 after being in power for some 47 years. Excavations at Tikal uncovered his tomb (identified from a small carved jadeite head forming Curl Nose's name glyph). Inside were the skeletal remains of Curl Nose and offerings showing close connections with the Early Classic rulers of Kaminaljuyu in the highlands to the south and even beyond, to the central Mexican city of Teotihuacan.

These ties indicate crucial trade and military alliances between Tikal and other important cities. The alliances continued during the reign of Tikal's 11th ruler, Stormy Sky, the son of Curl Nose. Stormy Sky was one of Tikal's greatest kings, successful in warfare and the expansion of Tikal's power in the face of its rival Calakmul. He is portrayed on Stela 31, a beautiful monument discovered enshrined and buried in the temple built over Stormy Sky's tomb. Dedicated in A.D. 435, Stela 31 shows Stormy Sky in traditional Maya regalia, complete with his name glyph on a headdress held above his head. Above this is depicted his father and celestial protector, Curl Nose. The text on the back records much of the Early Classic dynastic history of Tikal, naming the founder, Yax Moch Xoc, Scroll Ahau Jaguar, Moon Zero Bird, and the principals in the Uaxactun takeover, Great Jaguar Paw and Smoking Frog.

Stormy Sky's tomb was excavated deep beneath the temple containing

Stela 31. The tomb contained offerings linked to both Teotihuacan and Kaminaljuyu. The plastered walls of the tomb were painted with sacred symbols and a Long Count date equivalent to A.D. 456, the date of Stormy Sky's death or burial.

Tikal's Early Classic history continues with Stormy Sky's successor, the 12th king known as Kan Boar, whose carved portraits no longer display the war and captive motifs of his ancestors. This may indicate that Tikal was having trouble against Calakmul and its allies. We know very little about Kan Boar's successors (Rulers 13–20) except that most of their reigns were brief.

One of the few monuments surviving from this time is Stela 23, which mentions the first woman known to Maya history. Her palace has been identified near the center of the city, but her name is unknown, so she is called Woman of Tikal. She may have been the wife of the 14th ruler, Jaguar Paw Skull, and the mother of the twenty-first ruler, Double Bird (this would mean that Rulers 15–20 were probably the uncles and older brothers of Double Bird).

Double Bird's reign marked the end of the Early Classic period at Tikal. For the next century and a half Tikal suffered a severe decline in the wake of the triumph of Calakmul, its greatest rival. Over the years Calakmul had built an alliance against Tikal and as a result succeeded in nearly surrounding it with hostile cities. Evidence of destruction and abandonment for some 70 years (ca. 530–600) at Rio Azul indicates that this ally of Tikal was conquered by Calakmul before the major confrontation took place between the two Maya superpowers.

Confrontation and Defeat by Calakmul   Evidence discovered by archaeologists at Caracol indicates that Tikal's Early Classic expansion was ended by a bitter defeat. Caracol was one of Calakmul's key allies, located to the southeast of Tikal. The text of a monument from Caracol records the crucial events in a confrontation between Tikal and Caracol that was supported by Calakmul. In 553 a new ruler, named Lord Water, came to the throne of Caracol. Three years later Double Bird of Tikal took action against Caracol to defeat the alliance of its enemies. Tikal apparently won the first round, for the Caracol monument records the capture and sacrifice of someone from Caracol by the Tikal king in 556. But the conflict continued between Tikal and the Calakmul alliance, and in 562 Tikal was defeated and Double Bird was captured and sacrificed.

Now Calakmul and its victorious allies were able to overwhelm Tikal and destroy many of its rulers' monuments. The successors of Double Bird, the 22nd through 25th rulers of Tikal, were subordinate to Calakmul. They were probably prohibited from displaying monuments, and it is likely that the wealth once controlled by Tikal was siphoned off as tribute to the victors. Suppression of Tikal's power and fortunes contin-

View of Caracol, Belize, showing the central royal complex known as Caana, once occupied by the kings, who as allies of Calakmul defeated Tikal. (Courtesy of Arlen Chase, Caracol Project)

ued for over a century. Population growth at Tikal stopped, and many people in outlying areas resettled closer to the center of the city for greater security.

At the same time, the defeat of Tikal boosted the wealth and power of Calakmul and its allies. For example, Caracol experienced dramatic increases in size and prosperity. But the established order had been upset, ushering in a new era of political development in the Maya lowlands. For a time Calakmul was able to exploit its newly won power, but its rulers could not convert a military alliance into a permanent political domination of the southern lowlands. Indeed, the allied cities resisted domination and were able to maintain their independence. In addition, Tikal's defeat had created a power vacuum that was filled by the rapid expansion of other Maya cities.

LOWLAND STATES IN THE LATE CLASSIC (ca. A.D. 600–800)

The Late Classic period was a time of unprecedented expansion and vigor that saw the peak of Middle Maya civilization. We trace this period by discussing the development of several better-known Maya states in the southern lowlands, beginning with areas that expanded in the wake of Tikal's defeat. Then we return to Tikal in the Late Classic before discussing two distant lowland polities, Palenque and Copan.

The Petexbatun Kingdom
To the south of Tikal is a region of rivers and lakes known as the Petexbatun. A branch of the royal lineage of Tikal, escaping defeat by Calakmul, established a new capital here at the beginning of the Late Classic period. To do so they had to subdue a local royal family who ruled from their capital Tamarindito. Once in control, and drawing on their connections with the prestige of Tikal (the Tikal emblem glyph was used by the Petexbatun Kingdom, asserting its claim to be the "new Tikal"), the Petexbatun rulers embarked on an independent and aggressive course to expand their realm, even becoming allied with Calakmul to do so.

The new Petexbatun capital was at Dos Pilas, where the founder of the new kingdom, Flint Sky, was inaugurated in 644. He soon became one of the leading political and military figures in the Maya lowlands. Royal marriages cemented his alliances. Flint Sky also used warfare to increase his power, although his victims tended to be smaller centers within the Petexbatun region. But soon Dos Pilas became involved in a war with Tikal, just after it was recovering from its defeat by Caracol. Perhaps motivated by a claim to the Tikal throne, Flint Sky was eventually successful in this conflict. In 678 he captured and sacrificed Shield Skull, the 25th ruler of Tikal.

Flint Sky was succeeded by his son, Shield God K, in 698. During his reign the Petexbatun polity expanded further. The third ruler came to power in 726, using both conquest and marriage alliances to further increase his domain. Ruler 4 took the throne in 740, and the Petexbatun polity reached its zenith during his reign. However, at its height this powerful and expansionistic state was suddenly defeated. Dos Pilas was attacked and besieged by its old enemies, descendants of the deposed royal family of Tamarindito. Dos Pilas was defended with hastily erected walls that were built over the very symbols of its kings, including one of the hieroglyphic staircases recording the history and conquests of the Petexbatun dynasty. Stones were ripped from its buildings, including the royal palace, to support the palisades that encircled the center of the city. But revenge motivated the attackers, and in 761 Dos Pilas was overwhelmed. The victorious Tamarindito ruler recorded on his monuments how he had demolished the royal palace and destroyed the throne of the Petexbatun kings.

After 760, survivors of the Petexbatun royal family moved to a new fortified capital known as Aguateca. It is not known how long the last rulers were able to hold out behind their defenses, but ultimately warfare doomed the Petexbatun kingdom. One center was located at the end of a narrow peninsula in Lake Petexbatun that was converted into an island fortress by cutting a massive moat across its base. The level of violence became so great that not only were cities protected by walls, but small settlements and agricultural fields had to be fortified as well. In the end, warfare and the breakdown of authority led to the destruction of the Petexbatun kingdom. Much of its population fled the violence to settle in more secure and stable areas, and the region was nearly abandoned.

In addition to the birth of new polities, the Late Classic saw the expansion of older powers. For example, to the west of the Petexbatun region a string of important cities along the Usumacinta River reached their apex during the Late Classic. The largest and most important was the city of Yaxchilan, well defended within a nearly closed loop of the river. From this secure base its kings ruled a powerful and independent polity. Its inscriptions tell of a dynastic founding in 320, and its many carved monuments and temple lintels document the conquests and deeds of a line of kings that extended throughout the Classic era.

Yaxchilan and the Usumacinta Cities

An Early Classic ally of Tikal, Yaxchilan probably became embroiled in the conflict between Calakmul and Tikal. By 629 Yaxchilan had recovered, and then it went on to dominate the Usumacinta region under the aggressive leadership of three famous "Jaguar" kings who ruled for

The hieroglyphic stairway at Dos Pilas, the capital of the Petexbatun kingdom. The rubble to the right is the remains of a hastily built wall built to defend the city from its enemies before its conquest in A.D. 760. (Courtesy of Arthur Demarest, Petexbatun Project)

over 175 years: Shield Jaguar II (671–742), Bird Jaguar III (752–796), and Shield Jaguar III (796–808). These reigns show how important longevity and warfare were to the prestige and success of Maya kings. However, after the successes of these three great kings, Yaxchilan fell on hard times. The last known king of Yaxchilan came to power around 808, but there is little record of his reign or fate.

Two smaller Usumacinta cities, Bonampak and Piedras Negras, are also important to an understanding of Maya civilization. The small site of Bonampak is located about 30 km south of Yaxchilan, its superior in the local political hierarchy. Bonampak is famous for its beautiful murals, which are masterpieces of Classic Maya art. They cover the walls of three rooms in a small palace, and record the naming of the royal heir, one of the most important rituals of Maya kings. The heir-designate in this case was the young son of the Bonampak ruler, Chan Muan. The rituals took place over a two-year period (790–792) during which the king of Yaxchilan, the most powerful individual of the region, visited Bonampak to participate in some of the events. There are scenes recording the presentation of the royal heir, a violent battle to gain captives for sacrifice, the display of the captives, a great procession of dancers and musicians, and the bloodletting ritual by the royal family that sealed the heir-designation ritual.

Piedras Negras, a larger city, is located some 40 km down river from Yaxchilan. It managed to survive and prosper in the shadow of its more powerful neighbor. Its beautifully sculptured inscriptions and monuments detailing the lives of its rulers provided the first evidence that Maya texts dealt with political history. By studying an unbroken series of monuments spanning over two hundred years (608–810), the Russian-American scholar Tatiana Proskouriakoff was able to define a pattern that began with the portrait of a seated male figure associated with a date and a glyph read as "accession to power." Each of these examples was followed by monuments at five-*tun* (five-year) intervals until a new "seating" motif appeared. The span of time between such seating motifs did not exceed a normal human lifetime. This allowed Proskouriakoff to work out a sequence of six Piedras Negras rulers who were in power for most of the Late Classic era.

Back at Tikal, the period of Calakmul's dominance erased most traces of Double Bird's immediate successors, Rulers 21–25. Then, just as Tikal was beginning to recover under its 25th ruler, Shield Skull,   **The Revitalization of Tikal**

both king and kingdom fell victim to Dos Pilas. But Tikal's fortunes were dramatically revitalized by the son of the defeated Shield Skull. The new king was Tikal's 26th ruler, Ah Cacau, who took power in 682. His reign saw the renewal of Tikal's prestige and power through both warfare and the propaganda of recalling its past glories.

Drawing of Yaxchilan Lintel 8 showing King Bird Jaguar III capturing
an enemy lord assisted by a subordinate Yaxchilan lord (left).
(Ian Graham & Eric von Euw)

Stela 14 from Piedras Negras,
Guatemala, showing a young
newly inaugurated ruler seated in
a niche, accompanied by his
mother (lower left), A.D. 758.

Ah Cacau paid homage to the past by constructing a new temple that sealed the funerary temple of his illustrious predecessor, Stormy Sky. Stela 31, Stormy Sky's great monument, was carefully placed inside the rear room of the old temple before it was buried beneath the new temple. Ah Cacau also directed the reburial of the shattered remains of Stela 26—dedicated by another ancestor, Jaguar Paw Skull—within a new bench inside the old funerary temple built over the tomb of Curl Nose.

By sanctifying these relics of Tikal's past glories, Ah Cacau restored the prestige of his royal dynasty. His next step was to strike back at Tikal's old enemies to re-establish Tikal's power and position within the Maya world. In a series of raids he defeated several of Calakmul's allies. Then, in 695, Ah Cacau attacked the powerful state of Calakmul itself and took captive its ruler, Jaguar Paw. Some 40 days after the battle Ah Cacau recorded a victory celebration at Tikal, which must have included the sacrifice of Jaguar Paw.

Ah Cacau died after a successful reign of about 50 years. He was buried in a sumptuous tomb with a wealth of offerings of jadeite, shell, and pottery—including an exquisite jade mosaic vase and a set of beautifully carved bones—testifying to Tikal's renewed prosperity and power. Above his tomb his son and successor, Yax Kin, directed the construction of the most famous of all Tikal's buildings as his funerary shrine, now known as Temple I.

Yax Kin, the 27th Tikal ruler, was inaugurated in 734. He exceeded his father's efforts to restore Tikal as one of the most powerful capitals in the Maya world. Yax Kin ordered the construction of Tikal's largest temple, Temple IV, marking the western boundary of the civic and ceremonial center. He died around 768 and was buried in a sumptuously furnished tomb near that of his father. He was succeeded by the little-known 28th ruler and then by Chitam, the 29th and last-known member of Tikal's long and illustrious dynasty. Chitam apparently attempted to carry on his forefathers' programs. However, by now Tikal's prosperity and power were in decline. By the time of Tikal's latest known monument (dated 889), the ancient kingdom had broken up into smaller polities and the last members of Tikal's dynasty had disappeared from history.

Palenque and Tonina

The western region of the Maya lowlands was a frontier where both Maya and non-Maya groups lived on the Gulf coast and beyond. Research has been carried out at several Classic Maya cities in this region (Palenque, Tonina, and Comalcalco). Palenque's history is the best known because its texts have been studied for years. The Palenque inscriptions deal with mythology and dynastic succession in more detail than those from any other Maya site. Thus Palenque provides the best example of how Maya rulers used

Two jade mosaic vessels from Tikal, Guatemala. The vessel on the left is from
the tomb of the 26th king, Ah Cacau, whose portrait head decorated its lid.
The vessel on the right is from the tomb of his son and successor, Yax Kin,
whose portrait head is also on its lid. (Courtesy of Tikal Project, University of
Pennsylvania Museum)

both religious myth and history for political purposes.

The Palenque texts tell of a long sequence of rulers. Like other Maya rulers, the Palenque kings arrayed themselves in the trappings of power, performed rituals to ensure the continuance of the world order, led raids against neighbors, sacrificed captives, and accumulated prestige and wealth that set them apart from the rest of society. The later rulers of Palenque also credited a founding king, but they did not count themselves in a numbered sequence from this ruler. This is because the royal succession was interrupted twice by changes in the royal family.

The record of the earliest rulers of Palenque begins with a mythical figure, Kin Chan (Sun Snake), who is said to have ruled over a thousand years before the Classic period. The texts also record a more believable figure who became king in 431, named Balam Kuk (Jaguar Quetzal), later to be called a founder. The next six Palenque rulers were members of Balam Kuk's patrilineage. When the last male ruler in this line died in 583 without fathering a son, the throne passed to his daughter, Lady Kanal Ikal. She was the last of the original royal lineage and the first woman ruler of Palenque, reigning for 20 years until her death in 604. Because the Maya could not marry a member of the same lineage, Lady Kanal Ikal's husband was from a different lineage and her son, the royal heir, was a member of his father's lineage. Thus in 605 with the accession of Lady Kanal Ikal's son, Ac Kan, a new patrilineage (that of his father) held the throne.

But when Ac Kan died in 612 there was again no male heir, so the throne passed to Ac Kan's brother's daughter, Lady Zac Kuk. She was married to a man of another noble family named Kan Balam Mo. Lady Zac Kuk ruled for three years until her son, Pacal, at age 12 was considered old enough to assume the throne. With this event Pacal brought the patrilineage of his father to the royal succession, marking the second shift of royal families in Palenque's political history.

The Palenque texts credit Pacal with a reign of 67 years, until his death in 683. It is with his reign that the archaeological and historical evidence becomes much clearer, showing that Palenque became a major polity. The growth of its power and prestige was boosted by the political stability resulting from Pacal's long reign. (Prosperity was linked to the longevity of individual rulers in a number of other cases, as at Tikal under Ah Cacau and at Yaxchilan under the "Jaguar" kings.)

The records left by Pacal and his successors enable us to reconstruct the dynastic sequence but also provide unique information about the supernatural world and how it was used to support the status and power of Maya kings. The Palenque texts contain far more details about Maya creation myths than those found at other Maya sites. These accounts were used by Pacal to justify his legitimate right to rule because he was a member of his father's lineage, a family without any direct claim to

View of the Temple of the Sun at Palenque, Mexico, part of a royal complex
dedicated by Chan Balam, son and successor of Pacal, in A.D. 690.

the throne. Pacal's son and successor, Chan Balam, belonged to Pacal's
patrilineage and therefore inherited the same problem of political legit-
imacy.

The justification made by Pacal and his son was based on both history
and religious belief. The historical justification was the precedent of Lady

Zac Kuk's uncle, Ac Kan, who had succeeded his mother as ruler. The religious justification was that Pacal and his son claimed to be a living replication of the mythological events that occurred during the creation of the Maya world.

According to the creation myth, three gods inherited power from their mother, the mother of all creation. The birth of the sons of the First Mother created a new order, the present world; and the three gods became the special patrons of Palenque's kings. Pacal's texts associate his mother, Lady Zac Kuk, born of the previous royal lineage, with the First Mother. Pacal himself was identified with the three patron gods who inherited the right to rule over the present world from their mother. Through this religious justification, Pacal claimed a divine right to rule and a role as living replication of the creation of the present world.

Whereas his father lived a long life, Chan Balam, who was middle-aged when he took the throne, reigned for just over 18 years. Chan Balam's texts continue the case made by Pacal for a supernatural connection and justify his right to rule on the basis of his divine father. The records of a series of ceremonies performed by Chan Balam document re-enactments of the creation of the present world by the gods, his ancestors.

Chan Balam died in 702. His younger brother, Kan Xul, then 57 years old, became the new ruler 53 days later. During the reign of Kan Xul, Palenque's realm suffered its greatest setback. Initially Kan Xul began the construction of a new addition to the splendid royal residence, the Great Palace. To secure the necessary captive sacrifices to dedicate his new palace, Kan Xul led a raid on the neighboring city of Tonina. But fate dictated otherwise, for at Tonina there is a record of Kan Xul's capture by the Tonina king. Kan Xul was held captive for a long period, keeping Palenque in a leaderless limbo, before eventually being sacrificed.

After the sacrifice of Kan Xul, Palenque inaugurated a new king, Chacaal, in 721. Age 43 when he came to the throne, Chacaal ruled for only a short time. During his reign one of his subordinate lords, a man named Chac Zutz, rose to a powerful position within the Palenque political hierarchy. This signaled the weakening of centralized royal authority, a trend seen in other Maya kingdoms toward the end of the Late Classic era. After Chacaal the power of Palenque apparently declined. Its last historical figure is recorded in 799, but we know nothing of the fate of Palenque's dynasty after this date.

During the Classic period Copan was a powerful capital that dominated the southeastern Maya region. The Copan state, together with nearby Quirigua, controlled the frontier with Central America. Famous for their elaborate sculpture, Copan's buildings and monuments proclaimed Maya traditions in a city

Copan and Quirigua

nearly surrounded by non-Maya people. Even though it was far from the rivalries of the southern lowlands, Copan may have been drawn into the rivalry between Tikal and Calakmul.

The Copan Valley had been occupied since the early Preclassic era. By the end of the Late Preclassic, Maya rulers held sway over the valley (this assertion is based on later texts that recall events as early as A.D. 159). But all the known Copan rulers counted their succession from a ruler named Yax Kuk Mo (First, or Precious, Quetzal Macaw), who was given the title of founder. The entire Copan dynastic succession is summarized on an extraordinary monument, known as Altar Q, dedicated by the last ruler, Yax Pac (First or Rising Sun). The four sides of this carved stone display the portraits of the 16 Copan rulers seated on thrones formed by their name glyphs. The sequence begins with Yax Kuk Mo, whose name is visible in his headdress and who sits on an *ahau* ("ruler") glyph as he hands the royal scepter to Yax Pac. Behind Yax Kuk Mo sits the 2nd ruler of Copan followed by the rest of the successors, four to a side. On the upper surface of Altar Q are the records of two events in A.D. 426 associated with Yax Kuk Mo, his arrival or founding, and his display of the royal scepter.

No monument dedicated by a dynastic *founder* has survived, either at Copan or elsewhere. But excavations beneath the Acropolis (the location of the palaces and temples of Copan's rulers) have revealed (1) the buildings in use at the time of the dynastic founding, and (2) three inscriptions dedicated by Yax Kuk Mo's son, the 2nd ruler. All three refer to father and son and the events of their reigns. Thus it is certain that texts on monuments carved almost 400 years later, such as Altar Q, refer to the sequence of actual rulers and events in the history of Copan that began with the royal founder.

In the earliest levels under the heart of the Acropolis are a series of beautifully decorated temples. Inside the earliest is a small platform and tomb that may be the original house and burial place of Yax Kuk Mo himself. Built over this are (1) two temples commemorating the founder, and (2) another tomb containing a hieroglyphic text with a date of A.D. 437 and references to Yax Kuk Mo, his son, and a "place of burial." The second tomb is probably that of Yax Kuk Mo's wife, the mother of the second king. North of the early Acropolis, under the famed Hieroglyphic Stairway, are several other early buildings. In front of the earliest is another monument portraying Yax Kuk Mo and his son. This stone and another monument found inside a slightly later building, Stela 63, refer to important ceremonies performed by Yax Kuk Mo and his son in 435.

These royal constructions, which form Copan's first royal complex, indicate that centralized political power began at the very time the later

The carved front of Altar Q, Copan, shows Yax Kuk Mo, the ruler who founded the dynasty in A.D. 426, handing the royal scepter to the 16th king, Yaz Pac (right), the ruler who dedicated this "throne stone" three and a half centuries later (A.D. 775).

texts tell of the founding of the royal dynasty and the reigns of the first kings. Their reigns were marked by huge building efforts. Much of the Acropolis was created during the reigns of the first seven rulers (between ca. A.D. 430 and 550). The general size and layout of the Acropolis that remains today was established by the 7th ruler, Waterlily Jaguar (504–544). In fact, a royal tomb discovered beneath the Acropolis may well be that of Waterlily Jaguar. The tomb is located on the western side of the courtyard of a temple inscribed with a date (A.D. 542) and Waterlily Jaguar's name. Later this temple was rededicated by the 10th ruler, Moon Jaguar (553–578).

View of the ball court at Copan, Honduras, with the hills of the surrounding
Copan Valley in the background.

The nine kings who followed expanded on the basic plan begun by
the 7th ruler. The original sacred location in the center of the Acropolis
associated with Yax Kuk Mo and his son was further commemorated by
a splendid temple decorated with painted stucco masks. This temple,

named Rosalila by the archaeologist who discovered it, was eventually buried intact by an even larger temple. A later and final temple built by the last Copan King, Yax Pac, completed a sequence of seven temples erected on this spot and dedicated to the founder of the royal dynasty of Copan.

The 11th ruler, Butz Chan (Smoking Sky), expanded Copan's power during a reign of 46 years (578–626). The Copan polity was expanded further by Smoke Imix, the 12th ruler, whose 67-year reign was the longest of any Copan king (628–695). These lengthy and stable reigns allowed Copan to reach its maximum extent in area, power, and prestige. From its founding the Copan polity included Quirigua, a smaller center located some 50 km to the north. With Quirigua, Copan controlled both the lower Motagua Valley with its fertile agricultural resources and the "jade route" that followed the Motagua River.

After Smoke Imix's death, the ruler named 18 Rabbit took the throne in 695. He concentrated on constructions in the site center—especially the Great Plaza north of the Acropolis—as the setting for Copan's greatest assemblage of monuments. One of these, Stela A dating to 731, proclaims that 18 Rabbit's kingdom (Copan) ranked with Tikal, Palenque, and Calakmul as one of the four greatest polities of the Maya world. The final project of his reign was the rebuilding of the Great Ball Court in 738. But 18 Rabbit fell victim to the same fate as Kan Xul of Palenque: 113 days after dedicating his new Ball Court he was captured and beheaded by his vassal, Cauac Sky of Quirigua.

As a result, Copan's power was broken. Although Quirigua did not conquer Copan, it gained independence from Copan's control and prospered. For the remainder of Cauac Sky's 60-year reign at Quirigua, he used his newly won wealth and prestige to transform his capital through a major rebuilding effort. Copan itself suffered a severe economic setback by losing control over the productive lands and trade of the Motagua Valley. Just as important, it lost prestige and power, because to the Maya the capture and sacrifice of a ruler signified that the gods had withdrawn their blessings from king, kingdom, and their destinies.

Almost nothing is known about 18 Rabbit's successor at Copan. Cauac Sky claimed the title of 14th successor of Yax Kuk Mo and may even have controlled Copan for a time, installing or controlling a subordinate named Smoke Monkey. The damage to its power and prestige caused internal political changes at Copan. Ruling authority during this critical time came from the sharing of power among the leaders of the highest-ranking elite lineages who met in the *popol na* (council house) located next to 18 Rabbit's former palace.

The 15th Copan king, Smoke Shell, re-established much of Copan's prestige and power. This was dramatically symbolized by his dedication of the famed Hieroglyphic Stairway. Part of a new temple built over a shrine to the dynasty, it is in a sacred location next to the Ball Court. The staircase was carved with the longest known Maya inscription, some 2,200 glyphs recording Copan's royal history. Decorated with statues of Copan's most famous kings dressed as warriors, it negates the humiliation of Quirigua's victory and proclaims the restoration of the cosmic order and the return of Copan to its former importance in the Maya world. Capping his achievement, Smoke Shell formed an alliance with one of the most important Late Classic Maya cities by marrying a royal woman from Palenque.

This royal marriage produced a son, Yax Pac, who became the 16th ruler of Copan in 763. He dedicated two famous monuments to Copan's royal dynasty: Altar Q and Temple 16, the last temple built over the sacred center of the Acropolis established by Yax Kuk Mo. However, Yax Pac was destined to be the last ruler of Copan's dynasty, and his reign was marked by a weakening central authority. Despite Smoke Shell's achievements, he had not been able to reverse the power held by the nobles on the ruling council. As Yax Pac tried to keep the kingdom together by rewarding his officials with more titles and greater status, he unwittingly increased the power of the nobles. They proclaimed their power on the carved thrones in their palaces, where they held court like lesser versions of the Copan king himself.

In 810 the ceremonies marking the auspicious *katun* ending were not held at Copan but rather at Quirigua, where Yax Pac visited the new Quirigua ruler, Jade Sky. The end of dynastic rule at Copan is told on its last dated monument, Altar L. It is a poor imitation of Altar Q, showing Yax Pac seated opposite a noble named U Cit Tok, who attempted to be the 17th ruler of Copan. Altar L was never finished and its inscription was never carved. U Cit Tok failed to rule Copan, and the last remnant of centralized authority vested in the king disappeared. Thereafter, power at Copan was divided among the principal nobles who lived in compounds throughout the valley.

THE DECLINE AND REBIRTH OF MIDDLE MAYA CIVILIZATION (TERMINAL CLASSIC; ca. A.D. 800–900)

Maya polities throughout most of the southern lowlands suffered a dramatic decline at the end of Middle Maya civilization. This was followed by a rebirth of success and prosperity in several areas outside the southern lowlands. These developments occurred over a period of about one hundred years, defining the Terminal Classic period (ca. 800–900).

Archaeologists have noted changes over the southern lowlands, the area that supported some of the greatest cities of Middle Maya civilization. A combination of overpopulation, over exploitation of an already exhausted environment, destructive warfare, and loss of faith in a political system that could not solve these problems forced people to seek a better life elsewhere. By about 800, most cities in the southern lowlands were declining in population. By about 900, construction of great buildings and carving of stone monuments had completely stopped at most of the former capitals.

Why did this happen? There are many reasons, but in the end it was because people lost faith in their kings. The people no longer supported a political system that had failed—the deified rulers and the elite class could not solve their problems. This is evident in the decline of all things sponsored and directed by the Maya kings. No more temples andcurricular innovation palaces were built. No more monuments were carved with their portraits. Texts and dates that preserved their achievements were no longer recorded. The elaborate prestige and ritual goods used by rulers and the elite—objects made of pottery, jade, wood, bone, and shell—all but disappeared from the southern lowlands.

This political change was not sudden. It began with a gradual trend away from power concentrated in the hands of a single king within each polity. At Copan, for example, political change grew out of the power-sharing council formed by the successors of 18 Rabbit. Once increased power was granted to the council of nobles, it was extremely difficult to reverse the process. In fact, power sharing increased as later rulers bestowed even more titles and favors to buy the loyalty of the nobility.

The pressures on Copan's final kings were much the same as the problems faced by rulers at other Maya centers. The shifting balance of political power is evident in many Classic polities. Most Classic-period portraits show individual rulers bearing all the trappings of supernatural and secular power, alone and aloof, except for downtrodden captives. But in the Late Classic period the Maya kings began to share center stage with subordinate nobles, who appear on monuments, hold prestigious titles, and live in larger and more elaborate residences. During the Terminal Classic period the individualized portrait of the ruler is replaced by images of the new leaders of society: the nobility who shared power within each polity. Free-standing monuments all but disappear as well; thereafter, portraits of ruling nobles are usually carved or painted on their palaces.

The weakening of centralized political power led to a fragmentation of authority among the elite class. This down-scaling of political organization managed to keep some polities going. But in areas with the greatest problems—the southern lowlands especially—gradual depopulation continued to weaken city after city. People were attracted to newly rising and prosperous polities outside of the southern lowlands. When viewed across the entire Maya area, such shifting of population concentrations occurred over several centuries; it was not a sudden change.

The people who quarried stone, built temples and palaces, and performed other labor to support the Classic kings had spoken. For a hundred years or more the families of common people drifted away from the declining cities. They abandoned depleted fields that no longer provided enough food. They fled areas ravaged by violence and warfare. Some families stayed on and were successful because there were fewer people to feed. Especially favored areas, along the coasts and around certain southern lowland lakes, continued to support populations long after the Classic period. But the overall trend was set, so that eventually most of the great cities of Middle Maya civilization were completely abandoned to the forest.

People who left the southern lowlands moved to areas that promised a better life. Some went to the coasts; others went south into the highlands, or north into Yucatan. The influx created a renewal of Maya civilization and a new era of prosperity in these regions, especially the northern lowlands. In fact, many older northern centers reached their greatest power and prosperity as the cities to the south waned. New settlements sprang up in empty areas, and some of these became major cities within a century.

The great city of Coba, situated among several lakes in northeastern Yucatan, was one of the older polities that not only survived the changes of this era but gained population from the northward migrations. However, the most dramatic area for Terminal Classic growth was the Puuc region in northwestern Yucatan. Centered within the only hilly region of the northern lowlands, the Puuc area is best known for its distinctive architecture. Some of the most beautiful and appealing of all Maya buildings are found in this region. The building style features a plain lower zone contrasting with an upper zone decorated with intricate mosaic designs.

In the Puuc region a series of new cities—Uxmal, Kabah, Sayil, Labna, and others—were founded, grew, and prospered during the relatively brief Terminal Classic period. These were the direct outgrowth of movements of people from the south, not as a single migration but as a gradual population shift spread over a century or more. Prior to the Terminal Classic, the Puuc area was sparsely settled because of its long dry season and lack of surface water. But the soils of this hilly region are among the best in Yucatan; so with enough labor to construct underground cisterns to collect and store rain water, the Puuc became densely settled during the Terminal Classic.

Coba, Mexico, was one of the largest cities in the northern lowlands; one of its major buildings is the Nohoch Mul temple shown here.

Rather quickly the dense settlement and proximity of cities led again to competition and warfare. The largest Puuc site, Uxmal, has a low surrounding wall. A few surviving sculptures depict warriors and captive-taking. Because there are few hieroglyphic texts and portraits of the ruling elite, little is known about these cities' political organization. How-

The largest palace at the northern lowland site of Uxmal, Mexico, known as the Governor's Palace, is one of the best examples of the Puuc architectural style.

ever, it is clear that the political order did not emphasize the individual power and prestige of kings. Most likely these cities were ruled by councils of nobles that collected tribute and maintained political alliances.

Like El Mirador, Tikal, and Calakmul in earlier times, soon one city in the north would rise above the rest and gain dominance over an extensive area. This new capital was Chichen Itza, the largest and most powerful city in Yucatan. Chapter 6 presents a full discussion of Chichen Itza.

OVERVIEW OF MIDDLE MAYA CIVILIZATION

Middle Maya civilization emerged after the decline of most major centers that dominated the rapid growth of Early Maya civilization. The decline was more complete in the highlands and along the Pacific plain, where the tradition of erecting dated portrait monuments—and by extension, rule by kings as well—seem to have ended. But by this time the royal political system, together with monuments proclaiming the power of kings, had been passed to the southern lowlands. In this setting the demise of the greatest Preclassic city, El Mirador, was followed by the rise of Tikal, Calakmul, and other cities that prospered during the heyday of Middle Maya civilization.

With Tikal the thread of Maya history begins to supplement archaeological evidence, and an understanding of the developmental course of Maya civilization becomes more complete. During this period the southern lowlands experienced the greatest growth in population and number of states, accompanied by the blossoming of Maya art, architecture, and intellectual achievement. These developments define the Classic period, which is marked by dynastic political systems in each of the major lowland polities centered on a "cult of personality" of individual kings.

Middle Maya civilization was also a time of increasing competition and conflict, culminating in a great rivalry between the two largest lowland states of Tikal and Calakmul. After initial success in the Early Classic, Tikal was defeated by a coalition of states manipulated by Calakmul. But Calakmul was unable to unify its control and the coalition broke up. In the Late Classic, Tikal revived and defeated Calakmul under the leadership of its 26th king, thereby initiating a period of its greatest power and growth. By this time a series of powerful polities and their capitals had risen throughout the lowlands. The Petexbatun kingdom used conquest to dominate its region for a time, only to be overwhelmed by its former victims. Along the Usumacinta River, Yaxchilan was led to prominence by a succession of long-lived warrior kings. In the southwest, Palenque entered the limelight under the leadership of Pacal and his successors, only to suffer defeat at the hands of Tonina. In the southeast, Copan prospered during four centuries of royal rule by the successors of its founding king, Yax Kuk Mo. Its only setback was the breaking away of Quirigua under Cauac Sky, leading ultimately to greater power for Copan's nobility.

The decline of the dynastic political system marks the end of Middle Maya civilization. Causes for the decline are a complex mixture of environmental degradation, overpopulation, increasingly destructive warfare, and fatalistic beliefs that undermined morale and the authority of kings. At Copan events led to the decline of centralized royal power and the rise of the ruling council of nobles, a process that foretold political changes to come throughout much of the Maya area. The transition between Middle and Late Maya civilization was defined by a new economic and political order during the Terminal Classic era. This was a time of yet another rise of successful polities characterized by the Puuc region in the northern lowlands, even as the great cities to the south declined and were ultimately abandoned.

PRINCIPAL PUBLISHED SOURCES

The Late Classic: Culbert 1991; Fash 1991; Houston 1992; Miller 1986a; Sabloff 1994; Sabloff and Henderson 1993; Schele and Freidel 1990; Sharer 1990, 1994; Tate 1992; Urban and Schortman 1986.

The Terminal Classic: Chase and Rice 1985; Culbert 1973; Kowalski 1987; Lowe 1985; Sabloff 1994; Sabloff and Andrews 1986.

6

Late Maya Civilization

The final episode of Maya civilization, corresponding to the Postclassic era (ca. A.D. 900–1500), is characterized by increasing population and more prevalent warfare. In some cases the Postclassic has been described as a period of cultural decline or decadence because of shifts in artistic expression or other aspects of life. But such judgments reflect an application of our modern cultural standards to Maya society. It is better to view the developmental course of Maya civilization on its own terms.

During Late Maya civilization a new political orientation emerged, as seen at the large regional state controlled by Chichen Itza. The greatest and most powerful Maya capital in Yucatan, Chichen Itza was also the most cosmopolitan. Rising to power during the Terminal Classic, it set the stage for the Postclassic period as a time when distinctions between the regional cultures of Mesoamerica diminished. Populations continued to expand, and interregional contacts increased through commerce, alliances, migrations, and military conquests.

This time is often considered a period of "Mexicanization," when cultural traits from central Mexico were incorporated into Maya art, architecture, ceramics, and the like. However, such a label diminishes the leading role of Chichen Itza and other Maya cities in creating new institutions and styles by combining Maya and non-Maya traditions. The newly cosmopolitan culture of Late Maya civilization first arose during the Terminal Classic, nourished by the Putun Maya of the southwestern periphery of the Maya area (also known as the Itza Maya in Yucatan). The peripheral Maya people were heavily influenced by non-Maya cultures of the Gulf coast and central Mexico. Expansion of the coastal Maya groups into both Yucatan and the highlands brought other Maya into contact with new political ideas, military tactics, and religious practices, thereby ushering in social change and Late Maya civilization.

It was a time of profound changes. Many earlier traditions were transformed during the final centuries before the Spanish Conquest. The Maya of Yucatan saw their past as a time when people "adhered to their reason. . . . At that time the course of humanity was orderly." But like all peoples, they resisted change and saw the Putun Maya as bringing misfortune and instability marked by "the origin of the two-day throne, the two-day reign. . . . There were no more lucky days for us; we had no sound judgment."

These words, from a translation of a chronicle recorded by the Maya in the *Books of Chilam Balam* (Edmonson 1982, 1986), reflect a traditional Maya view of history. The Maya used the past to reconcile actual events with prophecy. In fact, Maya writings often modify, compress, or expand sequences of events to fit their prophecies. Thus the sequence of events recorded by the Maya do not always agree with the results of archaeological research. By compensating for the distortions, however, we can outline the major sequence of events as revealed by both archaeology and Maya history.

The most significant developments of Middle Maya civilization occurred in the southern lowlands. The most significant developments of most of Late Maya civilization occurred in the northern lowlands of Yucatan and the southern area, especially the Maya highlands. We will look at Yucatan first, then the southern Maya area.

STATES IN THE EARLY POSTCLASSIC (ca. A.D. 900–1200)

Political and social changes at the end of Middle Maya civilization paved the way for Late Maya civilization. The coastal Putun Maya used their expertise in trade and warfare to expand northward into Yucatan, probably beginning around 850. The invading Putun Maya are called the "Itza" in the Yucatecan chronicles. Because they spoke Chontal Mayan, a language related to but distinct from Yucatec Mayan, they are described as people "who speak our language brokenly."

The Putun Maya established their first foothold in Yucatan at Isla Cerritos, an island port just off the northern coast. Remains of a sea wall and stone piers define the ancient harbor used by Putun coastal traders. From here they expanded inland, first settling the boundary region between the powerful polity of Coba to the east and the more numerous states in the Puuc region to the west. The base from which they were to dominate the political, economic, and religious life of Yucatan was Chichen Itza. The later Yucatecan chronicles record that the Itza established a new capital at this city, probably around 850. From their new inland base the Itza expanded their power through trade, alliances, and conquest to control most of the northern lowlands during the Early Postclassic era.

One reason for the success of Chichen Itza in dominating the northern lowlands was its central location. It was situated to control overland trade networks in Yucatan as well as coastal commerce from the seaport at Isla Cerritos. Military success was another major factor, **Chichen Itza and Hegemony in Yucatan** as documented by the colorful murals on Chichen Itza's buildings that show warriors, captives, and human sacrifices. Its economic and military power was reinforced by religion: with its sacred cenote and imposing temples, Chichen Itza was believed to be a sacred and powerful place, one destined to be successful. Most important, its flexible and stable form of government was more successful in administering a conquest state than was the former Maya royal system.

Political authority at Chichen Itza was held by a group of nobles— "brothers," or heads of allied elite lineages. They were members of the ruling council; each held a specific office and may have administered specific territorial divisions within the state. This form of government was still being used by some Maya polities at the time of the Conquest, when it was called *multepal* (*mul*, "group"; *tepal*, "to govern"). In these later times colonnaded structures, one of the most distinctive of Chichen Itza's architectural features, were still being built and used as meeting places for ruling councils.

The multepal system was the culmination of a long evolution of Maya political organization. Among its predecessors was the royal council that gained power at Copan toward the end of Middle Maya civilization. The system of rule by council crystallized at Chichen Itza, providing a critical advantage in the often violent and competitive Postclassic era. The multepal removed Chichen Itza from the vulnerability of the traditional royal system, under which the capture and sacrifice of a king would paralyze a defeated polity. Joint decisions made by the ruling council also eliminated dependence on the abilities (or inabilities) and longevity of an individual king.

The name Chichen Itza means "the wells of the Itza," referring to the two large limestone sinkholes, or cenotes, at the site. The city's cosmopolitan character is reflected in its architecture, which blends Puuc style with Mexican traits including the use of colonnades. It fact, colonnaded buildings provided much more light and open space than traditional Maya buildings, but they were usually roofed with Maya-style corbel vaults. The most famous of Chichen Itza's colonnaded buildings is the Temple of the Warriors. Puuc-style buildings at Chichen Itza display typically fine Maya workmanship in their mosaic-decorated upper fa-cades. Mexican styles can be seen in a temple known as the High Priest's Grave built over a natural cave, suggesting that it marks a sacred en-trance to the underworld (like the cave beneath the Temple of the Sun at Teotihuacan). The Caracol, a distinctive round temple, resembles Mex-ican temples associated with the wind deity. The most famous of Chi-chen Itza's buildings is the Castillo. Like many Classic Maya structures, the Castillo has nine terraces; its four stairways recall the platforms in Tikal's Twin Pyramid Groups. It also has plumed serpent columns and a flat roof similar to those of Toltec temples in central Mexico. A cause-way leads north from the Castillo to the edge of the sacred Cenote of Sacrifice. During the city's ascendancy, and even after its downfall in the Late Postclassic, pilgrimages were made to this sacred cenote from all parts of the Maya area to cast offerings into its depths.

The Great Ball Court is the largest in Mesoamerica, and Chichen Itza has more ball courts (13) than any other Maya center. The famous carved frieze from the Great Ball Court depicts a victory by an Itza war leader and the decapitation of a vanquished foe, undoubtedly celebrated by a ritual ball game in time-honored Maya tradition. Being a famous pil-grimage center, the Great Ball Court certainly contributed to the prestige and economic well-being of Chichen Itza during its heyday.

From their capital at Chichen Itza, the Itza Maya dominated Yucatan for two hundred years. This domination ended the old order in which most of Yucatan was divided between Coba, the Puuc states, and other polities of the northwestern peninsula. The Putun invasion of Yucatan and the establishment of their new capital was greeted with hostility by the old masters of the land. In response, Coba constructed the longest of all Maya causeways to connect this powerful capital with the central boundary city of Yaxuna. This allowed Coba to consolidate its realm and, for a time, block further Itza penetration into central Yucatan. But soon Coba's outpost at Yaxuna was conquered by Chichen Itza. The fate of the other Maya polities in Yucatan remains unclear, although most de-clined in the wake of the Itza expansion. Even Coba, the most powerful of Chichen Itza's rivals, gradually declined until it was abandoned, cut off from economic and political allies in Yucatan, and bypassed by the new coastal trade routes controlled by the Putun Maya.

New Masters in the Southern Maya Area Among Maya chronicles recording the history of the Postclassic highlands, the most famous is that of the Quiche Maya, the *Popol Vuh* (Tedlock 1985). From sources such as this we can trace a history of Postclassic peoples in the southern Maya area that was similar to that of Yucatan. Several southern areas were invaded by outsiders, in-cluding Putun Maya groups from the Gulf coast lowlands who intro-duced non-Maya cultural elements from Mexico.

View of the Temple of the Warriors at Chichen Itza, Mexico: a) in order to climb to the summit temple, one had to pass first through a great colonnade;

(b) the central columns of the summit temple form great feathered serpents.

The Castillo at Chichen Itza is the largest temple in the city.

The Great Ball Court at Chichen Itza is the largest in Mesoamerica.

Earliest contact with the Mexicanized outsiders occurred on the Pacific plain during the Terminal Classic period. This introduced a new monumental sculptural tradition that combined Maya and Mexican elements. By Postclassic times much of the Pacific plain was occupied by peoples known as the Pipil, who were from central Mexico and spoke a Nahua language.

Expansion by the Putun Maya from their Gulf coast homeland brought some groups into the northern highlands, introducing new Mexican traits seen in artifacts, buildings, and site planning. This is marked in the archaeological record by changes that begin in the Terminal Classic, around A.D. 800. Some earlier sites were abandoned; others were rebuilt and expanded. Although many Terminal Classic highland centers continued to be located in open-valley settings, many were larger than sites of the Classic period.

Increasing warfare during the Early Postclassic era caused a dramatic shift in settlement location throughout the highlands. Open-valley sites were abandoned in favor of settlements in well-defended locations, such as hilltops or promontories surrounded by steep ravines, often reinforced by ditch-and-wall fortifications. The highland chronicles tell of conquests led by warrior elites with names that suggest Putun Maya groups from the Gulf coast.

Early Postclassic sites have been identified along the natural routes into the highlands via both the Motagua and upper Usumacinta drainages. The Usumacinta River was a direct route from the Putun homeland in the Gulf coast lowlands, and the Motagua Valley provided a route from the Caribbean coast to the east, where the coastal trading Putun had also established outposts. As they moved into the highlands, the invading warrior groups first occupied mountain strongholds from which they conducted raids and subjugated the local populace. As time passed, the initial bases became capitals of new kingdoms forged through warfare and alliances. Although they maintained their elite status as the masters of the land, later generations of the Chontal-speaking warrior elites gradually adopted the local languages of the original inhabitants.

STATES IN THE LATE POSTCLASSIC (ca. A.D. 1200–1500)

According to the Yucatecan Maya chronicles, Chichen Itza fell in A.D. 1221. The political intrigue that led to its downfall is related in the later Maya histories. It began with the kidnapping of the wife of the ruler of Chichen Itza by the ruler of the city of Izamal. In the ensuing war, another Itza city named Mayapan conquered Chichen Itza. There is supporting archaeological evidence that buildings at Chichen Itza were deliberately destroyed. Some survivors from Chichen Itza are said to have migrated south, taking refuge in the forests of the southern lowlands.

The conquest of Chichen Itza was led by Hunac Ceel, a member of the Cocom lineage from Mayapan. The Cocom were an Itza noble lineage also well established in the political hierarchy of Chichen Itza. After the destruction of Chichen Itza, Mayapan became the new capital of the Itza state with a multepal government and buildings modeled after its larger and more splendid predecessor. The chronicles indicate that Mayapan controlled a fairly unified state in central Yucatan for nearly 250 years. This was done through a strategy of alliances and the simple but effective means of keeping the heads of each local ruling family at Mayapan— thus under direct control of the Itza ruling elite.

Mayapan and Its Successors in Yucatan Mayapan was a smaller city than Chichen Itza, but it was better prepared to survive in an age of increasing conflict. The city was defended by an encircling wall with four gateways that were carefully planned against attack.

The settlement pattern inside shows a contrast with earlier Maya cities, where houses were dispersed with garden plots in the intervening spaces. At Mayapan the houses within the 1.5 sq. mi. area of the walls are more densely packed. The major buildings and a cenote are near the center of the city. Many of Mayapan's buildings were patterned after those at Chichen Itza but were not as well constructed. There are some 3,500 buildings inside the wall, and the population must have totaled over 15,000.

The best-preserved architectural remains of the Late Postclassic period in the north are at the walled city of Tulum on the eastern coast of Yucatan. Although smaller than Mayapan, Tulum's location gave it direct access to the Caribbean and seacoast trade. Other ports of trade lie off the eastern coast on the Isla de Mujeres and Isla de Cozumel. Cozumel was a major Putun port of trade for the sea routes reaching around the Yucatan peninsula. Shrines built during this period have been identified at Coba and several other Classic era sites, indicating that the earlier centers were reoccupied during the Late Postclassic.

Mayapan's dominance in Yucatan ended in violence shortly before the Spanish Conquest. In 1441 one of the noble lords held at Mayapan, Ah Xupan of the Xiu lineage, led a successful revolt against the Cocom. All members of the Cocom lineage were killed, except one who was away on a trading mission. Mayapan was sacked and abandoned, an event verified by archaeology. Excavations at Mayapan have revealed evidence of burned buildings, looted ceremonial deposits, and the bones of individuals who may have been killed during the revolt.

After the destruction of Mayapan, all the larger northern cities declined and many were abandoned. The Chels, a prominent noble lineage

The Cenote of Sacrifice at Chichen Itza continued to be the destination of religious pilgrimages long after the city declined.

View over the small walled city of Tulum, Mexico, which was still occupied at the time of the arrival of the Spaniards in the 16th century.

of Mayapan, established their principal settlement at Tecoh. The only surviving son of the slain Cocom ruler, gathering the remnants of his people about him, established his rule at Tibolon. The victors, the Xiu, founded a new capital called Mani ("it is passed"). With these events Yucatan fragmented into at least 18 petty kingdoms. The southernmost was Chetumal. Its capital or chief town, now known as Santa Rita Corozal in northern Belize, was recorded by the Spanish in the sixteenth century as being large and prosperous.

The final chapter in the Maya history of Yucatan occurred after the wars of the Spanish Conquest had begun. This was the pilgrimage of the Xiu ruler and his court to offer sacrifices at Chichen Itza's Cenote of Sacrifice in 1536. By this time the recently arrived Spaniards had withdrawn completely from Yucatan to prepare for a renewed invasion. Ah Dzun Xiu, ruler of the Xiu at Mani, thought it was an auspicious time for a pilgrimage to make offerings for success to the Maya gods. He asked for and received assurance of safe conduct from Nachi Cocom, the ruler of Sotuta, a province the pilgrims had to travel through to reach Chichen Itza. The Xiu ruler feared reprisals by Nachi Cocom because his great-grandfather, Ah Xupan Xiu, had slain Nachi Cocom's great-grandfather during the conquest of Mayapan.

Indeed, Nachi Cocom had not forgotten the death of his great-grandfather, so he welcomed the Xiu request as a chance for revenge. Ah Dzun Xiu, his son Ah Ziyah Xiu, and 40 other Xiu leaders set out for Chichen Itza. Nachi Cocom and a large delegation met them near the Cocom capital. The Xiu pilgrims were royally entertained for four days, but at a banquet on the evening of the fourth day the Cocom suddenly turned on their guests and slaughtered them all. This act of treachery divided the Maya further and pitted the two most powerful kingdoms in Yucatan against each other. Most tragically, this prevented a united stand against the Spaniards, who returned to the conquest of Yucatan in 1540. By then the Maya were divided, exhausted by civil war, decimated by disease, and unable to effectively resist the Spaniards. As a result, the European invaders finally triumphed.

There is a postscript to the history of Late Maya civilization that took another 150 years to complete. Remember that some survivors of the destruction of Chichen Itza in 1221 moved southward into the southern lowland tropical forests. There, on an island in the lake that still bears their name, Lake Peten Itza, the Itza refugees founded a new capital known as Tayasal. This last Itza kingdom remained independent long after the Spaniards conquered the rest of Mesoamerica in the early sixteenth century. Isolated by the dense rain forest, Tayasal remained beyond the reach of the Spanish power for nearly two centuries. Finally the Spaniards raised an army to invade the Peten; and after a dramatic naval battle on Lake Peten Itza, Tayasal was captured, sacked, and forcibly abandoned in 1697, almost 400 years after the fall of Chichen Itza.

By the Late Postclassic period the invading Putun Maya groups had established a series of kingdoms in the Maya highlands, many of which were described by the Spaniards during their conquest in the early sixteenth century. These highland kingdoms included the **The Quiche and Cakchiquel Highland States** Pokomam Maya (their capital was at Mixcu Viejo), the Tzutuhil Maya (their capital was at Atitlan on the famous lake of the same name), the Quiche Maya (their capital was at Utatlan), and the Cakchiquel Maya (their capital was at Iximche). From their bastions, the capitals of each kingdom competed for control over the people, products, and trade routes within the highlands. Warfare was used to settle disputes. Two of the most successful highland kingdoms, the Quiche and Cakchiquel, expanded as far as the Pacific coastal plain to control trade routes, cacao production, and other resources.

The *Popol Vuh* gives the best history of the development of the Quiche Maya kingdom. According to this account the ancestral Quiche warriors, led by Balam Quitze, came into the highland region shortly after A.D. 1200. There they began to forge a kingdom from a stronghold known as Jakawitz. A century later three Quiche elite leaders traveled to the east to gain the proper symbols of authority to rule over their expanded domain. It has been suggested that they went to Copan, by then all but abandoned but still a sacred and powerful place that represented the past glories of the Maya. With the proper symbols of authority secured, the three princes returned to their highland kingdom. After returning, one of the leaders, C'ocaib, assumed the title of Ahpop (He of the mat), the highest political office in the Quiche kingdom.

Around 1350 the Quiche consolidated their kingdom and, led by Ahpop Conache, founded a new capital, Ismachi. During the reign of his successor, Ahpop Cotuja, an unsuccessful revolt led to a further expansion of the kingdom. Early in the fifteenth century, during the reign of Gucumatz (Feathered serpent), a new and well-defended capital was founded at Utatlan. Gucumatz extended the power of the Quiche to the north and west and was glorified in the *Popol Vuh*:

> All the other lords were fearful before him. The news spread; all the tribal lords heard about . . . this lord of genius. And this was the beginning and growth of the Quiche, when the Lord Plumed Serpent [Gucumatz] made the signs of greatness. His face was not forgotten by his grandsons and sons. (Tedlock 1985: 213)

The kingdom was further expanded by Quicab, his successor. But around 1470, during the reign of Vahxaqui-Caam, the Cakchiquel

View of one of the temples at the Quiche Maya capital of Utatlan, Guatemala, located in the highlands and a target of the invading Spanish forces in the 16th century.

View of the Cakchiquel Maya capital of Iximche, Guatemala; after the Spanish Conquest this Maya city became the first colonial capital of Guatemala.

Maya—who had been subjects and allies of the Quiche—revolted and established an independent kingdom southeast of Utatlan. The Cakchiquel founded a new fortified capital, Iximche, from which they began a new cycle of conquests. The Quiche made several attempts to subdue the Cakchiquel but were unsuccessful. The Cakchiquel were still expanding their kingdom in the early sixteenth century when the Spaniards arrived. Deceived at first, the Cakchiquel initially allied themselves with the Spaniards in order to gain their assistance to defeat rival highland Maya kingdoms. By the time the Cakchiquel realized the true motives of the Spaniards, it was too late. Along with the rest of the highland Maya, they were subjugated by the Spanish conquerors.

OVERVIEW OF LATE MAYA CIVILIZATION

Late Maya civilization emerged in the Postclassic era from the failures and decline of Middle Maya civilization. Marked by a more cosmopolitan culture, the most active agents of the new order were a mercantile and warrior elite from the Gulf coast lowlands who successfully adopted both Maya and Mexican traditions and expanded into the vacuum left in the wake of the Classic decline. Known as the Putun Maya, these formerly peripheral peoples adopted a political system more suited to consolidating economic and military control. The heart of the new political system was collective rule by council. The Putun Maya used seacoast trade as their prime means to gain economic domination over much of the Maya area.

The Putun Maya expanded into two areas: the northern lowlands and the southern highlands. In the northern lowlands a powerful Putun group, the Itza Maya, established a new capital at Chichen Itza. From this base they replaced the former powers in Yucatan (Coba and the Puuc centers) and dominated most of the peninsula for several centuries during the Early Postclassic period. When Chichen Itza was destroyed, apparently by armed conquest, a successor capital, Mayapan, reigned supreme in the northern lowlands for most of the Late Postclassic period. After the fall of Mayapan around 1440, centralized authority was fragmented into a series of independent, petty states that continued until the Spanish Conquest.

A similar course was charted in the southern highlands, where during the Early Postclassic period invading warrior elites gradually consolidated a series of small polities. This process is best illustrated by the kingdom founded by the aggressive Quiche Maya, whose ruling elite originated from the Putun Maya heritage. By the Late Postclassic, from their new capital at Utatlan the Quiche had emerged as the supreme power in the highlands. By the end of this era the Quiche Maya and their chief competitors, the rapidly rising kingdom of the Cakchiquel Maya, jockeyed for political and military supremacy until they and the other highland kingdoms fell victim to the Spanish Conquest.

PRINCIPAL PUBLISHED SOURCES

Chase and Rice 1985; Diehl and Berlo 1989; Edmonson 1982, 1986; Sabloff 1994; Sabloff and Andrews 1986; Schele and Freidel 1990; Sharer 1994; Tedlock 1985; Tozzer 1941.

7

Maya Economy

The Maya economy was based on the production and distribution of food and a variety of goods, which were distributed throughout the Maya area and beyond.

FOOD PRODUCTION

The development and growth of all civilizations require efficient means for producing food. The most important is usually agriculture; the harvesting of domesticated plants and, to a greater or lesser extent, the use of domesticated animals for food (animal husbandry). Today Maya men cultivate corn fields but also hunt and fish. Women often gather wild foods and maintain the gardens found next to most houses. The ancient Maya were probably no different, for in addition to hunting, fishing, and gathering wild foods, they relied on agriculture to produce many different crops and on several varieties of domesticated animals to produce an array of food sources. These methods were well adapted to the variety of environments found throughout the Maya area.

As populations increase there is pressure for food production to increase: this process is known as intensification. Agricultural systems, for example, can be intensified by increasing the amount of land being cultivated or by increasing the yield of each unit of land under cultivation. Yields can be increased by developing more productive crops, irrigating, fertilizing, and so forth. The Maya used various means to intensify food production through time. As populations grew they opened new lands to cultivation and developed new methods to increase crop yields. Evidence also suggests that some lowland areas were used for large-scale food production, so the harvests must have been transported to major cities for distribution.

Diet   Foods consumed by the ancient Maya were similar to the traditional diet of Maya peoples of today. The major differences include domesticated plants and animals introduced after the Spanish Conquest (such as rice, wheat, chickens, and pigs). The core of the Maya diet—past and present—is maize, beans, and squashes. Maize is usually dried, removed from the cob, and soaked in water and lime to remove the casing around each kernel. The process releases amino acids that would otherwise not be utilized when maize is consumed; this boosts its nutritional value. After being dried and ground on a metate (grinding stone), the maize flour is mixed with water to form a dough that can be formed into flat tortillas and baked over a fire on a pottery griddle *(comal)* or wrapped in leaves and steamed in a clay pot to make tamales. Traces of hearths are sometimes found inside the remains of ancient Maya houses. In some cases the Maya may have cooked inside special kitchen structures next to their houses. On the basis of present practices, we can assume that food was prepared and cooked by women.

A variety of beans is still grown, but among the most favored are the black beans of the Maya highlands. A major source of protein, beans are cooked and served whole, or mashed and refried. In fact, the combination of either tortillas or tamales with beans provides most of the protein essential to human nutrition. A variety of squashes is also part of the traditional diet. Both the flesh and the seeds (often dried and roasted and used in sauces) are consumed. Several kinds of chilis were used fresh, roasted, or sun-dried as a condiment. A variety of root crops, such as cassava (manioc), were also grown. The diet was further supplemented by fruits that were either domesticated or collected wild from the forest, including avocados, papayas, guavas, and ramon (breadnut).

The major sources of animal protein were domesticated turkeys, supplemented by other birds and animals. A rich and spicy turkey soup remains an especially important festive dish among the Maya today. Because the Maya kept no other fully domesticated animals except for the dog, other meat came from wild animals and birds. A great variety of wild forest animals were hunted or trapped. The most important food animals included deer, rabbits, peccaries, tapirs, agoutis, armadillos, and monkeys (see Table 1). These could be roasted or stewed with chilis and other condiments. Rivers, lakes, and the sea were harvested for snails, shellfish, and fish that could be roasted or cooked in soups.

The Maya stingless bee was kept in hives, especially in Yucatan, and the honey they produced was used for sweetening. Cacao (chocolate) was prepared as a beverage, mixed with honey (and sometimes chili). Other beverages (such as *atole*) were made from maize and water and similar mixtures (one ceremonial drink was made from ground beans and squash seeds). A potent, intoxicating beverage was made from the bark of the balche tree; other fermented drinks were made from maize, honey, and fruits.

Honey, cacao, and salt were the most commonly traded dietary items, but almost any food product could be dried and transported. Salt was produced by evaporating sea water or water from salt springs. In Yucatan, extensive salt pans were constructed along the northern coast to harness the sun to evaporate sea water. In the highlands are several areas with salt springs; there and along the Pacific coast, the Maya boiled saltwater in large pots to produce salt.

Over thousands of years the Maya developed and perfected a rich and varied diet. It was maintained by hunting and gathering (wild-food resources), animal husbandry, and agriculture.

Hunting and Gathering

All pre-Columbian peoples relied in part on wild-food resources. After all, there were far fewer species adaptable for domestication in the Americas than in the Old World. Thus the Maya supplemented their protein diet by fishing and hunting. Hunting was done with bow and arrow, spear, and blowgun, as well as traps and snares. The most desirable food animals were deer, tapirs, agoutis, rabbits, monkeys, and birds. The use of snares to trap deer is depicted in an ancient Maya book. The blowgun was used to hunt birds, monkeys, and other arboreal animals. The most common forest animals used by the Maya are listed in Table 1. Not all hunted or trapped animals were eaten; some, especially the carnivores, were used for their pelts, teeth, claws, and other products.

Aquatic species were very important to the ancient Maya diet. Fired-clay net weights and bone fishhooks are often found at Maya sites. The Maya used dugout canoes, which are depicted on murals and artifacts. Fish and shellfish were a major source of food for people living along the coasts. It is likely that dried fish were traded far inland, just as is done today throughout the Maya area. Freshwater lakes and rivers throughout the highlands and southern lowlands provided a variety of fish and freshwater mollusks. The importance of both fish and shellfish is indicated by their frequent representations in Maya art.

A variety of useful wild plants are found throughout the Maya area. Today many are still collected for food, fibers, medicines, and other uses. Doubtless the same was true in the past as well. Among the common forest plants used by the Maya are papaya, annona, sapodilla, cheri-

Table 1
Common Wild Animals Hunted by the Maya

Agouti (*Dasprocta ssp.*)

Armadillo (*Dasypus novemcinctus*)

Brocket deer (*Mazama americana*)

Coatimundi (*Nasua narica*)

Cougar (*Felis concolor*)

Howler monkey (*Alouatta villosa*)

Jaguar (*Felis onca*)

Jaguarundi (*Felis jaguarondi*)

Macaw (*Ara macao*)

Manatee (*Trichechus manatus*)

Ocelot (*Felis pardalis*)

Opossum (*Didelphis marsupialus*)

Paca (*Agouti paca*)

Peccary (*Tayassu tajacu*)

Rabbit (*Sylvilagus brasiliensis*)

Spider monkey (*Ateles geofroyi*)

Tapir (*Tapirus bairdii*)

White-tailed deer (*Odocoileus virginianus*)

moya, coyol, allspice, vanilla, and oregano. Some of these trees and plants were also tended and cultivated in household gardens.

Animal Husbandry   Although the Maya did not rely on domesticated animals for food, they did raise a few species. The most important was the turkey, although doves and Muscovy ducks may have been raised for food as well. (The Muscovy duck was domesticated in South America but was probably known to the Maya before the Spanish Conquest.) As in many societies, dogs were the most important domestic animal. They were used as household guardians and hunting companions. Special species of dog may have been fattened and eaten, as was the custom elsewhere in Mesoamerica. The Maya also probably raised captured wild animals, such as deer, in pens for food. In addition, the drainage canals in raised field systems (discussed below) could have been used to raise fish and mollusks.

Today the Maya keep many different wild animals as pets, the most favored being parrots, monkeys, coatis, and kinkajous. In the sixteenth century, Bishop Diego de Landa wrote that the Maya of the Yucatan did likewise:

there is an animal which they call *chic* [coati, and] the women raise them and they leave nothing which they do not root over and turn upside down.... [Women] raise other domestic animals, and let the deer suck their breasts, by which means they raise them and make them so tame that they never will go into the woods, although they take them and carry them through the woods and raise them there. (Tozzer 1941: 204–5, 127; trans. of Landa's original manuscript of ca. 1566)

It is likely that the Maya used many more means to produce food than can be demonstrated by either archaeology or history.

Agriculture was the most important means of producing food for the Maya. Their most common food plants are **Agriculture** listed in Table 2. Over time, farmers perfected a variety of cultivation methods: nonintensive systems, in which fields are allowed to lie fallow between periods of cultivation; and intensive systems, in which fields are cultivated continuously.

Table 2
Common Domesticated Food Plants Grown by the Maya

Amaranth (*Amaranthus ssp.*)

Avocado (*Persea americana*)

Cacao (*Theobroma cacao*)

Cassava (*Manihot esculenta*)

Chili (*Capiscum annuum*)

Common bean (*Phaseolus vulgaris*)

Guava (*Psidium guajava*)

Maize (*Zea mays*)

Papaya (*Carica papaya*)

Pineapple (*Ananas comosus*)

Squash (*Cucurbita pepo*)

Sweet potato (*Ipomoea batatas*)

Yucca (*Yucca elephantipes*)

The most common form of nonintensive agriculture is swiddening. This involves clearing new fields from overgrowth or virgin forest, burning the debris, and planting for one or more years until the soil is depleted. In areas with better soils the fallow periods may last from one to three years for each year of cultivation. In areas with poorer soils the fallow periods may increase to three to six years for each year of culti-

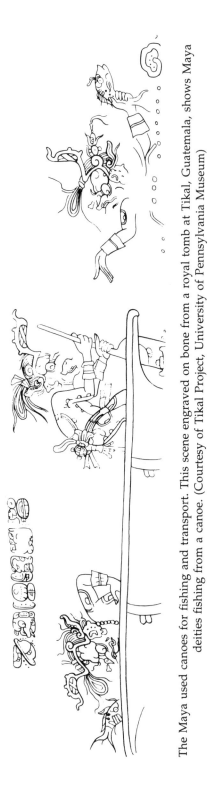

The Maya used canoes for fishing and transport. This scene engraved on bone from a royal tomb at Tikal, Guatemala, shows Maya deities fishing from a canoe. (Courtesy of Tikal Project, University of Pennsylvania Museum)

vation. Large trees and species that provided wild foods or other useful products were probably left to grow with the stands of maize, beans, squashes, manioc, and other planted species. In most areas the fields could be planted and harvested for several successive seasons, depending on rainfall and soil fertility. When a field was depleted, it was abandoned to lie fallow and recover its fertility while other areas were cleared for fields.

Swiddening was probably among the oldest forms of agriculture used by the Maya. This method was undoubtedly used in the original colonization of forested areas. But it produces low yields while requiring large areas of land and therefore can only support small and scattered populations. As populations increased, fallow periods were shortened and more efficient methods were developed. Fallow periods can be shortened by weeding and intercropping (growing several complementary species together, such as maize and beans). These techniques decrease competition for the food plants, reduce soil depletion, or even replenish nutrients in the soil.

Although Maya farmers today still raise traditional crops, they rely on steel tools such as machetes and axes. Machetes are used to clear overgrown (fallow) fields with relative ease, axes to clear new lands of large trees. Because the ancient Maya did not have steel tools, they used sharp blades of flint or obsidian and flint axes. Without steel cutting tools, the clearing of new forest or second growth in fallow areas requires more energy and time. Thus, once the time and effort had been invested in clearing a new field, Maya farmers probably maintained it by constant weeding to prevent new growth from taking over.

Indirect evidence for the use of swiddening by the Maya comes from analyses of pollen samples in sediment cores from the beds of several southern lowland lakes. These show that the earliest settlers of that region grew maize. Remnants of ash fallout, possibly from field burning, indicate swiddening. Traces of ancient field systems are found mostly in the northern lowlands, consisting of stone boundary walls and water-flow deflectors; these could have been cultivated by swiddening.

Other relics of past agricultural uses have been found by archaeologists. Remnants of stone terraces have been identified in several areas of the lowlands. These were used to artificially level areas of sloped landscape and help retain water in the soil to increase productivity. Archaeological excavations indicate that these terraces were constructed during Middle Maya civilization. Such agricultural features require a heavy investment of labor, which implies that they may have been used for intensive agricultural methods.

The Maya used several intensive agricultural methods, including continuous field cultivation, household gardens, arboriculture, and hydraulic modifications. Continuous field cultivation involves growing crops

Many Maya families continue to raise maize and other crops next to
their houses today.

with little or no fallow periods, so that the fields never become overgrown. This requires constant weeding and maintenance. Continuous
cultivation could have been used in areas with fertile soils and plentiful
rainfall, such as the alluvial valleys in parts of the southern and coastal
lowlands. Alluvial valleys provide especially fertile soils on natural river
levees and bottom lands where periodic flooding replenishes soil fertility
by depositing new alluvial soils.

There is only indirect evidence to indicate that the Maya used continuous cultivation. It is likely that some constructed agricultural features,
such as terraces, were used for continuous cultivation. Estimates of peak
sizes and densities of Maya populations in the southern lowlands suggests that continuous cultivation may have been a necessary part of the
ancient system. The high potential yields from alluvial soils suggests that
continuous cultivation could have transformed these areas into "breadbaskets" supplying large amounts of maize, beans, and other staples to
feed the great Maya cities.

Household gardens are a common form of intensive agriculture in
Maya communities today. Gardens are cultivated in the open spaces adjacent to each house. These gardens usually provide a great variety of
foods from annual root crops, maize, beans, and other field species as
well as perennial shrubs, vines, and trees. Because weeding and other
maintenance is minimal and the rate of soil depletion is low, household
gardens continuously supply large quantities of foods per unit of land.

At the site of Ceren, El Salvador, a sudden volcanic eruption buried and preserved the houses and gardens of a farming village; shown here are the burned remains of maize cobs and fragments of the cane crib where they were once stored (ca. A.D. 550). (Courtesy of Payson Sheets, El Ceren Project)

Soil depletion is minimized by intercropping; fertilization comes from plant residues and human and animal wastes from the household.

In one extraordinary case, archaeologists have found portions of preserved household gardens buried by volcanic ash from a sudden eruption. These have been carefully excavated at Cerén, El Salvador. The ash preserved the casts of a variety of crops, some grown right next to the remains of houses. There are carefully tilled rows for cotton and several food plants, including maize and manioc, separated by furrows that facilitated drainage. The volcanic ash also preserved fences made of sticks that protected fields from pests, and storage facilities for the harvested food.

There are sixteenth-century Spanish descriptions of Maya household gardens. There is also indirect evidence for such gardens. Settlement studies show a nearly uniform spacing of residences throughout most sites. Spaces between the house remains, not large enough for agricultural fields, are just the right size for household gardens. At many lowland archaeological sites there are unusually heavy stands of food-producing trees, especially ramon. They probably represent the descendants of stands grown around the houses of Tikal and other lowland cities. Some food trees—such as ramon, cacao (chocolate), and avocado—may also have been cultivated in extensive groves in areas of low population. Studies of the yields from ramon trees show that they produce ten times more food per unit of land than maize. Ramon is a starchy food that can be processed and used like maize to make tortillas. Tree crops require little labor, and the fruit or nuts of some species may be collected from the ground as they fall. By mingling different food tree species, the Maya would have discouraged pests or diseases that thrive on a single species.

Both archaeological evidence and ethnohistorical accounts indicate that tree crops were once important to the Maya. Cacao was a highly valued tree crop in lowland environments. In addition to its use as a beverage, cacao beans were used as money in economic exchanges (even counterfeit cacao beans made of clay have been found). Pottery images of cacao pods have been found at Copan, Quirigua, and other Maya sites, indicating these cities controlled important production areas for chocolate.

The Maya used hydraulic modifications to intensify food production. They dug extensive networks of ditches to irrigate crops and to drain excess water from saturated soils, thereby allowing better growth. Edzna in the northern lowlands has an impressive canal and reservoir system capable of irrigating at least 450 hectares of cultivated land. The Edzna hydraulic system was constructed during Early Maya civilization (ca. 300–50 B.C.) and probably was used for several centuries thereafter.

Even more extensive are the remains of raised fields constructed in low-lying areas. These provided fertile and well-drained growing conditions for a variety of crops, including maize, cotton, and possibly cacao. Raised fields are built by digging narrow drainage canals in water-saturated soils and heaping the earth to both sides, forming raised plots for growing crops. By periodically dredging the muck from the drainage channels, farmers replenished the raised plots with fresh soil and organic debris, allowing continuous cultivation. The canals also may have been used to raise fish, mollusks, and other aquatic life.

Traces of raised fields have been detected by aerial photography in several areas of the Maya lowlands. Although more research is needed to verify the function of detected canal networks, it is obvious that hydraulic agriculture was a major source of food in the lowlands beginning during Early Maya civilization and, increasingly, during Middle Maya civilization.

DISTRIBUTION OF FOOD AND GOODS

The diversity of environmental conditions allowed the Maya to develop local economic specializations. After all, the environmental differences throughout the Maya area provided many different food products and a variety of important non-food resources as well. The forests produced firewood, an essential fuel for cooking, firing pottery, making lime

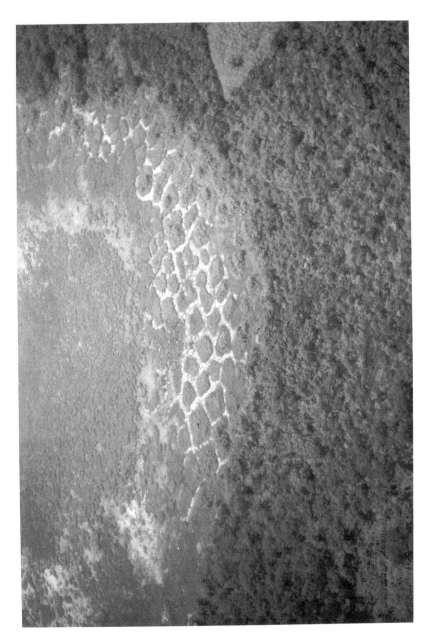

The ancient Maya made swamps and shallow lakes into productive agricultural fields by digging drainage canals between plots of land, forming raised fields as can still be seen here at Pulltrouser Swamp, Belize. (B. L. Turner, *Science* ©1981 AAAS)

plaster, and similar purposes. By preserving forested areas the Maya could maintain supplies of wood, thatch, and fibers for buildings, baskets, rope, nets, and bark cloth. The most important cultivated fiber, cotton, was spun into thread, colored with a rich variety of vegetable and mineral dyes, and woven into clothing and textiles. Hunted animals provided bone, teeth, and pelts used for adornments and ritual objects. Aquatic species were used in similar ways, especially coral and seashells. The varying local economic specialization throughout the Maya area created the need for transportation and exchange networks to distribute these resources, goods, and services.

Markets   Maya farmers to this day produce most of the food needed to feed their families, and any surplus is sold to others. Many women tend household gardens to grow fruits and vegetables, selling surpluses in the local market. Both men and women produce other goods for sale (such as salt and lime) and manufacture a variety of crafts (such as charcoal, pottery, and textiles). In both the highlands and in Yucatan today, markets allow the exchange of foods and other goods between producer and consumer. This gives everyone a central place at which to obtain products from different areas that otherwise would be unavailable (see p. 7).

Markets are usually held on one or two days each week (often on Sundays in conjunction with religious services in many rural communities), or daily in larger cities. In the past, markets may have been scheduled by the ritual calendar to coincide with major ceremonies or pilgrimages to local religious shrines, as at Chichen Itza. During Late Maya civilization there were important shrines on Cozumel Island, off the Yucatan coast, that attracted many visitors. The pilgrims were also a source of consumers, and it is no accident that Cozumel was a major port for the seacoast trade around the Yucatan peninsula.

Thus it is likely that ancient Maya families obtained at least some of their food and a variety of products from markets like those described by the Spaniards in the sixteenth century. The largest market described by the Spaniards was in the capital city of the Mexica (Aztecs) in central Mexico (present-day Mexico City). The market was surrounded by an arcade; stalls were arranged in a grid of streets around a central elevated platform used for making public announcements and executing thieves. A court where disputes were settled stood at one corner. Goods from all over Mesoamerica were sold, including a variety of foods and beverages, baskets, mats, pottery, obsidian blades and other tools, clothing, jewelry, medicines, rubber, paper, and building materials.

But it is difficult to find archaeological evidence of markets. Maya markets were probably held in open plazas, with only pole-and-thatch stands for shelter. Such a facility would leave little trace for the archaeologist to find. A more permanent facility, an enclosed quadrangle of multi-doorway structures, has been proposed as the location for the central market at Tikal. Near the intersection of several causeways, it is easily accessible. However, there is no direct evidence to prove that these structures were used as a marketplace.

Highland capitals such as Iximche and Utatlan may also have had permanent plaza areas for the market, and government officials to enforce rules, settle disputes, and collect taxes. Larger markets probably even had facilities to house foreign merchants. Well-organized markets, with designated areas for various commodities like those of the Aztecs, had an advantage in attracting more buyers and sellers, thus contributing to the prosperity of the entire community.

Beyond the local level, the Maya have always traded a variety of products to more distant destinations. The traditional **Trade** trade networks in the Maya highlands are maintained by in- **Networks** dividual traders who buy products in one area; carry loads of goods on their backs, secured by tumplines (cords running from the backpack around the forehead); and then sell in another area. Similar individual traders undoubtedly operated in the past. The Spaniards also found wealthy elite merchants who managed the transportation and distribution of goods overland and via waterways. On land, teams of porters transported cargoes on their backs (the Maya did not utilize beasts of burden or wheeled vehicles). On the rivers and lakes, and along the seacoasts, goods were carried by fleets of canoes.

A network of trade routes kept the ancient Maya in contact with neighboring societies throughout Mesoamerica. Trade networks were a conduit not only for goods but also for the movement of people and ideas. Indeed, the management of people to acquire, transport, and distribute goods required organizations. Control of at least some of these organizations was in the hands of the elite for whom the economy was an instrument of power. How effectively the elite used their economic power influenced the ebb and flow in the fortunes of each polity and the prosperity of their inhabitants.

The Maya and other societies in Mesoamerica were never united by a single political system, but they were integrated by commerce. Both archaeological evidence and documents (such as surviving native tribute lists and Spanish accounts) indicate a complex system of trade routes throughout Mesoamerica. Goods were exchanged by bartering (one type of goods exchanged for another) or by payment with cacao beans, which had uniform value.

Two kinds of trade are usually distinguished: utilitarian (food and tools) and nonutilitarian (ritual, wealth, and status goods). Generally speaking, utilitarian goods were handled by the nonelite and were not traded great distances—except for some products that were only available in a few areas, such as metates made from volcanic stone. Trade over great

Table 3
Important Trade Goods from the Maya Area

Utilitarian Goods		
Pacific Plain	*Highlands*	*Lowlands*
Agricultural products	Agricultural products	Agricultural products
Balsam	Hematite	Cotton
Cotton	Manos & metates	Flint
Dyes & pigments	Obsidian	Lime (plaster) Flint
Fish & sea products	Pottery	Pottery
Pottery	Salt	Salt
Salt	Talc	Shell
Shell	Textiles	Sugar (honey & wax)
Tobacco	Volcanic ash	Textiles
Nonutilitarian Goods		
Pacific Plain	*Highlands*	*Lowlands*
Bark paper	Amber	Bark paper
Cacao	Cinnabar (mercury)	Cacao
Feathers	Feathers (esp. Quetzal)	Copal
Shark teeth	Jadeite	Coral
Spondylus shell	Pyrite (mirrors)	Feathers
Stingray spines	Serpentine	Jaguar pelts & teeth

distances, such as between central Mexico and the Maya lowlands, was most often devoted to nonutilitarian goods. Certain critical resources with limited and specific sources, such as obsidian, served both utilitarian needs as tools and nonutilitarian purposes in bloodletting rituals. Restricted use of certain nonutiliarian goods—those with special purposes for religious ritual or as symbols of superior status—helped define social differences. Control by the elite class over items such as jade, magnetite (used for mirrors), and feathers marked and reinforced their elevated status.

Trade that supplied the populous Mexican states with goods from Central America and beyond had to pass through the Maya area. This enabled Maya merchants to control much of the commerce and become an important part of Mesoamerican long-distance trade networks. The Maya area was also blessed with critical resources that not only could be used by local inhabitants but could be traded throughout Mesoamerica (Table 3). Some goods were traded to even more distant areas: pyrite mirrors and macaw feathers from the Maya area have been found as far north as the southwestern United States.

The Maya area was economically linked by many overland north-south trade routes. At the same time the longest routes ran generally east-west, linking the cities in Mexico, the Maya area, and beyond into Central America. Many of the earliest routes appear to have been land-based, including those that connected the Gulf coast with the Mexican highlands and those that ran eastward along the Pacific coastal plain to the resources in the Maya highlands and Central America. Other routes extended more directly east-west through the Maya lowlands, using both land and river-canoe transport. These could reach the resources in the Maya highlands via the Usumacinta River, and in Central America via the Caribbean.

During some past eras, certain societies dominated trade networks by controlling supplies of critical mate- **Consequences** rials and forming trading alliances to manage distribu- **of Trade** tion. It is possible that Olmec centers on the Gulf coast dominated commerce in jade and other status goods that came from the Maya highlands, at least for a time. Growing powers in the Maya highlands and along the Pacific coast may have competed for this trade, leading to the eventual loss of control of these status goods by the Olmec. One reason for the growth of several centers of Early Maya civilization, especially Kaminaljuyu and El Mirador, was undoubtedly the control of trade goods and routes. During Middle Maya civilization a series of states dominated segments of the Mesoamerican economy, including the great city of Teotihuacan in central Mexico, which controlled several major sources of obsidian. At the same time, the highland power of Kaminaljuyu controlled much of the Maya trade in obsidian and was probably allied to Teotihuacan. Concurrently, Tikal and Calakmul inherited the position of El Mirador in controlling east-west trade across the lowlands. During Late Maya civilization a succession of powers, beginning with Chichen Itza, controlled important segments of trade in the Maya area and in parts of Mesoamerica until the Spanish Conquest.

Eventually the rise of sea trade based on larger and more efficient canoes expanded the water routes around the Yucatan peninsula at the expense of many trans-lowland routes. Water transport was an ancient tradition among the Maya. Canoes followed riverine routes across the lowlands and exploited the islands off the eastern coast of Belize and the coastal margins of Yucatan. But the Putun Maya, from their homeland along the Gulf coast of Tabasco, rose to power largely through their control over seacoast commerce. The key to the Putun Maya's prosperity and power was their strategic location and the development of large seagoing canoes capable of transporting huge loads of goods at less cost than by land. A single large seagoing canoe could carry more goods and needed less manpower than land-based porters or even river craft, which required large crews for portages.

We know far more about Maya trade at the time of the Spanish Conquest due to the accounts written by Europeans. One famous encounter with a Maya trading canoe off the northern coast of Honduras near the Bay Islands was recorded by Columbus on his fourth voyage. The canoe was described as being as long as a European galley and 8 feet wide, with a cabin amidships and a crew of some two dozen men, plus its captain and assorted women and children. It carried a cargo of cacao, copper bells and axes, pottery, cotton clothing, and *macanas* (wooden swords set with obsidian blades).

The rise of sea trade resulted in profound changes for Maya society. It may even have contributed to the decline of the southern lowland cities, especially those (like Tikal) that were located far inland and dependent on the older trans-Peten trade. But cause and effect in past societies are not always clear. It is also possible that the breakdown of Middle Maya civilization disrupted the older riverine and land-based trade routes, thereby giving rise to seacoast commerce. At any rate, it appears that during Late Maya civilization sea trade created a shift in settlement toward the seacoasts of the Yucatan peninsula.

Even though sea trade was critically important to the economy of Late Maya civilization in Yucatan, porter-borne overland trade continued. Following the Conquest, Maya coastal trade soon disappeared. During the sixteenth and seventeenth centuries, unconquered Maya groups such as the Tayasal Itza maintained a vestigial overland trade network through the central and southern lowlands. Because of the terrain, overland trade has always been primary in the Maya highlands. Today, the last vestiges of traditional Maya commerce are being replaced by modern transport with bus and trucks, and traditional Maya markets are being replaced by supermarkets.

PRINCIPAL PUBLISHED SOURCES

Flannery 1982; Freidel and Sabloff 1984; Harrison and Turner 1978; Hirth 1984; Jones 1977; Sheets 1983.

8

Maya Society

Although their ancient civilization is gone, the Maya people and their cultural tradition continue in today's world despite 500 years of conquest, disease, and oppression at the hands of Europeans who first invaded and then took over most of their homeland. What we know about the organization and lifeways of ancient Maya society comes mostly from indirect sources, for the Maya's own writings say little about this subject. What *is* recorded deals almost exclusively with kings and the elite class; nothing is said about the majority of ancient Maya society, the common people. Thus in reconstructing all levels of ancient Maya society we rely on ethnohistorical sources, that is, records made after the Spanish Conquest either as transcriptions of Maya documents or as accounts written by Europeans. We also rely on archaeological interpretations of the surviving remains of ancient Maya houses, palaces, temples, burials, middens (refuse heaps), and other features that have been excavated.

Before describing these sources of information and what they can tell us about past Maya society, we discuss one of the most important traditions that define the Maya as a people: their languages.

MAYAN LANGUAGES AND GROUPS

In the Maya area today live at least 4 million people who speak one of the 28 closely related languages that make up the Mayan family of languages (the term *Mayan* is used to refer to the languages spoken by

Maya people). Although most of these people also speak Spanish (the official language of Mexico, Guatemala, and Honduras) or English (the official language of Belize), their native language continues to define them as Maya people, holders of a proud cultural tradition.

The various Mayan languages are similar because they are descended from one ancestral language spoken thousands of years ago. Scholars who study the process of language divergence estimate that the ancestral Mayan language was spoken earlier than 2000 B.C., or about the time the Maya first settled in permanent communities. After this time the ancestral language began to separate into three major subgroups: Southern Mayan, Yucatecan, and Huastecan. These subgroups became distinct between ca. 2000 B.C. and A.D. 100, during the era of Early Maya civilization. Although the process of divergence has continued to the present, producing the many language differences of today, most Mayan languages have remained in contact with each other and often blend into each other just like the environmental zones of the Maya area.

Using comparisons among languages today, scholars can reconstruct aspects of the ancestral language. In such cases the meanings of reconstructed words can tell us about early society and culture. For example, the ancestral Mayan language had a rich vocabulary for weaving and farming, indicating these were important activities. Maize agriculture, in particular, had separate words for generic maize, the green ear, the mature ear, the cob, three stages of maize flour, maize dough, the tortilla, a maize drink, and the maize grinding stone.

Similar research has identified languages spoken in the southern lowlands during the era of Middle Maya civilization. This has long been an issue of debate, because the vast region—the central Peten and upper Usumacinta drainage—was largely depopulated by the time of the Europeans' arrival. Evidence from Classic period texts at the southernmost sites such as Palenque, Dos Pilas, Aguateca, and Copan shows that closely related languages of the Southern Mayan subgroup, known as Cholan, were spoken at these sites. But further north in the southern lowlands, texts at Tikal, Piedras Negras, Bonampak, Yaxchilan, Seibal, and Naranjo indicate that Yucatec Mayan, the primary member of the Yucatecan subgroup, was spoken at these cities. Thus it appears that the Maya lowlands was populated by speakers of several Mayan languages at the time of Middle Maya civilization.

ETHNOHISTORICAL SOURCES

After the Conquest the Spaniards taught Maya scribes to use the Spanish alphabet to write their own languages. This allowed the Maya to transcribe many of their own older documents, histories, prophecies, myths, rituals, and the like. Although only four pre-Columbian Maya books are known today, many additional colonial period transcriptions have survived. These documents were often recopied over the years, but they provide an invaluable source of information about ancient Maya society.

The most important transcriptions come from Yucatan and the Maya highlands. From Yucatan we have several of the *Books of Chilam Balam* ("Books of the Jaguar Shaman"). These were kept by local religious leaders in many towns of Yucatan. Of those that have survived, the most important are the *Books of Chilam Balam* of the towns of Mani, Tizimin, Chumayel, Kaua, Ixil, and Tusik. They include historical chronicles known as the *u kahlay katunob*, or "count of the katuns" (the Maya period of 20 360-day years), which reconcile past events with prophecy and the Maya belief in the cyclic nature of history. Also from Yucatan we have a variety of colonial Spanish compilations of information about the Maya. The most important are Bishop Diego de Landa's *Relación de las cosas de Yucatán* (a sixteenth-century "ethnography" describing many facets of Maya life), and the *Diccionario de Motul*, a colonial dictionary of the Yucatec Mayan language.

From the highlands of Guatemala we have the history of the Quiche Maya recorded in the *Popol Vuh* ("Book of the Mat"). The most outstanding surviving Maya literary work, it preserves the mythology and traditional history of one of the most powerful peoples of the highlands (see Chapter 6). The elegance and style of the *Popol Vuh* is sad evidence of the loss the Maya and the rest of the world have suffered through the destruction of most of the original Maya books during the colonial period. Also from the highlands come the *Annals of the Cakchiquels* (a shorter history of the Cakchiquel state) and the *Rabinal Achi* (a Quiche dance-drama).

These and related documents are priceless sources of information about Maya language, history, social and political institutions, religion, and other aspects of the vanished ways of life. For example, from documents we know that Mayan languages in colonial times had well-developed vocabularies for personal names, hereditary and occupational titles, and titles of place of origin. Mayan languages did not distinguish gender by pronouns, as does English, but they did so in titular expressions and in kinship terms. Some of the earliest colonial dictionaries were the most comprehensive; these preserve terms that have been lost in the spoken languages since the colonial era. Studies of preserved vocabularies tell a great deal about ancient Maya kinship terminology and organization, numerical systems, botanical and zoological nomenclatures, and color terms.

Of course, the Maya of today also preserve many ancient traditions. Thus the Maya themselves can teach us about their past. Overall, our understanding of ancient Maya society is based on many kinds of research: archaeology, epigraphy, ethnohistory, and ethnography. Archaeology can enhance our knowledge through settlement studies. Settlement archaeology defines the geographical distribution of the remains of ancient occupation, from the smallest house to the largest city. The distribution and patterning of remains reflect ancient social, political, and environmental relationships. For the Maya, archaeological research is complemented by ancient texts that include accounts of the alliances, marriages, and kin-based relationships of Maya kings.

SIZE AND ORGANIZATION OF MAYA SOCIETY

The location and size of all human settlements are determined by availability of critical resources such as water, good agricultural soils, wood, and other natural materials. Patterns of settlement allow us to reconstruct ancient social organizations. For instance, information about the size and organization of a Maya family can be obtained by studying the patterns of remains from households—cooking vessels, utensils, storage and disposal areas, and the size and shape of the houses themselves.

Moreover, the patterning of all household remains within a village or city reflects the social ties that once defined the community. Patterns of houses and differences in size, elaborateness, or type of construction reflect aspects of social organization. And patterns of houses in relation to nonresidential buildings (temples, storage facilities, administrative structures, etc.) provide information about political organization.

Population Reconstructions To understand how past Maya society was organized, we need to determine the size of the population; how many people made up a typical family, or how many people lived in Maya villages, towns, and cities. Archaeological studies of population size begin by identifying and counting houses or other features that reflect size of population. Ancient houses are identified by the remains that over the years have formed low but distinctive mounds. At some sites, population can be estimated from the number and size of water storage facilities (wells, cisterns, or reservoirs). Regardless of what is counted, there is always an unknown proportion of features that have been completely destroyed or gone undetected. At Maya sites it is estimated that the actual number of ancient houses ranges anywhere from 10 to 100 percent greater than the total identified through archaeological study.

Reconstructing ancient population size from archaeological remains provides only approximations. Nonetheless, the results of settlement studies at lowland Maya sites gives a basis for comparing the numbers and densities of structures at these sites. Such studies reveal that lowland sites usually vary between 200 and 450 houses per sq. km. Central Copan is outside of this range, having the greatest constructional density of any Maya site (1,450 structures/sq. km), due to the unusually close confinement of the Copan Valley. Mayapan shows the second highest density (996 structures/sq. km), in this case due to crowding within its defensive wall. At the low end of settlement density are both Quirigua (129/sq. km) and Uaxactun (124/sq. km).

To estimate population on the basis of house counts, we need to know the average number of people in a Maya family. Census figures from shortly after the Conquest show that in several Maya communities the size of the family ranged from 5 to 10 people. Ethnographic studies show that average traditional Maya families today number between 4.9 and 6.1 people.

To arrive at population estimates for Maya cities for which settlement data are available, a reasonable average of 5.5 people per family can be used. These figures show that Tikal was the largest surveyed lowland city, with a Late Classic peak of some 65,000 people within the site proper (defined by the 120 sq. km area bounded on the north and south by earthworks, and east and west by swamps, or *bajos*). The rural hinterland (an area within a 10 km radius of the site center) was occupied by about 30,000 more people, giving "greater Tikal" a population of between 90,000 and 100,000 people during the Late Classic. For comparison, "greater Copan" was about one-quarter the size of Tikal, with an estimated peak population of 20,000–25,000 people during the same period. These are estimated population sizes for cities, not total polities. Because there is no way to gauge the size of political territories, the total number of people who were subjects of the kings of Tikal, Copan, or any other Classic Maya capital remains unknown.

Recent studies of lowland Maya settlement between cities shows that the rural areas also supported large numbers of people. For example, the hinterland in the Central Lakes region of the Peten supported about 190 people per sq. km during the Late Classic. This means that at its peak, occupation density in parts of the southern lowlands was comparable to areas of China and Java, the most densely settled preindustrial societies of the world. Such high population density illuminates the pressure exerted on the lowland environment and the critical role of over-exploitation in leading to the drastic decline of Middle Maya civilization.

These reconstructions also show the patterns of growth and decline of population through time. Two peaks of highest population are apparent: one at the end of Early Maya civilization (ca. A.D. 250) and another at the end of Middle Maya civilization (ca. A.D. 800). The later peak was far higher than the former. Both were followed by population decreases, but the one following the decline of Middle Maya civilization was the most severe. Research has also shown that substantial occupation continued after A.D. 800 (Late Maya civilization) in some southern lowland areas, notably the Central Lake regions and many regions of Belize.

The Organization of Maya Settlement Low mounds can usually be recognized as the remains of ancient Maya houses. These are the remnants of low earthen or rubble platforms that once supported oblong or rectangular houses of one or more rooms. The ancient Maya house *(na)* was very much like those in use today. Some were built with stone or adobe (mud) walls roofed with pole and thatch; others were built entirely of perishable pole and thatch. They were about the same size as modern Maya houses; like today, they undoubtedly sheltered a nuclear family—wife, husband, and children.

In the past there was more variation in house materials and size based on status. Houses of the Maya elite were much larger than those of the common people and were often built completely of masonry blocks, had vaulted roofs, and were supported by higher masonry platforms. The houses of Maya kings were so large and elaborate that they are usually referred to as palaces.

The remains of ancient Maya houses often reflect the range of past household activities. These include food storage, preparation, and cooking (chultunes, manos and metates, flint or cutting obsidian tools, hearths, and even food remains). Houses were also used for craft manufacturing, with workshop areas where textiles were woven, pottery was made, and chipped-stone tools and a variety of other products were produced. When family members died, they were usually buried beneath the house. The sudden volcanic eruption that buried a Middle Maya civilization village at Cerén, El Salvador, provides a rare view of the buildings, tools, and activities within a rural Maya community as they were at the moment of the disaster. Careful excavation of the buried areas at Cerén have exposed several adobe houses and even the charred remains of their pole-and-thatch roofs, outbuildings, workshops, storage areas, household articles, and adjacent fields where maize and a variety of crops were grown (see p. 103).

Maya houses are seldom found in isolation. Most often they are in clusters *(nalil)* of from two to six units arranged around a central patio. Based on similar situations in modern Maya communities, we can assume these nalil were occupied by an extended family, that is, two or more related nuclear families. The extended family groupings are often composed of grandparents, parents, and married children living in separate but adjacent houses. The head of the extended family may be indicated by the largest or most elaborate house in the group. Ancillary buildings—used for storage, workshops, or other purposes—may be included. A repeated pattern in the nalil clusters at Tikal consists of a central patio bordered on three sides by houses and a smaller but higherplatformed building on the east side. This was probably the extended family's household shrine, where the founder of the residential group was buried and which serves as the focus of rituals to venerate the important ancestor.

Clusters of nalil often form wards or barrios *(china)*. These may have been occupied by larger kin groups, such as lineages. But not all residents of the typical china may have belonged to the lineage. Some houses may have been occupied by retainers, servants, and other clients of lineage members.

Although they could be organized in various ways, the sum total of people living together in one place defined the *cah*, or Maya community. The cah could be of any size, from the smallest agricultural village *(chan cah)* to the largest political capital *(noh cah)*. Yet even the largest Maya cities included the same residential components—some much larger and more complex than others, of course. At the heart of a capital such as Tikal was the *noh nalil* (palace complex) of the royal family, along with those of the other elite extended families. The larger Maya cities also included many more public buildings and facilities than the smaller communities. Regardless of its size, the cah was the setting for the organizations that gave society its basic structure. Many were based on kinship: nuclear family, extended family, and lineage bonds.

THE INDIVIDUAL LIFE CYCLE

The day-to-day activities and the entire life cycle of each person was set by custom and governed by religious beliefs, much as they are among the Maya of today. The Maya kept their lives in harmony with their world—their family, their community, and their gods. The key to this harmony was the calendar that tracked the cycles of time, beginning with the 260-day sacred almanac (discussed in Chapter 11). Every person's destiny, from birth to death, was tied to his almanac.

The date of each person's birth in the 260-day almanac had different attributes—some good, some neutral, some bad. In this way each person's birth date controlled his or her temperament and destiny. To this day many highland peoples, such as the Cakchiquel Maya, are named after their date of birth in the 260-day almanac. In Yucatan at the time of the Spanish Conquest, each child's *paal kaba*, or given name, was determined by a divining ceremony conducted by a shaman. Like Americans and Europeans, the Maya are given multiple names. In Yucatan these are the paal kaba, the father's family name, the mother's family name, and an informal nickname.

Childhood

Children are greatly desired and receive a great deal of love and affection by the Maya. At the time of the Conquest, women would ask the gods for children by giving offerings, reciting special prayers, and placing an image of Ix Chel, the goddess of childbirth, under their beds. Today, having many children is seen as beneficial and as security for the family. Sons assist their fathers in the fields, and older daughters assist their mothers in taking care of younger sisters and brothers. Children take care of their parents in their old age. These roles were probably little different in the past.

The Maya still perform ceremonies marking a child's acceptance into society. In Yucatan this ceremony is the *hetzmek*, performed when the baby is carried astride the mother's hip for the first time. For girls the hetzmek is held at three months; for boys, at four months. The girl's age of three months symbolizes the three stones of the Maya hearth, an important focus of a woman's life. The boy's age of four months symbolizes the four sides of the maize field, the important focus of a man's life. Participants in the ceremony, besides the infant, are the parents and another husband and wife who act as sponsors. The child is given nine objects symbolic of his or her life and is carried on the hip nine times by both sponsoring parents. The ceremony closes with offerings and a ritual feast.

In colonial Yucatan, and today, children are raised by their mothers until the age of 3 or 4. At about age 4, girls were given a red shell that was tied to a string around their waists. At the same age, boys received a small white bead that was fastened to their hair. Both symbols of childhood were worn until puberty, when another ceremony marked the transition to adulthood.

There is no evidence that the ancient Maya had formal schools. But it is certain that children selected on the basis of social status or aptitude were trained for specialized roles in society by an apprentice system. Scribes, priests, artists, masons, and other occupational groups recruited novices and trained them. Today, among some highland Maya peoples, shamans continue to recruit and train the future generation of specialists. In all Maya communities the girls learn women's roles from their mothers throughout childhood, doing household chores, buying and selling in the market, and assisting with specialized activities such as making pottery or weaving textiles. Boys are taught by their fathers the skills of farming, hunting, fishing, and other male tasks.

Adolescence   In colonial Yucatan the 260-day almanac was consulted to select an auspicious day for the community puberty ceremony marking the end of childhood and the beginning of adulthood. It was held every few years for all children deemed ready to take this step. The ceremony was conducted by a shaman; four assistant shamans, or *chacs* (after the Maya rain god); and a respected elder man of the community. The parents, children, and their sponsors assembled in the patio of the community elder's house, which was purified by a ritual conducted by the shaman. The patio was swept and covered by fresh leaves and mats.

After the chacs placed pieces of white cloth on the children's heads, the shaman said a prayer for the children and gave a bone to the elder, who used it to tap each child nine times on the forehead. The shaman used a scepter decorated with rattlesnake rattles to anoint the children with sacred water, after which he removed the white cloths from their heads. The children then presented offerings of feathers and cacao beans to the chacs. The shaman cut the white beads from the boys' hair, and the mothers removed the red shells from their daughters' waists. Pipes of tobacco were smoked, and a ritual feast of food and drink closed the ceremony. After this both the girls and boys were considered adults and eligible to marry.

Until they married, young women continued to live with their parents and were expected to follow the customs of modesty. When unmarried women met a man, they turned their backs and stepped aside to allow him to pass. When giving a man food or drink, they were to lower their eyes. In colonial times the young unmarried men of the community lived in a house set apart for them; this was probably an ancient custom. They painted themselves black until they were married but did not tattoo themselves until after marriage.

In colonial times marriages were often arranged between families while the boy and girl were still very young. The wedding took place when they came of age, usually when the couple was around 20 years old. Today in most Maya communities the average age of men at marriage is about **Adulthood and Marriage** the same, and the average age of women at marriage is 16 or 17 years.

In colonial Yucatan it was customary for a father to approve of the prospective spouse for his son, being careful that the young woman was of the same social class and of the same village. According to marriage taboos it was incestuous to marry a girl who had the same surname, or for a widower to marry the sister of his deceased wife or the widow of his brother. However, because they would always have different surnames, cross-cousin marriages were fairly common (marriage between the children of a brother and sister). A professional matchmaker (*ah atanzahob*) was often hired to make the arrangements, plan the ceremony, and negotiate the amount of the dowry, a custom that survives in some Maya communities today.

For the dowry the groom's father usually provided dresses and household articles for the bride, and the groom's mother made clothing for both her son and prospective daughter-in-law. Today in Yucatan, the groom or his family usually covers the expenses of the wedding, including the bride's trousseau.

The wedding ceremony was traditionally held at the house of the bride's father. It was performed by a shaman, who began the ceremony by explaining the details of the marriage agreement. After this he burned incense and blessed the new couple. Everyone enjoyed a special feast that concluded the ceremony.

Monogamy was and remains the most common form of marriage, but in pre-Columbian times polygyny (multiple wives) was permitted. Because of its greater economic demands, it was probably much more widespread among the elite than the nonelite. Divorce was uncomplicated, consisting of a simple repudiation by either party. By custom, widowers and widows remained single for at least a year after the death of their spouses. They could then remarry without ceremony; the man simply went to the house of the woman of his choice; and if she accepted him and gave him something to eat, they were considered married.

After the marriage the groom lived and worked in the house of his wife's parents (uxorilocal residence). His mother-in-law ensured that her daughter gave her husband food and drink as a token of the parental recognition of the marriage; but if the young man failed to work, he could be put out of the house. After a period of no more than six or seven years the husband would build a new house adjacent to that of his father and move his new family there (patrilocal residence). According to ethnohistorical sources, the family slept in one room on mats set on low platforms of poles. Today in the highlands mats are still used, although hammocks are often favored in the hotter lowland regions.

Roles of Men and Women

Although archaeological evidence for gender roles in the Maya past is sparse, we can reconstruct some role differences on the basis of present-day society. We can assume that in the past, as today, girls were trained to take on the traditional roles associated with wife and mother in the Maya family. In nonelite families they undoubtedly played an essential part in subsistence by collecting firewood, wild foods, and condiments. We can also assume that the processing and preparation of food was the responsibility of women. In addition, nonelite women probably engaged in a variety of household crafts, weaving textiles for clothing and making containers of pottery, gourds, and other materials. Women probably took surplus food and goods to local markets, where they exchanged them for other products. It can also be assumed that women undertook several community-level specializations, such as being midwives and matchmakers. Finally, we can assume that many nonelite women served as cooks and servants for the noble and royal families within each kingdom.

Beyond this we do not know how many occupations were open to women in the past. But at the elite level of society we know from both the texts and portraits of Middle Maya civilization that the wives and mothers of royalty played essential roles in the rituals and other duties of Maya kings. Mothers of kings were vital to the ceremonies held for the designation of the heir to the throne and at the inauguration of the new ruler. The royal histories of Palenque record that two royal daughters assumed the throne in the absence of a male heir and held the position of ruler until their sons were old enough to become king.

We can also assume that nonelite Maya boys were trained to take on the traditional roles associated with husband and father. They played another essential part in provisioning the family by hunting and trapping animals, fishing, and tilling the fields. Men also probably engaged in a variety of household crafts, making basalt grinding stones and obsidian cutting tools, for example. Outside the home it can be assumed that men took on a variety of roles. Most men were obliged to provide a portion of their time and labor to their community and king. Like women, many nonelite men must have been servants to noble or royal families. During the dry season when their agricultural duties were minimal, the men of each lineage were recruited to help construct and maintain buildings, causeways, reservoirs, and other essential facilities. Of course, in time of war they were also called to serve in the lower ranks as soldiers. Some men probably became peddlers and merchants, engaged in manufacturing specializations, or became shamans or priests. The various low-level political offices were filled by the men of each community selected on the basis of their abilities or kin ties.

Elite men held the multitude of upper-level political and religious offices in each Maya kingdom, advancing according to age and ability within the governmental or priestly hierarchy. Other elite occupations were probably concerned with economic affairs, such as collecting and recording tribute, managing plantations for growing valuable crops such as cacao, or directing major trading expeditions over land or water. Warfare also created roles for elite men in positions of military command. In addition, certain elite men became artists, artisans, and scribes, sometimes even signing their names to their works.

The Maya marked social status through personal appearance, clothing, and adornments. One way of doing this **Personal** was to alter their physical appearance. For example, **Appearance** crossed eyes were considered a mark of beauty for the ancient Maya. In colonial times mothers induced crossed eyes by tying little balls of resin to their children's hairs so they would hang between their eyes. Other marks of beauty included piercing the ears, lips, and septum of the nose to hold a variety of ornaments that indicated the individual's status. Flattened foreheads were also considered a mark of beauty and status. This was done by binding babies' heads between a pair of boards, one at the back of the head, the other against the forehead. These were left in place for several days. Once the cranial bones had set, the desired flattened appearance remained for life. Carved and painted representa-

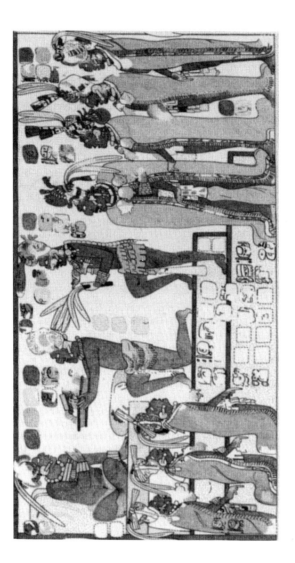

The costumes and adornments worn by elite Maya men are often depicted in Maya art; this scene depicts the presentation of tribute to the king and is on a painted pottery vessel from a royal tomb at Tikal, Guatemala. (Courtesy of Tikal Project, University of Pennsylvania Museum)

tions of profile heads show that this practice was often used in the past to indicate elite status.

Clothing marked gender and status differences among the ancient Maya. Men wore loincloths *(ex)*, a band of cotton cloth that went between the legs and was wrapped around the waist. The ex is represented in Maya art, ranging from elaborately decorated examples worn by kings and other elite men, to simple, undecorated versions worn by commoners. Elite men often wore a large square of cotton cloth *(pati)* around the shoulders, elaborately decorated with different patterns, colors, and featherwork according to the wearer's status. Simple versions of the pati were worn by commoners and also served as a bed covering at night.

Men wore sandals made of untanned deer hide that were bound to the feet by two thongs, one passing between the first and second toes, the other between the third and fourth toes. The sandals worn by kings and elite men seen on carved monuments were very elaborate. Although the ex and pati are no longer worn, and today most Maya men wear Western-style clothing, many still wear sandals similar to the ancient examples (except they are tied by a single thong).

Ancient Maya men wore their hair long, usually braided and wound around the head except for a queue that hung down behind. Body paint was often used to mark special groups. Priests were painted blue, the color usually associated with sacrifice; warriors painted themselves black and red. War captives are sometimes shown painted black and white. Paint was also used in tattooing, the painted designs being cut into the skin with an obsidian knife. This was done only after marriage.

The principal garment worn by Maya women was a woven cotton skirt *(manta)*. According to Bishop Landa's colonial-era account, "The women of the coast and of the Provinces of Bacalar and of Campeche are more modest in their dress, for, besides the (skirt) which they wore from the waist down, they covered their breasts, tying a folded manta underneath their armpits" (Tozzer 1941: 126; trans. of Landa's original manuscript of ca. 1566). Women also covered their head and shoulders with a cotton shawl *(booch)*.

Today the traditional Maya women's garment is the *huipil*, a Nahuatl word from central Mexico. In the Guatemalan highlands the huipil is a blouse worn over a wrap-around skirt. Each highland community has its unique design, so a woman's home town can be recognized from the huipil she wears. In Yucatan the huipil is a white, loose-fitting cotton dress with arm holes and a square opening at the neck. Huipils are beautifully embroidered in cross-stitch. A long white petticoat *(pic)* is worn underneath to hang below the huipil. Today, Maya women often go barefoot or wear slippers of European style, but formerly they may have used sandals.

The costumes and adornments worn by elite Maya women are often depicted
in Maya art; here a group of royal women are shown in the murals from
Bonampak, Mexico. (K. Rupert, J.E.S. Thompson, & T. Proskouriakoff)

Today as in the past, women and girls wear their hair long, arranged
in various ways. Married and unmarried women each had distinctive
hair styles. Both women and men anointed themselves with a sweet-
smelling red ointment, the odor of which lasted for many days. Like
men, married women also tattooed themselves—except for their
breasts—with delicate designs.

Clothing reflected status. The costumes worn by the highest-status
men in society, Maya kings, were the most elaborate and decorated with
the symbols of supernatural power. Portraits of Classic period kings
show them wearing beautifully decorated loincloths, capes, sandals, and
huge headdresses. The belt holding the ex was adorned with jade masks
(probably derived from earlier versions that used real human trophy
heads), from which jade celts were suspended. Earlier belts often included a chain dangling a small image of a god. A large jade god mask
was often worn on the chest, along with necklaces of jade beads. Jewelry
of jade, shell, and other materials was formed into beads, pendants, and

mosaics; these were worn in the ears, nose, and lips and around the neck, arms, wrists, and ankles. The king's pati was a magnificent cape of embroidered cotton, accompanied by jaguar pelts and featherwork. On his feet the king wore elaborately decorated sandals.

Completing the royal display was a huge headdress adorned with an array of iridescent tail feathers from the sacred quetzal bird. The headdress framework was probably made of wood, including a front piece carved to represent one or more heads of Maya gods. The headdress was also adorned with mosaics and carved jades. Specialized headdresses were used by kings for special events, including one associated with warfare. On early representations the ruler wore a headband with a trilobed element, sometimes personified by three heads of the so-called jester god. At Copan, each ruler of the royal dynasty is often shown wearing a distinctive textile headdress wound like a turban.

Even commoners wore jewelry—usually simple nose plugs, lip plugs, and earrings of bone, wood, shell, or stone. Adornments worn by the elite were much more elaborate and were made of jade, stone, obsidian, coral, and shell. The most precious were delicately made mosaics and inlays. The elite also wore collars, necklaces, wristlets, anklets, and knee bands made of feathers, jade beads, shells, jaguar teeth and claws, crocodile teeth, or—in later times—gold and copper.

In Maya society each person's time and labor was critical to ensure that the daily needs of life were maintained. Once **Recreation** each family's needs were met, adults had obligations to fulfill for their king or kingdom: surplus food and other goods were given as tribute, and labor was given to build and maintain the great temples and palaces. Thus there was little leisure time for most of the Maya population, and recreation as we know it today was almost nonexistent. Even children, as soon as they were old enough to help their parents, had to put work before play.

Nothing is known about the games children played in the past; but we can assume that at least some games made use of balls made from the elastic gum of the rubber tree, cultivated and widely traded by the Maya. We can also assume that people found time between their labors to relax and enjoy themselves. Certainly the great religious feasts and festivals held periodically throughout the year broke the difficult routine of daily life. We can also assume that both children and men (when they could find free time) played various ball games.

This Maya ball game is known from both archaeological evidence and carved representations, although these tell mostly about a formal version played in the major capitals of Maya kingdoms. We speculate that a more everyday version of the game was played by nonelite people in their communities.

The formal version was played in a specially constructed ball court. One or more of these are found at most larger Maya cities, usually near the center. The ball courts have a level paved surface between two masonry platforms and an open end zone at both ends of the playing alley. In most cases there are no provisions for large crowds, although at both Copan and Quirigua the ball courts are placed near extensive stepped terraces that could have accommodated several thousand spectators. The size of the playing alley varied from court to court but was generally smaller than a baseball infield (the playing alley of the Great Ball Court at Chichen Itza, the largest known, was about the size of a football field). Most Classic period ball courts have sloping side walls, whereas most Postclassic ball courts have vertical side walls with a single vertically set stone ring placed high up at the center point of each wall (see pp. 71 and 86).

The game was played between two teams with a hard rubber ball that could be struck with the body but not the hands or feet. For protection, ball players wore special padded garb around the waist and on the head. There were at least two versions of the game.

The Classic era game was played with a large heavy ball, larger than a basketball. The rules are unknown, but it seems that the objective was to keep the ball moving back and forth between the two teams, each defending one end zone. Points were probably scored on the opposing team if they failed to properly strike the ball or if the ball landed in their end zone. The Postclassic version was played with a smaller rubber ball. The rules are also unknown, but the objective was probably similar to the Classic game. We do know from Bishop Landa's description that the game would be instantly won by the team that managed to direct the ball through one of the stone rings. This was a rare event, so much so that the winning team and its spectators could seize the clothing and possessions from the losing team and its spectators—provided they could catch them!

We also know that the Maya ball game was closely associated with religious belief and ritual. The Hero Twins of Maya myth (see Chapter 10) were expert ball players who defeated the death gods in a game. Because of this religious association, a ritual version of the ball game was played out to dramatize military victories. We can be certain that the ritual had no recreational value for the losing side! In such rituals the defeated captives, including kings on those rare occasions when a Maya ruler was captured in battle, were forced to play a ball game with the victors. The result of the contest was preordained, and after the defeated captives lost the game they were sacrificed. Defeated kings were decapitated, just as the Hero Twins decapitated the defeated death gods in the Maya myth. We actually know more about this ritualized aspect of the ball game than we know about the game itself. We assume that the original ball game played in every Maya community was a far less fatal contest.

Bishop Landa's colonial-era account describes Maya shamans "who cured with herbs and many superstitious rites. . . . The(se)   **Health** . . . physicians performed their cures by bleedings of the parts which gave pain to the sick . . . (the Maya) believed that death, sickness and afflictions came to them for their wrong doing and their sin; they had a custom of confessing themselves, when they were already sick" (Tozzer 1941: 106, 112; trans of Landa's original manuscript of ca. 1566).

As in other matters, the Maya still believe their personal well-being depends on harmony with the world about them. Illness is a sign of disharmony. When a person is ill, a shaman is summoned. Shamans use a variety of techniques to reveal the cause of illness. The prescribed cure includes measures to correct the cause of the illness discovered by the shaman—usually some harm done to another person, animal, or deity. Curing rituals include praying and burning incense, along with taking medicines made from local plants. There are many medicinal herbs and plants in the Maya area, and shamans to this day preserve an extensive knowledge of these cures. Several colonial-period Maya manuscripts list a series of illnesses and their cures, and many of these remedies are considered effective.

The Maya believed the dead went to Xibalba, the underworld beneath the earth, just as the sun did when it "died" at sunset   **Death** before being reborn each dawn. Xibalba was a place of rest, but not a paradise. There is evidence that Maya kings promoted special rituals to grant divine status to their dead predecessors. Several examples of this ritual apotheosis are recorded in Classic period texts. Once deified, it was believed that the dead kings escaped Xibalba to dwell in the sky thereafter.

Common people did not have the luxury of deification. According to Bishop Landa, the Maya expressed deep and enduring grief over the death of a loved one: "During the day they wept for them in silence; and at night with loud and very sad cries, so that it was pitiful to hear them. And they passed many days in deep sorrow. They made abstinences and fasts for the dead, especially the husband or wife" (Tozzer 1941: 129; trans. of Landa's original manuscript of ca. 1566).

The body was wrapped in a shroud and the mouth was filled with ground maize and one or more jadeite beads. Commoners were buried under the floors or behind their houses. Into the grave were placed idols of clay, wood, or stone and objects indicating the profession or trade of the deceased. Archaeologically excavated Maya burials usually contain offerings that vary according to the sex and status of the deceased but almost always include a jade bead in the mouth.

Burials of the elite were the most elaborate. Bishop Landa reports that

As in ancient times, Maya shamans continue to offer incense as part of curing rituals, as in this case from the Maya highlands.

in colonial-era Yucatan the bodies of high-status individuals were burned and their ashes placed in urns beneath temples. The construction of funerary shrines over tombs is well documented by archaeology. But although evidence of cremation is not often found, there is evidence of burial ritual involving fire. At Copan, for example, one elaborate tomb was re-entered on several occasions for rituals that included fire and smoke, and the painting of the bones with red cinnabar.

During Late Maya civilization the ruling lineage of Mayapan, the Co-com, reduced their dead to bones by boiling. The front of the skull was used as the base for a face modeled from resin, and this effigy was kept in the household shrines. Held in great veneration, on feast days offerings of food were made to them so they would remain well fed. When the Cenote of Sacrifice at Chichen Itza was dredged, a skull was recovered that had the crown cut away. The eye sockets were filled with wooden plugs, and there were remains of painted plaster on the face.

KIN GROUPS

In Maya communities today, the life and destiny of every person is bound to family, kin, community, and the supernatural world. Steps in the life cycle are marked by ritual, as they were in ancient times. This is also true of marriage, which allows the individual and his or her family to establish ties with another family group.

The nuclear family is the foundation of Maya society, but the Maya have long defined social groupings larger than the nuclear family. Membership in these groups is based on descent through the male line. Recognition of membership in patrilineal descent groups is by the father's family name, transmitted from generation to generation just as in our society. People with the same last name, therefore, are at least potentially members of the same patrilineage and thus are prohibited from marrying. More than a last name is inherited from the father; property, titles, status, and even offices may be transmitted from one generation to the next. In the past, these Maya patrilineal kin groups may have had their own patron deities and social obligations as well.

In ancient times, social and political offices were probably transmitted within patrilineal descent groups from father to son, brother to brother, or uncle to nephew. During the Classic period the succession of kings is sometimes specified as from father to son. There are also examples of younger brothers succeeding older brothers as king. But succession in even the highest offices was not according to a single inflexible rule. At some sites historical texts stress descent through both the male and female lines, as at Palenque; other sites emphasized the male line, as at Tikal and Copan. There are prominent portraits of elite women associated with kings at Piedras Negras, Yaxchilan, and several other sites, and paired male and female portraits at both Calakmul and El Peru. There are accounts of women rulers at Palenque.

A flexible system for the royal succession may have allowed the most talented individual from a very select pool (a royal lineage) to become king and may have diminished disastrous power struggles. When there was no male candidate from the patrilineage of the former king, a female member was chosen. This apparently happened twice in Palenque's history.

Archaeologists seek independent evidence to verify the deciphered accounts of ruling genealogies. For example, the histories commissioned by kings—such as Pacal at Palenque—cite the names of founders and other early members of the royal succession. As with all historical accounts, there is often reason to suspect distortions and fabrications that boost the prestige of the later kings. Yet archaeology has produced hard evidence to support the claims made by later kings about their predecessors. At Copan, for example, excavations beneath the royal Acropolis have produced the actual buildings and texts commissioned by the founding king, Yax Kuk Mo, and his son and successor. In this case at least, the kings of Copan living hundreds of years later recorded accurate accounts of the early history of their kingdom and its first rulers.

SOCIAL STRATIFICATION

Before the Europeans' arrival, Maya society was stratified into two classes: elite and nonelite. In Yucatan these were known as the *almehenob* (elite) and the *ah chembal uinicob* (commoners). Among the Quiche Maya of the highlands, the elite class was called the *ahawab* and the nonelite was called the *al c'ahol*. Social stratification means that the two groups have different rights, roles, and obligations. The most obvious distinction is based on wealth and power. In ancient Maya society, as in other stratified societies, the elite had a monopoly on wealth and power. The nonelite had little of either.

Stratified societies often define gradations of status within each class. In Maya society we are certain that the elite class was divided into positions of higher and lower status. Obviously the king held the highest position within the elite class. Of course, not all kings and their kingdoms were equal. At any point in time there were wealthy and powerful kings and polities, and there were less wealthy and powerful kings and polities.

Below the king and the royal lineage were a variety of other elite positions. Some probably were determined by lineage membership; a member of the elite class might have inherited his or her status and position in society from his father. Bishop Landa distinguished a title for priests, *ahkinob*, who were members of the elite class. The Quiche Maya distinguished several occupational groups, such as merchants *(ahbeyom)*, professional warriors *(achij)*, and estate managers *(uytzam chinamital)*.

The nonelite class was less formally ranked. Gradations in their burials and houses suggest that there were internal divisions of wealth and status. Some distinctions probably derived from occupations—for example, skilled craftsmen may have been held in higher regard than unskilled laborers. The largest occupational group were the farmers, whose toil supported both themselves and the king. Most Maya farmers worked their own land, held in common by their lineage. In some areas there was also a group of landless peasants (known as the *nimak achi* among the Quiche Maya) who worked estates owned by the elite and were inherited along with the land.

Commoners lived outside the central areas of the towns and cities, the core areas being reserved for the elite. Generally speaking, the greater the distance a family lived from the central plaza, the lower its position on the social scale.

The lowest status was that of slaves or captives owned by the elite. These were known as *p'entacob* in Yucatan or *munib* among the Quiche Maya. They included commoners captured in war, sentenced criminals, and impoverished individuals sold into slavery by their families. Elite captives were usually ritually sacrificed. Nonelite captives were either enslaved for labor or adopted by families to replace members lost to war or disease. Thieves were sentenced to be enslaved by their victims until they could pay for what they had stolen. Children of slaves were not considered slaves but were free to make their way into society based on their abilities. But unwanted orphans were often sacrificed, especially if they were the children of slave women. Slaves were usually sacrificed when their masters died so they could continue in their service after death.

All commoners had obligations to pay tribute to their rulers, their local elite lords, and the gods by offerings made through the priests. Tribute consisted of all kinds of agricultural produce, woven cotton cloth, domesticated fowl, salt, dried fish, and hunted game. The most valuable offerings were cacao, *pom* (copal) incense, honey, beeswax, jade, coral, and shells. Each commoner lineage also had an annual labor obligation, which went toward building the great temples, palaces, and other buildings as well as the causeways *(sacbeob)* that connected the principal Maya cities. Bishop Landa wrote: "The common people at their own expense made the houses of the lords (and) did their sowing for the lord, cared for his fields and harvested what was necessary for him and his household; and when there was hunting or fishing, or when it was time to get their salt, they always gave the lord his share" (Tozzer 1941: 87; trans. of Landa's original manuscript of ca. 1566).

THE DEVELOPMENT OF MAYA SOCIETY

What we know of ancient Maya society comes from documents, archaeology, and studies of Maya peoples today. Through these sources of information we can imagine the size and organization of ancient Maya society, how individuals lived, and the ways groups were defined by status and occupational specialties.

The foundation of Maya society, yesterday and today, is the nuclear family. In this kind of family today, the father or eldest male member is the authority figure; the same can be assumed for the past. But the domestic authority of the mother or eldest female member of the family is also important in the Maya social system. Not surprisingly, both the male and female lines of descent have long been important in Maya society. The clustering of houses seen at most Maya sites probably corresponds to groupings of related nuclear family residences.

Lineage was also important to Maya social organization. Lineage groups defined by patrilineal descent (patrilineages) were important in both Yucatan and the Maya highlands. Overall, Maya society was stratified into a smaller elite group that controlled most of the wealth and advantages, and a larger nonelite group of producers. Through tribute in goods and labor, the nonelite supported the elite and constructed and maintained the infrastructure of Maya cities, great and small.

Before civilization developed, Maya society was egalitarian. There were no permanent differences in status and authority except those based on age and gender. Maya communities today are also essentially egalitarian. Many are organized around a system whereby positions of authority and status are rotated among all members of the community. Each position is held for one year. By holding a different office once every few years, each individual advances with age in the community hierarchy so that the positions of highest authority are held by the elders. All levels of status and authority are shared. There is no permanent ruling class. A similar system may have operated among the ancient Maya—both before social stratification developed and even after, as the basic organization for small farming communities.

Stratified society emerged with Early Maya civilization. This may have begun as groups in the most favored locations gained wealth and power and needed to ensure that they would keep their advantageous position. Soon a pattern developed, with growing cities dominated by a small but permanent elite class along with their servants and retainers, and the outlying towns and villages almost exclusively occupied by peasant agriculturalists. The nonelite also made up the bulk of the population of the cities, living in the most humble dwellings generally located on the peripheries (except for the service personnel needed by the elite). The commoners supported the ruling class through tribute in goods and labor. In return, the elite class gave the commoners leadership, direction, and security with their knowledge of calendrics and supernatural prophecy. This knowledge gave rulers control over the times for planting and harvesting crops, thereby ensuring agricultural success for the common good of society.

In time, with continued population growth and social complexity, more groups emerged that reflected differences in wealth, authority, and status. By the time of Middle Maya civilization, many Maya cities were populated by large numbers of nonagricultural specialists representing numerous occupational groups and divisions within the two social classes. The ruling elite was subdivided into many different ranks and specialties. The same process of differentiation took hold of the nonelite as well, although the basic producers of food, the farmers, probably were always the largest group within Maya society. The division between ruling elite and commoner classes was subsequently filled by an emerging "middle" class, defined by occupational groups derived from higher-ranking commoners and lower-ranking elite. The incipient middle class included full-time occupational groups such as administrators or bureaucrats, merchants, warriors, craftsmen, architects, and artists. They probably lived close to the core of the major cities and were clients of the kings and more powerful elite. Otherwise, the core of Classic Maya cities continued to be inhabited by the ruler, his family, and other members of allied elite lineages that held the major positions in the political, religious, and economic hierarchy of society.

PRINCIPAL PUBLISHED SOURCES

Chase and Chase 1992; Edmonson 1982, 1986; Sharer 1994; Tedlock 1985; Tozzer 1941; Vogt 1969; Wilk and Ashmore 1988; Willey 1987.

9

Maya Government

The foundations of Maya society lay in ties of kinship, class, and community. Although all political organization beyond the community level was destroyed by the Spanish Conquest, most Maya communities during Early Maya civilization and throughout both Middle and Late Maya civilization were a part of larger independent Maya polities. The organizations of these larger political systems were also tied to kinship. The supreme ruler of each polity in the southern lowlands, the k'ul Ahaw ("divine king"), was a member of an elite lineage, in most cases chosen from a specific royal lineage. Maya kings usually ruled with an advisory council. By Late Maya civilization in many polities the council (multepal), composed of the heads of the major elite lineages within the state, ruled alone. Each elite lineage head held title to a specific office within the state hierarchy. Many lesser administrative offices right down to the local community level were probably passed from generation to generation within lineages.

Maya kings were very interested in advertising their achievements. The monuments, buildings, and texts they left behind provide the most explicit evidence for reconstructing the Maya political system, especially as it existed during Middle Maya civilization. But we must remember that these sources were not unbiased, being political propaganda designed to impress others with the successes and power of the king.

BASES OF POLITICAL POWER

The foundations for political power held by the Maya elite lay in the social and economic differences in the class structure of Maya society.

Because these distinctions were common to all Maya polities, other factors must account for the different degrees of power and success enjoyed by some polities over time. One factor stemmed from differences in the political organization itself. But more basically, differences in the environmental and economic potentials of each Maya settlement help explain why some cities grew to be the capitals of powerful states while others were always weaker and dominated by their more successful contemporaries.

The location and prosperity of all human settlements are conditioned by access to essential resources such as water and food, trade routes, and security in times of conflict. Thus it is no accident that the largest and most successful Maya cities were positioned to take advantage of good soils and dependable water sources. In addition, many Maya sites were located along major rivers (Yaxchilan, Piedras Negras, and Quirigua, to name only a few) that served as important communication and trade routes, besides providing water and productive alluvial soils for agriculture. El Mirador, Tikal, and Uaxactun, all located on the divide between major lowland drainage basins, were able to control the canoe portages for transport across the Peten. Most sites in this region are associated with *bajos,* shallow seasonal lakes that provided water and yielded rich harvests when modified by raised fields. Other sites, such as Cerros, Lamanai, and Tulum, are located to control seacoast trade along the eastern coast of the Yucatan peninsula.

Major resources with widespread demand influenced the location and prosperity of Maya cities. Examples include Kaminaljuyu in the southern highlands (control of obsidian), Dzibilchaltun in northern Yucatan (access to coastal salt), Colha in Belize (control of good-quality flint), Guaytan in the middle Motagua Valley (control of jadeite sources), and Quirigua in the lower Motagua Valley (control of cacao production).

Yet the location and prosperity of Maya settlements cannot be entirely explained by environmental and economic factors. Religious considerations were also critical. Cities enjoyed increased prestige from their cosmological and mythological associations, such as being an eastern capital associated with the rising sun. The locations of many Maya cities adjacent to bodies of water and caves were important because these landscape features were important in Maya cosmology—both were associated with Xibalba, the watery underworld. Maya cosmological principles are also reflected in the ways Maya sites were planned and grew through time.

Factors such as these help explain why Maya cities varied in size, arrangement, and style. The smallest covered less than a square mile; the largest, such as Tikal and Calakmul, extended over an area of some 50 square miles. The relative political and economic power held by these two cities was also evident in their elaborate buildings, their myriad monuments and hieroglyphic inscriptions, and the numerous times each was mentioned by other cities in historical texts.

Differences in size and complexity indicate that some Maya cities exerted political dominance over others. Economic, social, and political alliances provided varying degrees of control by more powerful cities over smaller centers. Dominant capitals such as Tikal sponsored the founding of colonial centers in outlying regions. Calakmul used alliances with smaller cities to nearly surround and finally defeat Tikal. The kings of many cities waged raids and open warfare to defeat their neighbors, followed by the extracting of tribute to maintain their domination.

The distribution of Maya road *(sacbe)* systems are evidence of the degree of political centralization of authority, as well as the extent of past political realms. The earliest example is the radiating causeway system that defines El Mirador's connections with its hinterland. Recent research at Caracol has discovered that this capital is connected to a series of satellite centers by causeways. The most extensive system is at Coba, where a network of roadways connects the site core with a series of outlying sites including Yaxuna some 60 miles distant, clearly reflecting the extent of Coba's ancient centralized authority.

MAYA POLITIES

The Maya were never politically unified, always being divided into numerous independent polities. But scholars have long been concerned with the factors that contributed to the growth and decline of these independent states and, in particular, how large the most successful examples grew in both territory and population. Maya sources give little direct information; the best historical information comes from the Spanish Conquest period. These sources enable scholars to reconstruct a great deal about the relationships between kingdoms and the approximate number of ancient Maya political realms at that moment in time (some 18 in Yucatan), but they offer little information about territorial boundaries and population size.

Networks of radiating causeways define the extent of political control exerted by some Maya capitals. However, determining the size of ancient Maya polities is difficult, especially when there are no records of actual boundaries. **Territorial Size** Archaeologists have attempted to estimate the extent of individual polities' territory by drawing hypothetical boundaries at the midpoints between cities. Midpoint boundary lines form polygons around each capital that define the rough limits of territorial control. But this assumes that boundaries were maintained equidistant from each capital and does not allow for differences in power between polities that would have been

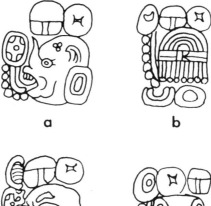

Examples of Maya Emblem Glyphs that represent
major Classic era polities: a) Copan; b) Tikal; c)
Calakmul; d) Palenque. Each is actually a royal
title that reads "divine ruler of (name of city)."

reflected in differences in territorial extent as well. The average distance
between larger sites ranges from 12 to well over 20 miles, whereas
smaller centers are found at lesser intervals. Also, the two largest southern lowland capitals, Calakmul and Tikal, maintained greater realms of
control than would be apparent from this method of estimating boundaries.

The southern lowland texts of Middle Maya civilization offer an ave-
nue for estimating the number of independent polities at various points
in time. This is done by analyzing the distribution of emblem glyphs in
the inscriptions found at many Maya cities. Emblem glyphs, royal titles
that essentially represent claims of sovereign political authority, are usually associated with Maya calendrical notations and therefore can be
dated accurately. Studies of the use of emblem glyphs as an indicator of
sovereignty show increasing numbers of independent polities over the
entire span of Middle Maya civilization. The maximum number, some
60 polities in the southern lowlands, was reached late in the eighth century. Thus we can conclude that there were many small-scale independent states by this time, the result of some 600 years of growth. But like
the polygon method, reliance on emblem glyphs cannot discriminate be-

tween degrees of power and territorial control. Nor can it differentiate between claims of sovereignty and actual independence—in some cases there may be reasons to suspect that a king who claimed to be ruler of a sovereign polity was in fact under the control of another state.

One of the oldest methods for estimating size and number of polities is based on the size rankings of sites. Studies of this kind assume that the largest sites represent capitals, the second-largest sites represent secondary administrative centers, and so forth. The clustering of size-ranked sites around each of the largest sites, which clearly represent political capitals (verified by inscriptions), suggests the political hierarchies and territorial extents of independent states. When compared to emblem glyph studies, size-ranking studies define far fewer—but far larger—regional states in the southern lowlands. Between six and eight regional states in the southern lowlands can be identified by size ranking, each greater in extent than those defined by emblem glyph distributions.

But there are problems with site-size hierarchy studies as well. Overall size is not always correlated with political capitals in preindustrial (or even modern) states. Site-size hierarchies cannot reflect important changes in the political landscape because changes in the sizes of sites are not accurately dated. Although emblem glyph distributions do reveal accurately dated patterns of change in the number and distribution of polities over time, neither type of study can detect relative differences in sovereignty and power.

Regardless of size, each of the independent Maya polities experienced growth and decline. A variety of events and circumstances contributed to the successes and failures of each kingdom. Some were internal and unique to each polity. For example, success might depend on the personal abilities and life spans of individual kings, or the efficiency of the king's administrators, or the success of local farmers and merchants in providing essential food and goods for the population. Other factors were external and involved a much wider network of relationships with other states. These included social and economic exchanges, competition, and warfare. And these were not only social, political, or economic relationships; as with most aspects of Maya culture, they were also imbued with levels of religious motivation and meaning.

Economic and Social Relationships

Maya lowland polities maintained many social and economic ties. For the most part these reflected the economic and social interactions between kingdoms, such as (1) visitations and marriage arrangements between lineages, or (2) goods and services exchanged, and tribute extracted, from one polity to another. It is likely that most social interaction, including visits and marriage alliances, occurred between people from the same or nearby communities, although some undoubtedly involved more distant regions. We know from inscriptions that Maya kings

The most vivid representation of Maya warfare comes from the Bonampak
murals; in the center of this scene we see the victorious ruler holding a spear
and grasping a captive by the hair. (K. Rupert, J.E.S. Thompson, &
T. Proskouriakoff)

used royal visits and marriage exchanges between elite families to ce-
ment alliances between polities. At the time of the Spanish Conquest,
there are records of reciprocal arrangements between Maya communities—some separated by several days' travel by foot—whereby each
town provided women marriage partners for the men living in the other
town.

       Not all interaction between Maya kingdoms was peaceful.
Warfare Warfare was an important determinant of the relative power
         and prestige of individual polities. But for most of Early and
Middle Maya civilization, conflicts were limited in scale and scope. The
most common results recorded on monuments were the taking of sacrificial captives from neighbors, used to sanctify events such as the inauguration of a ruler or the dedication of a new temple. Successes in
taking captives and gaining tribute were important for the prestige of
Maya kings; therefore warfare of this kind contributed to the growth of

royal authority, especially in establishing the power of new dynasties as the number of Maya polities expanded.

Warfare also had religious meaning. The timing and degree of success was seen as determined by the will of the gods. The most important conflicts between kingdoms were re-enacted in ritual ball games, held in the victorious city, in which the leaders of the losing side (the captives) were sacrificed after playing out the preordained scenario. The timing of the raids and the captive sacrifice rituals were scheduled to coincide with important anniversaries of past events, or with auspicious positions of the sky deities (planets), especially Venus, in keeping with Maya beliefs in predestiny and the cyclic nature of time (discussed further in Chapter 10).

However, some conflicts were motivated by more practical purposes, such as commercial rivalries. It is quite likely that Quirigua attacked and gained victory over its former master at Copan to secure independent control of the Motagua jade route. Regardless of motivation, successes in warfare often created economic prosperity. But they also created tempting targets for rival powers. Thus it is no surprise that several prominent Maya cities were fortified. Indeed, the greatest rivals of Middle Maya civilization were well defended: Tikal by earthworks and Calakmul by an encircling canal.

Warfare between Maya kingdoms clearly had several purposes. The prevailing mode was a ritualized conflict or raiding undertaken for economic and political purposes—to increase the wealth and power of the victor, and to diminish the wealth and power of the vanquished. Tribute was extracted by the winner in the form of goods and captives. But the aims and scale of warfare changed over time. Some winning kingdoms, such as the Petexbatun, expanded their territory by conquest. The reverse was also true, with new polities created by breaking away from older kingdoms, as when Quirigua gained independence from Copan. Conflict grew in intensity as competition for resources, prestige, and power increased, becoming even more frequent by the end of Middle Maya civilization. By then warfare was endemic. The wars of conquest that became even more common during Late Maya civilization undoubtedly contributed to the decline of Middle Maya civilization in the southern lowlands.

The Maya kingdoms experienced a constantly changing political landscape. Some Maya cities, obviously **The Cycles of** larger and more powerful than others, likely controlled **Political Unity** larger territories and exercised dominance over their smaller neighbors. (Chapter 5 discusses some of the best-known southern lowland polities, showing how each enjoyed one or more cycles of growth and prosperity followed by decline and depression.) Some polities expanded their realms through takeover, as Tikal did in annexing

Uaxactun and the Petexbatun did in annexing territory from its neighbors. Calakmul may have come close to unifying much of the southern lowlands under its dominion through alliance and warfare. But following Calakmul's failure to consolidate its victory and Tikal's eventual triumph over its adversary, the number of independent polities expanded once again. New capitals were founded and some formerly subordinate sites, such as Quirigua, broke away and became the capitals of independent polities.

During Late Maya civilization in the lowlands of Yucatan to the north, there was a similar ebb and flow of fortunes. Initially Yucatan fragmented into small polities until a large portion was united under the control of Chichen Itza. After its downfall, central Yucatan was dominated by a new capital at Mayapan, only to fragment again into at least 18 independent polities by the time of the Spanish Conquest. Collectively these trends can be seen as fluctuations between times of political consolidation (fewer and larger polities) and times of political fragmentation (more numerous and smaller polities).

POLITIES DURING MIDDLE AND LATE MAYA CIVILIZATION

The earliest monuments and texts indicate that rule by powerful individual kings *(ahaw)* began during the era of Early Maya civilization in the southern area. By the beginning of Middle Maya civilization the kings were also in power throughout the lowlands, where they took on the title of *k'ul Ahaw*, or "divine (or supreme) ruler." In the royal inscriptions later kings often referred to the earliest ruler in each polity as a "founder" and counted the line of succession from this hallowed individual. Especially successful kings accumulated additional titles honoring their achievements in battle ("captor of . . ."), their age ("four katun lord"), and their identification with supernatural powers ("sun or sun-faced lord"). The elite class and the various secondary offices held by elite men grew in numbers. The hierarchy of authority continued to expand, and in some Maya states the king designated subordinates with formal titles such as *Cahal* or *Sahal* ("subordinate ruler").

An overriding feature of Maya state organization was the reliance on kinship ties for lines of authority that radiated out from the king and his elite council to the hinterlands. These lines were enforced by economic and religious factors. The ruler and his elite officials provided security and protection for their subjects, but people were also motivated to be obedient because they received economic and religious benefits as a result. From the king on down, officials rewarded good deeds with gifts of food and goods. Religious belief reinforced the system by holding that everyone's success and health depended on staying in harmony with the

Maya kings, in this case Cauac Sky of Quirigua
who defeated Copan in A.D. 738, are usually
portrayed as magestic figures accompanied by the
symbols of their political and religious powers
(costuming, headdresses, and scepters).

Maya universe, an important part of which meant obeying the king and
his officials. Sanctions for disobedience would be loss of economic benefits and the wrath of the gods, bringing misfortune and even death.

In Maya government there was less authority based on true political
power than is common in today's world. Maya kings had less ability to
do physical harm to those who disobeyed than is found in modern industrial states. Political power in most modern states is based on the
threat or use of coercive force through laws, courts, and police dedicated
to the enforcement of authority. The Maya state relied instead on economic and religious sanctions—although we can be sure that when all
else failed, severe punishments were given to individuals who dis-
pleased the king.

By the same token, the authority and prestige of each Maya king depended on the economic and supernatural success of his polity. Power was transmitted by promoting economic benefits, agricultural success, and ready access to markets and religion—especially the sponsoring of public ceremonies that were believed to ensure favor from the gods. Of course, such bases of power are less reliable than more overt and coercive measures. Agricultural failures could weaken a king's prestige and cripple his ability to bestow favors on officials and subjects. Disasters such as a defeat in war could undermine the authority of the king and his royal lineage by being interpreted as the anger of the gods. As a result the Maya political landscape was composed of many relatively unstable and competitive kingdoms that were dependent on each other because they shared cultural values, subsistence technology, economic systems, and religious beliefs.

Each polity had a capital where the king, his court, and the advisory council lived. A loose hierarchy of subordinate centers surrounded the capital. The size of the kingdom, and the number of subordinate centers, shifted over time according to the personal success of each king in promoting his followers' loyalty or defeating his neighbors in war. At the same time, some of the more self-sufficient subordinate centers attempted to break free of the control of the capital or shift their alliances to other centers, especially when a weak king was on the throne. Aggressive and powerful kings attempted to expand or centralize their power, which often created further instability in the system. For example, Calakmul used a network of alliances to defeat Tikal, its chief rival. Tikal's fortunes were at low ebb until an especially effective and powerful king took power and defeated its former enemies.

In a government where the power and success of each polity was dependent on the personal performance of its king, a Maya ruler had to be a successful war leader, a successful diplomat to organize alliances, and a successful religious leader to conduct successful ceremonies. He also had to personally control his subordinates, especially in the collection of tribute in goods and labor. Thus it was the charismatic leadership qualities of the king more than anything else that allowed a Maya polity to expand and prosper.

This kind of political system has an obvious weakness. The personal failures of the king, whether caused by inability or bad luck, could bring misfortune to the entire kingdom. Most critical, the capture and execution of a king by a rival could mean subjugation or complete takeover of the defeated polity. One case in point was the aggressive kings of the Petexbatun kingdom who conquered more and more territory by defeating and beheading their rivals, until the tables were turned. When Tikal and Palenque lost kings to their enemies, even though they remained too powerful to be completely subjugated, both polities suffered declines—far more serious in the case of Tikal. In other cases, as when the former subordinate ruler of Quirigua captured and beheaded the king of Copan, the result was political independence for Quirigua and a severe blow to the prosperity and prestige of Copan. Even though the Copan kingdom eventually regained prestige and power, the power of its kings never recovered from this defeat. The power vacuum was filled by the elite lineage heads of the *multepal*, or advisory council, who assumed more power in the wake of the defeat.

When an ever-increasing number of Maya kings failed to solve the problems of overpopulation, degradation of the environment, and escalating violence, their prestige and power rapidly evaporated. By the end of Middle Maya civilization, the problems in many areas of the southern lowlands were severe beyond recovery. Even in less devastated regions, such as Yucatan and the highlands, the old system of divine kings was discredited and a new political order emerged. The new political order relied less on the personal achievements and charisma of the king and more on the collective wisdom of the *multepal*, or elite council. The multepal proved to be far more flexible and responsive than the former royal system.

The most effective and powerful of the new lowland states ruled by a multepal system was Chichen Itza. This form of government enabled Chichen Itza to control far more territory and resources than its predecessors. Chichen Itza was succeeded by a new capital at Mayapan; but when this last attempt at centralized authority was destroyed, the political landscape of Yucatan was fractured. What resulted were the many small and diverse polities that the Spaniards encountered: some ruled by the multepal system, some by single rulers, and others that operated as a loose confederation of towns.

POLITIES AT THE DAWN OF SPANISH CONQUEST

By the time of the Conquest, the many independent states in Yucatan and the highlands were organized in various ways. Overall, these systems continued the traditions of Maya political organization, balancing the concentration of power in the hands of individual kings with the dispersal of power among elite councils and a multitude of offices.

Much more is known about the political systems in these areas because of rich documentary sources. In Yucatan we have the Maya chronicles of the *Books of Chilam Balam* and the detailed account written by Bishop Diego de Landa in the sixteenth century. In the Quiche Maya area of the highlands we have the *Popol Vuh*, as well as other Maya and Spanish chronicles.

The Northern Lowlands
At the time of the Spaniards' arrival, the 18 independent Maya states in Yucatan had three forms of political organization. In fact, there were a great deal of shared features between these systems; but all but a few were ruled from a capital city *(cah)* with a ruling lord and a council of elite lineage leaders. The elite council met in the *popolna* ("house of the mat") and functioned (1) as an advisory body to the ruling lord, or (2) in the absence of a single ruler, as supreme authority within the state. In addition, several polities without a central capital relied on a loose confederation of allied cities, each controlled by elite lineages.

Nine of the 18 polities were ruled by a single lord, called either *ahaw* or *halach uinic* ("true man"). Although this system was the descendent of the old royal political system, it differed in important respects. The later ruling lords did not advertise their achievements and prestige on monuments or in texts, as their predecessors during Middle Maya civilization had done. In fact, they possessed less personal power, shared more authority with their advisory councils, and did not link their personal prestige with the fate of the kingdom. In these ways the lords of Late Maya civilization avoided the central weakness of the more powerful but vulnerable kings of Middle Maya civilization.

Landa reports that both civil and religious offices were hereditary and were derived from the elite class. However, there were important exceptions. The ruling lords of Yucatan were *usually* succeeded by their oldest sons, although Landa himself says that brothers or the best-qualified candidate could become king if there was no qualified son.

> If the lord died, although his oldest son succeeded him, the other children were always very much respected and assisted and regarded as lords themselves; . . . if, when the lord died, there were no sons [old enough] to reign, and [the deceased lord] had brothers, the oldest of the brothers, or the best qualified, reigned . . . and if the deceased lord had no brothers, the priests and principal people [elite council] elected a man proper for the position. (Tozzer 1941: 87, 100; trans. of original *manuscript* of ca. 1566)

The power of each halach uinic was far from absolute. He formulated foreign and domestic policies only after consulting his council. He received annual tribute in goods and labor from his subjects. He appointed his subordinates, the town and village overseers *(batabob)*, who were usually his close kin, and governed the major provinces of his kingdom. In addition, the halach uinic was the highest religious authority in his kingdom.

There were several other important officials in the small Yucatecan states. The *holpop* ("he at the head of the mat") was an ancient and important title among the Maya. In most polities of Yucatan groups of these officials (*holpopob*) formed the council that met in the popolna and advised the halach uinic on foreign and domestic policy. They also served as intermediaries for subjects who wished to approach the ruling lord. In at least two cases the holpop was the title of the ruler of the town. The supreme ruler of the sixteenth-century Quiche Maya in the highlands also held a title equivalent to the holpop.

A subordinate elite official, or *batab*, oversaw each subdivision within the state and reported to the ruling lord. The glyph for batab has been identified in texts from the southern lowlands, so this official probably served a similar role in some polities of Middle Maya civilization. In any case, during Late Maya civilization these officials were usually based in an outlying town where they held administrative, judicial, and military authority. Each batab saw to it that the subjects under his control paid their tribute in goods and labor to the halach uinic. The batab ensured that his town was kept clean, its buildings kept in repair, and that the farmers cut and burned their fields at the proper time. As a judge he sentenced criminals and decided civil suits, always consulting the halach uinic in serious cases before passing judgment. Each batab commanded his own warriors, although in times of war all batabob served under a single military commander.

Each batab presided over a local council composed of town councilors, the *ah cuch cabob*. These councilors were the heads of the next level in the government hierarchy, the *nalil* or subdivisions within each town. The batab also had two or three assistants, the *ah kulelob*, who accompanied him wherever he went and carried out his orders. Finally, each town had constables, the *tupiles*, charged with keeping the peace.

The supreme military commander (*nacom*) for each polity was an elected position, not determined by kinship. The nacom was elected for a period of three years by elite council, presumably based on merit. According to Landa the nacom was held "in great veneration . . . they bore him in great pomp . . . to the temple where they seated him and burned incense to him as to an idol" (Tozzer 1941: 122). The elected nacom formulated war strategy and commanded the batabob, who led their contingents into battle.

Each kingdom had a high priest, the *Ahawcan* ("Lord Serpent"), who received offerings from subordinate priests and other members of the elite. Landa describes the Ahawcan as "the key of their learning," referring to the high priest's role as keeper of the calendar and the sacred chronicles. Through divination and consulting the chronicles (the *Books of Chilam Balam*), the Ahawcan determined days for festivals and ceremonies and foretold auspicious events for the ruling lord and his kingdom. The high priest was responsible for teaching and passing on the history of his people, including knowledge of the writing system itself. Everything from the cures for diseases to the history of the kingdom was in his charge. Thus it is no surprise to learn from Landa that the high priest "gave advice to the lords and replied to their questions" (Tozzer 1941: 27).

Below the high priest were the regular priests, the *ahkinob* ("they of the sun"), who conducted most public rituals. According to Landa, the Ahawcan "provided priests for the towns . . . examining them in the sciences and ceremonies and . . . the duties of their office . . . and provided them with books and sent them forth" (Tozzer 1941: 27). Some priests had specialized duties; for example, one ahkin served as a famous oracle at the shrine on Cozumel Island, and another at the sacred cenote at Chichen Itza. An ahkin received the hearts of sacrificial victims and offered them to the Maya gods.

There was a specialized priest for making human sacrifices, used to appease the gods in times of greatest need. Landa says the sacrificer was held in low esteem. He dramatically describes how the sacrificer "with a knife of stone, and with much skill and cruelty, struck [the sacrificial captive] with the knife between the ribs of his left side . . . and seized the heart like a raging tiger, tearing it out alive, and having placed it on a plate, he gave it to the priest, who . . . anointed the face of the idols with fresh blood" (Tozzer 1941: 119). The human sacrifice ceremony was assisted by four *chacs*, elders chosen for each occasion, who held the victim. The chacs also assisted in the ritual used to make new idols, the puberty ceremony (see Chapter 8), and the kindling of new fire at the beginning of the Maya calendrical year.

The religious official most in touch with the people was the local shaman *(chilan)*, who used divination to cure illnesses, foretell events, and communicate with the gods. This is the only ancient religious specialist to survive into modern times. Among the Maya of Yucatan the shaman (known today as *ahmen*, or "he who understands") conducts traditional rituals such as the hetzmek (see Chapter 8) and treats illnesses through traditional medicines and divination.

The Maya Highlands   At the time of the Spanish Conquest the Maya of the highlands were organized in ways similar to that of Yucatan. The best-documented Postclassic highland government is that of the Quiche Maya.

The Quiche commoners *(al c'ahol)* were the farmers and laborers making up the bulk of the population. They lived outside the fortified centers in thatched wattle-and-daub houses, were not associated with the sacred origins of the elite, and provided food and tribute. The elite class, or *ahawab* (plural of *ahaw*, or "great lord"), claimed descent from the original founding Quiche conquerors, who were probably Putun Maya from the Gulf coastal lowlands. They lived a life of privilege, controlled most of the wealth by collection of tribute, and resided in masonry palaces located in fortified cities. The ahawab patrilineages held rights over the most valuable land. Each elite lineage held one or more *chinamit*, a territorial and residential unit with an administrative palace or "big house" *(nimha)*, and a population of landless peasants *(nimak achi)* that worked the land for its masters.

The head of each elite lineage held the principal office of that lineage and was the ultimate authority over its members. All ahawab lineage heads, together with other specialists including several high priests, formed the advisory council that met in the popolna ("house of the mat") and helped formulate policy for all Quiche society.

The elite lineages resident in the capital city, Utatlan, were organized into four larger descent groups. In order of descending status, they were named the Cawek, Nihaib, Ahaw Quiche, and Sakic. The Cawek and Nihaib descent groups were composed of nine lineages each, whereas there were four Ahaw Quiche lineages and two Sakic lineages. Because the head of each lineage held one of the major offices in the advisory council, there were nine Cawek officials, nine Nihaib officials, four Ahaw Quiche officials, and two Sakic officials in the council.

The supreme ruler of the Quiche Maya was the *ahpop* ("he of the mat"), the head of the highest-ranking Cawek lineage. Besides possessing the power to make political appointments and leading the religious rituals held for the well-being of the population, the ahpop was the military commander and the most important speaker in the ruling council. He was usually succeeded by his son, who as heir to the throne held a military command as *nima rahpop achij* ("great military captain"). The head of the second-ranking Cawek lineage was the *ahpop c'amha* ("he of the mat of the receiving house"), serving as assistant to the ruler, and the official who received visitors in the name of the ruler. The head of the highest Nihaib lineage held the title *k'alel* ("courtier"), being responsible as a judge and counselor. The head of the highest Ahaw Quiche lineage served as *atzij winak* ("speaker"), who proclaimed the council's decisions to the populace.

Each of the major descent groups had a special patron god. The Cawek patron was Tohil, the male sun deity. The Nihaib patron was Awilix, the female moon deity. The Ahaw Quiche patron was Jakawitz, the male sky deity. Most of the priests *(chalamicat)* came from a special lineage. They were highly esteemed, although they held little secular power. Like their Yucatecan counterparts, they conducted public ceremonies (often including bloody sacrifices) and acted as caretakers of the sacred chronicles that recorded the Quiche Maya histories, prophecies, ritual calendar, and divination tables.

Outside the capital were two adjacent secondary centers (Chisalin and

Ismachi), each with ruling elite lineages and a nonelite population. The elite of these secondary centers were allied to Utatlan by marriage alliances. Such kin-based alliances, and the acknowledged military supremacy held by the ahpop in Utatlan, forged the unity of the Quiche state. Yet the kingdom had a built-in weakness, for it was possible for any lineage and its leader to gain the military strength to challenge the power of the ahpop. This happened during the successful revolt of the Cakchiquel, who subsequently founded an independent state centered at Iximche (see Chapter 6).

On the eve of the Conquest there were a series of independent Maya polities in the highlands, many with political organizations similar to the Quiche. The Quiche state expanded to subdue some of its neighbors, such as the Mam Maya to the west. But the neighboring Cakchiquel and Tzutuhil, sworn enemies of the Quiche, remained independent. Despite these conflicts the Quiche and the other highland kingdoms maintained mutual relationships through peaceful commerce, religious pilgrimages, gift exchanges, and marriage alliances. Thus, although far from politically unified, the Postclassic Maya highlands were held together by economic, religious, and kinship bonds.

PRINCIPAL PUBLISHED SOURCES

Aveni 1975; Fox 1978; Marcus 1992a; Sabloff 1994; Sabloff and Henderson 1993; Schele and Freidel 1990; Tozzer 1941.

10

Maya Religion

Maya religion was based on a body of beliefs about supernatural powers that explained life and the universe. These concepts reinforced the social and political order and were used by kings and the elite to maintain their power and control. Indeed, the political system included priests who oversaw rituals and knowledge that allowed them to both communicate with the supernatural and, through the keeping of historical chronicles, interpret events. Maya religious beliefs were held by all levels of society: commoner, king, elite, and priest.

Like all aspects of human culture, Maya religion changed over time. By the time of the Spanish Conquest, the Maya had been influenced by customs introduced from other parts of Mesoamerica. These included a greater emphasis on worship of the images of deities (idolatry) and increased human sacrifice. But Maya religion was changed more drastically when Christianity was imposed, sometimes forcibly, by the Europeans. To the Spaniards, Maya priests were agents of the devil and accordingly were converted, killed, or driven underground.

The disappearance of the Maya priesthood, the most visible aspect of "paganism," produced great changes in Maya religion. Public shrines and their "idols" were destroyed, and public ceremonies were banned. Along with the disappearance of Maya priests and the public aspects of Maya religion went much of Maya learning, including the writing system. Maya books were confiscated and burned. Fortunately a few native accounts survived, preserving a partial record of ancient Maya religion and recorded knowledge.

Less public elements of the Maya belief system often escaped detection and managed to be perpetuated within Maya family and village life through the present. When Spanish pressure for conversion was intense, Maya beliefs and rituals were kept secret and apart from Christianity. Although baptized and officially "converted," many Maya people learned to accept the public aspects of the new religion inside the Catholic church but continued traditional family rituals inside their houses and agricultural rituals in their fields. Some Christian and Maya symbols were similar; this made it easier for the Maya to accommodate the new religion by seemingly accepting Christian concepts while preserving their old beliefs under a new guise. For instance, the cross was a Maya symbol for the "tree of life," the sacred ceiba supporting the heavens; thus the Christian cross was readily accepted, although it was often venerated for its traditional Maya meaning.

The Spanish Inquisition was brought to Yucatan in the sixteenth century to extinguish all vestiges of "paganism." Many Maya people fled from Spanish oppression in response, establishing refugee settlements deep within the forests of southeastern Yucatan. Under the leadership of shamans, Maya religious traditions were preserved in these communities amid a fierce tradition of independence. The religious traditions centered on the veneration of a Maya "talking cross" that served as an oracle. In the nineteenth century the Mexican government tried to gain control over these independent Maya communities, resulting in the War of the Castes. Although peace came early in the twentieth century, many such communities remained isolated and independent of outside control until recently.

Another group that remained isolated until recently are the Lacandon Maya in the southern lowlands of the state of Chiapas, Mexico. Many vestiges of ancient Maya religion have survived in their beliefs and rituals. For example, they continue to make and use pottery incensarios (incense burners) that are similar in form and use to those of the pre-Columbian era. Lacandon rituals are still held in sacred caves and, until recently, in the ruined temples of several lowland Maya cities.

In other areas Christianity was peacefully introduced—largely through curricular innovation the efforts of Father Bartolomé de Las Casas, who defended the Maya against exploitation by Europeans wherever he could. One such area was the Alta Verapaz in the highlands of Guatemala, where Maya and Christian elements have blended into a religion that preserves both traditions. Over the years in the remote communities of the highlands, in the absence of Catholic priests, Maya shamans assumed control of public ceremonies (such as baptisms and masses held in churches) while continuing their traditional roles of divining and curing illnesses. Maya highland shamans have also preserved elements of the ancient calendrical system such as the 260-day almanac, used to determine the birthday names of infants and the proper days for ceremonies.

Thus, although 500 years of European efforts profoundly changed the more public aspects of Maya religion, many traditional beliefs have been passed from generation to generation within Maya families, and from generation to generation of Maya shamans. In traditional Maya communities today there are shamans and other people who continue to hold concepts and beliefs from the pre-Columbian past. Ancient Maya religion can be reconstructed in part from present-day Maya beliefs and practices, combined with archaeological evidence and accounts from the time of the Conquest. This chapter explores certain reconstructed aspects of Maya religion as it existed before the Conquest.

COSMOLOGY

The basic Maya concepts of life and the universe are quite different from Western views, which see the world as being composed of separate natural and supernatural realms. Westerners use science to understand the natural world as defined by everything that can be observed, including both the living realm of creatures on this earth and the nonliving realm of planet earth, the solar system, the Milky Way galaxy, and the entire universe. Western science does not attempt to understand the supernatural realm as defined by everything that is unobservable, from luck and superstition to codified religions.

Maya cosmology, the concepts that described and explained their world, did not distinguish between natural and supernatural realms. For the Maya, all things, animate or inanimate, were part of a single existence both visible and invisible. Everything in the Maya world was imbued, in different degrees, with an unseen power or sacred quality. Rocks, trees, mountains, sun, moon, stars, and all living creatures—including humans—were animated by this sacred essence. The Yucatec Mayan word for this essence is *k'ul* (*ch'ul* in many highland languages), meaning "divine" or "sacredness." This comes from *k'u* (or *ch'u*), meaning "sacred entity" or "god." For humans and other living creatures, the Maya apparently believed the k'ul essence dwelt in blood; thus blood was a crucial sacred substance in their rituals.

Sacredness was also manifested in the concept of the *way* (pronounced "why"), the co-essence or spirit companion associated with living and divine beings. Every person had a way, or spirit companion, whose destiny was intertwined with the individual's. The most powerful *wayob* were embodied in what we call "gods" or "deities," best defined as beings who controlled aspects of the universe. Maya deities had different manifestations—sometimes very visible (such as the sun), sometimes invisible (such as the rain god). Both gods and wayob could be represented by forms that were animal-like (zoomorphic) or human-like (anthropo-

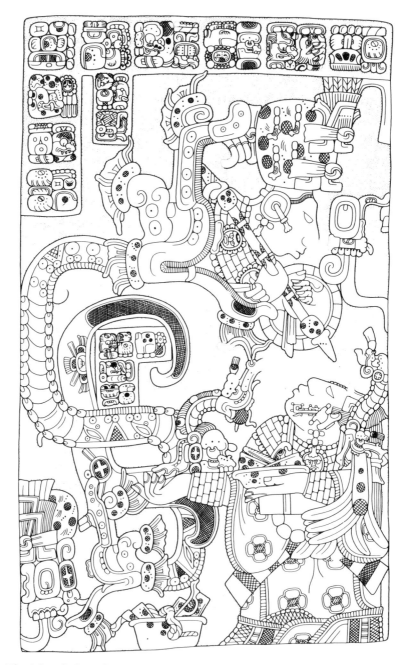

The Maya believed in a spirit companion (*way*); by one interpretation this
scene from Yaxchilan Lintel 25 shows Lady Xoc, wife of the king (lower right)
in the presence of the *way* of the Yaxchilan founder, Yat Balam, depicted as
emerging from a great serpent. (Ian Graham & Eric von Euw)

morphic). The Maya today continue to believe each person has a spirit companion, often called the *nagual*—a word of Mexica (Aztec) origin—whose life and destiny parallel that of every individual.

The Maya universe encompassed (1) the earth, the visible domain of the Maya people, (2) the sky above, the invisible **The Maya** realm of celestial deities, and (3) Xibalba below, the invisible **Universe** realm of the underworld deities. The earth was the back of a huge reptile, represented as a caiman or a turtle, that swam in the primordial sea. Mountains *(witz)* were seen as the ridges on the back of this giant reptile. The celestial realm had 13 layers, each presided over by one of the *Oxlahuntik'u* gods (*oxlahun*, "thirteen"; *ti*, "of"; *k'u*, "god" in Yucatec Mayan). Xibalba had nine layers, each presided over by one of the *Bolontik'u* gods (*bolon*, "nine").

There were five directions in the Maya world. Center was the axis of the world where the great sacred tree of life, a giant ceiba with its roots in Xibalba, supported the sky, symbolized by a cross. East was the direction of the sun being reborn each morning. West was the direction of the dying sun falling into Xibalba. North was straight up: the zenith, the direction of the sun in the fullness of life in the sky each day at noon. South was straight down: the nadir, the direction of the dead sun that battled the lords of Xibalba in order to be reborn.

Caves found throughout much of the Maya area were considered entrances to Xibalba. These were especially sacred and dangerous places where the dead were buried and special rituals for the dead were conducted. Doorways in some of the great Maya temples were symbolic cave entrances that allowed kings and priests to enter the *witz,* or sacred mountain (the temple platform), and communicate with the lords of Xibalba.

Many powerful celestial deities dwelt in the sky. During the day the sky was dominated by the all-powerful sun. At night it was filled with countless deities: the moon, the "sky wanderers" (the visible planets), and the stars. The great celestial reptilian god extended across the entire sky (the Milky Way) as a two-headed beast, one head associated with life, the other with death. Many Maya kings carry in their arms a representation of this cosmic deity, known as the double-headed serpent bar.

On earth, buildings and entire cities were imbued with unseen power and were constructed as symbolic reflections of the Maya universe. Individual buildings were "born" with dedication rituals, had a span of life, then died and were buried with termination rituals. Some arrangements of ritual buildings replicated the Maya concept of the universe; for example, the Twin Pyramid Groups at Tikal built for cyclic calendrical ceremonies (*katun*, or 7,200-day cycles). Four structures, one on each side, were built around a central plaza that represented the center

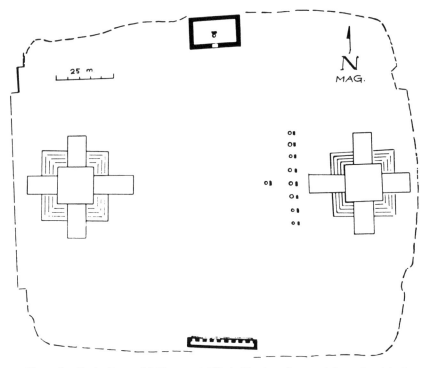

Plan of a Twin Pyramid Group at Tikal, Guatemala; used for calendrical ceremonies, they replicated the Maya universe with four buildings (four directions) built around a plaza (center of the world). (Courtesy of Tikal Project, University of Pennsylvania Museum)

of the world. Twin pyramids, one on the east and one on the west, marked the birth and death of the sun. The nine-layered underworld was represented by a nine-doorwayed building on the south. The celestial domain was represented by a walled enclosure on the north, open to the sky, that contained a paired stela and throne stone dedicated to the king who sponsored the katun ceremonies.

Although Maya cities were not laid out according to a single master plan, their arrangements reflected the Maya cosmos. Each city grew over time, but the positions of buildings remained properly aligned with the primary directions of the Maya world. These symbolic associations provided the cities' inhabitants with the security of living in a sacred and properly ordered place, protected by a powerful king and even more powerful deities. The earthly realm at the center of the world was represented by the palaces of the living ruler in the center of the city. To the north, and often in a higher location, were the funerary shrines and tombs of the dead kings, associated with the celestial realm where the royal ancestors dwelt after their apotheosis (rebirth from Xibalba as deities). The intervening threshold between this world and the celestial realm was the location of the ritual ball court, where the sacred ball game and sacrifices celebrating the creation myth were conducted.

The Maya believed there had been several worlds before the present one, and that each had been destroyed by a great flood. The Maya of Yucatan today believe there have been three worlds previous to this one. The first was inhabited by dwarfs, the second by people called "offenders," and the third by the ancient Maya. The fourth, or present, world is peopled by a mixture of all previous inhabitants of the peninsula. Eventually this world will also be destroyed by a flood.

The most complete and beautifully written record of Maya myth and history is preserved in the *Popol Vuh*, the sacred book of the highland Quiche Maya. It also relates that there had been multiple creations before the present world and that the people of the present world were created out of maize. The central drama in the creation myth of the *Popol Vuh* is the saga of the first humans, the Maya Hero Twins. Their names in Quiche Mayan are Hunapu and Xbalanque (or Hun Ahau and Yax Balam in Yucatec). These names have constrasting associations, recalling both sun and Venus, and life and death. Hunapu ("First Lord") is associated with Venus and celestial life. Xbalanque ("Sacred Jaguar") is associated with the jaguar sun and death in the underworld.

The Origin Myth

The father of the Hero Twins was also a twin. He and his brother were ball players who had played ball in Xibalba and then were sacrificed by the gods of death. The brother was buried under the Xibalba ball court; the father was decapitated and his head hung in a calabash tree. From the tree his head impregnated one of the daughters of the death gods by spitting into her hand. Fleeing this angry death god, the pregnant girl came to the earthly realm. There she gave birth to the Hero Twins, who grew up and discovered their father's old ball game equipment. Realizing their heritage, they followed their father and uncle by becoming such famous ball players that they too were invited to play ball in Xibalba with the lords of the underworld.

In Xibalba the gods of death subjected the Hero Twins to a series of daily ball games and nightly trials, but they outwitted the death gods each time. However, the only way they could escape Xibalba was by jumping into a pit of fire. After the death gods ground up their bones and threw them into a river, the Hero Twins were reborn and returned to Xibalba seeking revenge. They succeeded by showing the death gods an amazing feat. One twin decapitated the other, then brought him back to life. The death gods were so amazed by this that they demanded the

Hero Twins to perform the trick on them. This is what the Hero Twins were waiting for, so they decapitated the gods of death but of course did not bring them back to life. Following their victory over death, the Hero Twins escaped from Xibalba and were transformed in the sky as the sun and Venus, destined to re-enact their descent into Xibalba and their escape and rebirth forevermore.

The central themes of the Maya creation myth were replicated in religious rituals and the lives of individuals. The account of the Hero Twins entering Xibalba, outwitting the gods of death, and returning to life was a metaphor for the sun, the greatest power in the universe. It also showed that rebirth came through sacrifice. The rebirth of the Hero Twins after being sacrificed is a metaphor for human rebirth after death, a theme celebrated by the Maya ritual of human sacrifice. The ball court was the setting for the confrontation between the Hero Twins from this world and the death gods of Xibalba. In many Maya cities, the ball court symbolized the threshold between the earthly realm and Xibalba. The ritualized ball game played in this arena re-enacted the original confrontation between the Hero Twins and the death gods. Maya kings had the closest associations with the Hero Twins. Kings had the power to enter Xibalba and confront the death gods, play the sacred ball game, and perform human sacrifice. When a Maya king was captured by another in war, he was taken to the ball court to be defeated and sacrificed by decapitation. Thus he was sent to Xibalba to be born again in the sky in a ritual that re-enacted the myth of the Hero Twins.

Dualistic symbolism is an important feature of Maya creation myth. Two sets of twins struggled with the lords of death. The struggle was between the forces of good (life) and evil (death). The Maya conceived of their world as an eternal replication of these two forces in conflict. For example, benevolent forces bring rain to make the fields grow to ensure that the people will have food. But evil forces cause drought, hurricanes, and plagues, which can destroy the crops and bring famine and death. Other dualistic themes reflected male-female and day-night contrasts. In fact, Maya deities had many constrasting sets of attributes.

Life after Death   Xibalba, the underworld, was the dwelling place of the dead. Its nine levels may have been associated with differences in life. After the Conquest, Bishop Landa reported that the Maya believed the underworld was divided into places of rest and places of suffering—although there may be European influence in this account. Priests and kings were said to go to the place of rest after death. Women who died in childbirth, warriors killed in battle, and suicides also went there. All who went to the place of rest could dwell in the shade and be free from labor. There was an abundance of food and drink, and no pain or suffering. Those who led evil lives went to the place of suffering in the ninth and lowest underworld, *Mitnal.*

The *Popul Vuh* creation myth also relates a Maya concept of rebirth after death. Evidence from inscriptions and excavations of royal tombs at Palenque, Tikal, and other cities suggests that after death and journeying to Xibalba, Maya kings were believed to be transformed into deities. This royal apotheosis replicated the myth of the rebirth of the Hero Twins and the daily rebirth of the sun rising out of the underworld. Apparently after their rebirth, the Maya kings were believed to dwell in the sky. But there is no evidence that any other people were believed to escape Xibalba after death.

The Maya universe was both a living and an ordered place. Order could be seen in the predictable movements of the great celestial deities—the sun, moon, planets, and stars—that marked the passage of time. Their movements **The Concept of Time** represented repeated cycles of life (movement), death (setting or disappearance), and rebirth (rising or reappearance). In the Maya universe, time itself was alive, expressed by a series of deities that governed each recurring cycle.

The sun, or *kin* (also "day"), established the basic order of the Maya universe. The kin life cycle was the interval in which this deity passed out of the underworld to be reborn at dawn, then swept across the sky only to be swallowed at dusk by the underworld once again. Another cycle was 20 kins, each represented by an anthropomorphic deity, that formed another anthropomorphic deity known as *uinal*. This word derives from the word for "human," *uinic* in Yucatec Mayan, because humans with their 20 digits (fingers and toes) are beings who "know the rhythm of the days in themselves" (from the *Book of Chilam Balam* of Chumayel). The ever greater cycles of kins formed the solar calendar, and the various cycles of the other sky wanderers formed "calendars" based on the moon and visible planets (discussed further in Chapter 11).

The Maya held a series of ceremonies associated with the solar calendar. One of the most important centered around the Maya New Year. The ceremonies began in the closing five days of the preceding year (which were unlucky days when everyone was concerned about misfortune) and culminated on the first day of the New Year. Another important calendrical ceremony was held at the end of each katun, a period of 20 tuns (360-day "years") equivalent to 7,200 days, which was marked by the carving of a new stone monument. There were 13 differently named katuns, each with its own patron deity and special rites. Katun-ending ceremonies were celebrated for nearly 12 centuries (ca. A.D. 350–1520). The most elaborate version was celebrated at Tikal, not only with sculptured monuments but with the construction of an entire architectural complex, the Twin Pyramid Group for each katun. At some lowland cities the ritual was celebrated twice each katun, or every 3,600 days. At Quirigua and Piedras Negras the quarter-katun endings (each

1,800-day period) were also commemorated. By the time of the Conquest, however, the ritual was celebrated only on the katun endings.

MAYA DEITIES

According to Maya belief, the most powerful supernatural beings controlled aspects of the universe. The Maya referred to these beings as *k'u*, best translated as "sacred or divine entity." (*K'u* is the root of the word *k'ul*, referring to the sacred quality or essence in all things.) The Maya saw the beings we call "gods" as the most powerful embodiments of this sacred quality in the universe, but it would be a mistake to assume they had distinct or anthropomorphic (human-like) qualities like the gods of ancient Greece or Rome.

Maya deities were not finite. They were complex and contradictory beings. They possessed multiple aspects that blended together, often making precise identification difficult. Some aspects were visible, like the sun god seen in the sky each day. But other aspects of the same deity were invisible, like the sun after being transformed when it entered Xibalba at night. In this aspect the sun took on the attributes of the most powerful nocturnal animal of the tropical forest and became the jaguar sun of the underworld. Any Maya representation of the sun god, whether carved on a stone monument or painted on a vessel, might emphasize any one of these multiple aspects, so that each depiction may appear to us as being very different. Moreover, the portraits of Maya rulers often show them wearing costumes, masks, and headdresses with attributes of one or more of the gods. This makes it difficult to identify who is actually being depicted.

Any Maya deity could take on a multitude of other aspects and be transformed as a result. There were different aspects based on sex (male or female), direction (east, west, north, south, and center), age (old or youthful), color, and so forth. Direction and color were usually linked, so that one aspect of the rain god (Chac) was referred to as Chac Xib Chac, the "Red Chac of the East." Gods also could possess one or more inner essences, or wayob, adding even more variability. Because of these diffuse qualities there is general agreement about the identity of some Maya deities but disagreement about the remainder and the total number of such deities. However, we can briefly describe several of the most important Maya deities.

Itzamna ("Reptilian House") may have been the central deity of ancient Maya religion. One famous Maya scholar, Sir Eric Thompson, proposed that all other deities were but aspects of Itzamna, making Maya religion in a sense monotheistic. At least two aspects of Itzamna are often defined as gods in their own right: *Hunab K'u* (*hun*, "first"; *ab*, "living"; *k'u*, "god"), creator of the universe; and *Kukulcan* (*kukul*, "feathered"; *can*, "serpent"), patron of writing and learning. In his various aspects Itzamna was lord over the most fundamental opposing forces in the universe: life and death, day and night, sky and earth. As lord of the celestial realm he was the Milky Way, which the Maya usually depicted as a two-headed reptile or serpent. There his body represented the sky, from which other sky deities (stars) were suspended. His front head faced east, symbolizing the rising sun (day), the morning star (Venus), and life. His rear head faced west, symbolizing the setting sun (night), the evening star (Venus), and death. The two-headed ceremonial bar held by kings on many Classic Maya portraits represents Itzamna as this manifestation of the celestial realm.

Kinich Ahau was the sun god, one of the Hero Twins, who possessed several aspects corresponding to phases of the sun's daily journey. During the day the face of Kinich Ahau was represented with crossed eyes and a distinctive curl at the corners of his mouth. At dusk he was the dying sun. In his night aspect he became *Yax Balam* (or *Xbalanque*, his Hero Twin name), the jaguar sun of the underworld in his journey through Xibalba. At dawn he was the reborn sun. These aspects were closely associated with concepts of life, death, and rebirth. Maya kings associated themselves with Kinich Ahau and his power; in fact, his name often appears in the titles and names of rulers, and representations of him are frequently found on the headdresses and shields borne by kings in their carved portraits.

Hunahpu was the Venus deity, the other Hero Twin, and closely linked to his brother, the sun god. This link was visible in the sky because Venus, as morning star, precedes the sun at dawn, pulling the sun out of Xibalba. As evening star Venus follows the sun at dusk, pushing the sun into Xibalba. The Venus deity was closely associated with warfare. In addition, a calendar based on its cyclic movements was used to fix important events in the history of kingdoms such as Copan.

Bolon Tzacab, "He of Nine (Many) Generations," was a reptilian deity also known in the Classic Period by the name of Kawil. Bolon Tzacab was usually shown with an upturned snout and a smoking ax in his forehead. He was a special patron of Maya kings. The image portrayed on the so-called manikin scepter, often held as a symbol of office by kings, is that of Bolon Tzacab. In fact, the ritual of acquiring or presenting the manikin scepter was essentially the inauguration ceremony for Maya rulers. Bolon Tzacab's name often appears in the titles or names of kings.

Chac, the rain deity, is also represented with reptilian features—including a downward-curling snout and two downward-projecting fangs—indicating that he may also be an aspect of Itzamna. Many aspects of Chac have been identified, including four associated with colors and directions: Chac Xib Chac ("Red Chac of the East"), Ek Xib Chac

("Black Chac of the West"), Sac Xib Chac ("White Chac of the North"), and Kan Xib Chac ("Yellow Chac of the South"). An image of Chac Xib Chac was often shown dangling from the belt of Maya kings. The benevolent aspect of Chac was associated with creation and life. For Maya farmers, Chac was an all-important deity who nourished the fields and made life possible.

Yum Ka'x, as he is known in Yucatan, was an agricultural deity whose most important aspect may have been the maize god, represented as a youth with an artificially elongated head (a mark of beauty) and sometimes with a headdress formed of an ear of corn. He was benevolent, representing life, prosperity, and fertility. Occasionally Maya kings were depicted impersonating the maize deity scattering grains of maize (or drops of blood).

Yum Cimil is the name in Yucatan for the primary god of death. He was depicted either as a skeleton or as bloated and marked with black circles, suggesting decomposition. He was often adorned with bells fastened in his hair, arms, legs, and collar. He had several aspects: one associated with human sacrifice; another that presided over Mitnal, the lowest of the nine underworlds. To this day the Yucatan Maya believe that Yum Cimil prowls around the houses of the sick, looking for victims.

Buluc Chabtan, "Eleven Faster," was a god of war and human sacrifice and was probably closely related to Yum Cimil. Buluc Chabtan's face was adorned with black lines encircling his eyes and extending down his cheeks. In the codices he was shown burning houses with a torch in one hand and a spear in the other.

Ah Chicum Ek, "The Guiding Star," was the benevolent god of the North Star. He was shown with a snub-nosed face and black markings on his head. The North Star was the guide of merchants, who offered *pom* (copal) incense to him at roadside altars.

Ek Chuah, "Black Scorpion," was the patron of merchants. He was usually shown painted black with a large, drooping underlip and carrying a bundle of merchandise on his back, like an itinerant merchant. Ek Chuah was also the patron of cacao, one of the most important crops produced and traded by Maya merchants.

Ix Chel, "She of the Rainbow," was a rainbow deity who probably had both malevolent and benevolent aspects. Her benevolent aspects were associated with healing, childbirth, and divination. At the time of the Conquest, Cozumel Island (off the eastern coast of Yucatan) was a major place of veneration for Ix Chel.

Ixtab was a suicide deity, depicted in the Maya codices in a gruesome manner: hanging by a rope around her neck, her eyes closed in death, with a black circle representing decomposition on her cheek. Suicide was considered an honorable death by the Maya, and a qualification for residing in the place of rest in Xibalba.

There were a multitude of other deities, including (1) the Oxlahuntik'u, gods of the 13 levels of the sky, and (2) the Bolontik'u, gods of the nine levels of the underworld. Each number and unit of time that made up the various calendrical counts used by the Maya was also considered a god.

SHAMANS AND PRIESTS

Maya religion was guided and controlled by two kinds of specialists: shamans and priests. They had powers to communicate with the deities and thereby understand the universe.

Shamans undoubtedly represent a tradition with origins long before the development of Maya civilization. Most were commoners who looked after peoples' well-being in local communities throughout the Maya area. Shamans provided medicines based on their knowledge of illness, and they used divination rituals to determine the meanings of events, foretell the future, and cure the sick. These skills gave them prestige and a measure of power over other members of society. Shamans undoubtedly helped establish the basics of the Maya calendar and were considered essential to the world order because they knew how to track the cycles of time reckoned by the movements of the "sky wanderers." With this knowledge the annual coming of the rains could be predicted and the proper time to plant the crops could be chosen. This boosted the shamans' prestige and power in farming communities.

As Maya society became larger and more complex, priests who were full-time specialists in religious matters emerged. The Maya priesthood undoubtedly evolved from the older tradition of shamanism, which was primarily associated with the nonelite farming population. But because the management of religious matters was a fundamental concern of the ruling elite, Maya priests were associated with the elite class. By managing religion, the elite could reinforce and support their own elevated status and ensure their prosperity. Thus aspects of Maya religion that involved social and political concerns beyond the local level were taken over by elite-class priests. They managed the calendar, divination, books of history and prophecy, and public ceremonies—all of which ensured success and prosperity for the king and his polity.

The Maya priesthood was a self-contained group of specialists that was perpetuated through the recruitment and training of acolytes. Because there were not enough political offices for every member of the elite class, the priesthood served an important function as an alternative occupation for the increasing number of younger sons of elite families, including the many children of the royal families.

Over time Maya priests developed a considerable amount of esoteric knowledge that was codified and recorded in books (known as codices; see Chapter 11). This body of knowledge—records of myth, history, prophecy, ritual, and astronomical observations—had both practical and religious purposes. Some of the information was used to develop an increasingly complex calendrical system to record events and cycles of time. The calendrical cycles were used for astrological purposes, that is, to predict events and determine the destiny of the king, his polity, and ultimately the entire Maya world.

Elaborately costumed Maya priests conducted spectacular public ceremonies calculated to inspire awe and obedience on the part of the king's subjects. These religious ceremonies included music, processions, dancing, incense burning, and making offerings to the gods. Offerings were made of food and drink, sacrificed birds and animals, and the blood of priests and even the king, drawn by sharp bloodletters for the occasion. On especially important occasions, human sacrifices were made. Maya kings often served as the chief priest for their subjects, conducting rituals to protect them from disease and misfortune, divining the future and the gods' will to ensure the success of the state, and maintaining the harmony of the Maya universe through their own blood sacrifices.

CEREMONIES

To keep the universe harmonious and to prevent disasters or the end of the world, deities had to be placated by rituals and offerings. The Maya concept for this was "feeding" the gods. Nourishment came directly from offerings, or indirectly from devoting time and energy to the deities. When something did go wrong, it was thought to be due to the anger of gods who had not been properly nourished. Thus a drought was explained as the anger of an offended rain god.

The Maya conducted a variety of private rituals and public ceremonies to secure individual and collective success. Religious rituals were a part of everyday life: a mother might offer a bit of tortilla to Ixchel for the health of her child, or a farmer might make a quick prayer to Chac to begin his day in the fields. In contrast, the larger public ceremonies sponsored by king and state often extended over several days and nights. Whether small or large, most ceremonies included offerings to the gods. The most potent offering was life itself, or the *k'ul* ("divine" or "sacred") essence represented by blood.

An excellent depiction of Maya ceremonies is shown in the Bonampak murals, in this case the events marking the designation of the heir to the king (see Chapter 5). Kings performed many rituals while costumed as a god, perhaps because it was believed they assumed the identity of a supernatural power at these times. But a range of ceremonies involved people at every level of Maya society, not only the king and his court but merchants, craftsmen, farmers, and individual members of families.

Whether private or public, or conducted by farmer or king, most Maya religious ceremonies contained similar ritual episodes. Divination determined in advance the auspicious day for the ceremony, and one of several means of divining the gods' will might be included in the actual ceremony. Most ceremonies were preceded by fasting and abstinence that symbolized spiritual purification. The ceremonies included (1) specific rituals to expel evil powers, (2) music and processions, (3) the burning of incense, and (4) the offering of food or sacrifice of something living. If blood was offered, it could be burned like incense. At the time of the Conquest, blood was smeared on the idol of the god being appealed to in the ceremony. According to the Spaniards the priests were also smeared with blood, their hair becoming clotted, gory mops. Celebrations with music, dancing, feasting, and drinking brought most ceremonies to a close.

Fasting, burning of copal, offerings of food and blood, feasting, and ritual drinking all survive in Maya rituals today. One is the *hetzmek* ceremony described in Chapter 8. Today, however, if offerings of blood are called for, sacrificed chickens are used instead of human blood.

The Maya used divination to communicate directly with the supernatural and to determine future events, including **Divination** finding an auspicious day for a ceremony. It was also used to determine the causes for events, such as understanding why crops failed. Because it was seen as communicating with the supernatural, divination ritual might be included within a larger public ceremony.

The ancient Maya used a variety of divination methods, some of which are still used today. For example, in the Maya highlands shamans interpret events according to the ancient 260-day almanac and the random casting of sacred red beans (sortilege). In the past the many permutations of the complex Maya calendar foretold future events, and there are depictions of Maya kings in the "scattering gesture" that may represent divination by sortilege as well.

The ancient Maya also used a variety of substances that altered the individual's normal state of consciousness as a part of divinatory ritual. The taking of narcotics, hallucinogens, and other psychotropic substances by shamans was seen as a way to transform themselves and communicate with the supernatural realm. Experiences in these altered states were understood as messages from the gods that could be interpreted to answer questions and determine future events. Some active substances—especially alcohol and tobacco—were consumed by the general populace, but most of the more potent hallucinogens and psychotropic agents were reserved for specialists and for ritual divination.

Fermented alcoholic beverages were most often used to alter states of consciousness. One important ritual beverage was balche, made from fermented honey and the bark of the balche tree (*Lonchocarpus longistylis*). Wild tobacco (*Nicotiana rustica*) was also used; it is more potent than today's domestic varieties, and when rolled into cigars and smoked it can produce a trance-like state. Several mushroom species that contain hallucinogens were probably used in divination as well. In the highlands stone replicas of mushrooms are found, often accompanying burials. The names of several mushrooms in the Mayan languages of the highlands clearly indicate their use in divination, such as *xibalbaj okox*, "underworld mushroom" (it was believed to transport the taker to Xibalba).

Ritual Purification   Bishop Landa recorded that most important ceremonies in Yucatan began with fasts and sexual abstinence before the event. These were scrupulously observed by the priests and those who assisted them but were voluntary for other participants and observers. For some ceremonies, all new equipment and articles of clothing were made. Water used in ceremonies had to be pure; virgin water collected from caves was the most important. Incense made from the resin of the copal tree (*pom*)—less frequently of rubber, chicle, and other substances—was burned and used to purify objects such as images of the gods. Incense was burned in specially shaped pottery vessels with the head or figure of a deity modeled on the outside (these are called "incensarios" today). Until recently the Lacandon Maya burned pom incense in pottery burners at the ruins of Yaxchilan, and the Maya of eastern Yucatan did the same at the ruins of Tulum. Smoke rising from incensarios is still believed to convey requests directly to the gods in the sky.

Music and Processions   The Maya made music from a variety of instruments, not as a means of entertainment but as a fundamental part of religious ritual. Archaeologists have found remains of various musical instruments, and others are depicted in Maya art. The most famous is the painted scene of musicians on the Bonampak murals. Percussion instruments predominated: wooden drums, two-toned *tunkul* drums (made from hollowed-out logs), turtle-shell drums, bone raspers, and gourd rattles. Wind instruments included trumpets made from conch shells, and whistles, ocarinas, and flutes made from fired clay or wood.

We can assume that music was believed to be pleasing to the gods and thus facilitated the success of religious ceremonies. Music undoubtedly (1) accompanied the impressive processions of priests that opened most public ceremonies, (2) punctuated the steps in each important ritual, and (3) enhanced the general celebration that closed most ceremonies.

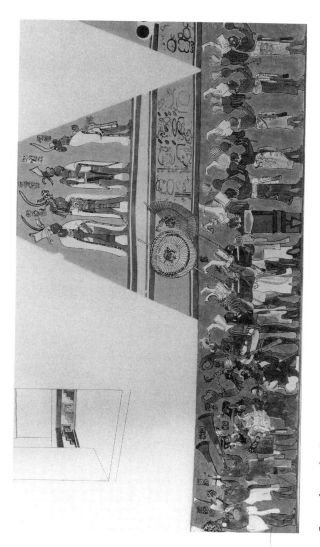

Scene from the Bonampak murals showing musicians accompanying a ceremony by playing a variety of instruments; visible (left to right) are large trumpets, turtleshell raspers, a large drum, and rattles. (K. Rupert, J.E.S. Thompson, & T. Proskouriakoff)

Offerings to the Gods   Sacrifices varied according to the urgency of the occasion. They included offerings of food, small birds, animals, and precious substances—even human blood. Sacrifices to cure illness or solve a minor problem might require offerings of food, birds, or small animals. Larger ceremonies might require the sacrifice of a deer, which also contributed to the feast that followed. The dedication of Altar Q by the 16th king of Copan included the sacrifice of 15 jaguars, each symbolizing the powerful spirit essences *(wayob)* of the 15 predecessors of Yax Pac. For especially important ceremonies—such as those conducted to bring rain or to end a drought for the common good—one or more human sacrifices might be required.

The sacred essence, or *k'ul,* was in the blood of living things. Blood from animals was—and still is—one of the most important offerings used by the Maya. In the past, human blood drawn with sharp obsidian blades was the most important personal offering that could be made to the gods. Several scenes carved on monuments show the wives of kings and other elite women drawing blood, often from the tongue. Maya kings offered sacrifices of their own blood to ensure the continuity of the cosmos. Rulers were sometimes depicted holding implements identified as bloodletters, made from stingray spines, used to draw blood from the penis, a ritual of symbolic meaning for human fertility. Drawn blood was absorbed by strips of bark paper in pottery vessels and then was burned as an offering to the gods. In later times in Yucatan, the Spaniards recorded that blood was sprinkled over idols of gods inside temples. An offering found at the base of the Hieroglyphic Stairway at Copan included a spondylus shell containing a residue identified by chemical tests as human blood.

Human Sacrifice   The ultimate offering of the sacred *k'ul* essence came from human sacrifices. This was the practice that most horrified the Spaniards. It was used not only by the Maya but by many other peoples of the Americas in their most crucial ceremonies. (Ironically, in their claims of horror the Spaniards overlooked their own practice of burning people alive in the name of religious orthodoxy.)

Among the Maya, human sacrifice was not an everyday event but was considered essential to sanctify major rituals, such as the inauguration of a new ruler, the designation of a new heir to the throne, or the dedication of an important new temple or ball court. Warfare usually provided the victims. After all, taking captives was a major goal of warfare; whereas those of low status might be adopted or enslaved, those of elite status were sacrificed. The heads of decapitated captives were worn as trophies by Maya kings or were buried with dead rulers in their tombs, beginning during Early Maya civilization. The most prized of all sacri-

In this scene from Yaxchilan Lintel 24 the king, Shield Jaguar (right), protects his wife as she draws blood from her tongue. The blood will be absorbed by the bark paper in the basket in front of her before being burned as an offering.
(Ian Graham & Eric von Euw)

This bone engraving from Tikal, Guatemala, depicts a bound captive lord from Calakmul, stripped of all vestiges of his power and prestige, destined to be sacrificed. (Courtesy of Tikal Project, University of Pennsylvania Museum)

fices was another king. Although relatively rare, the sacrifice of a Maya ruler by another king required a special ceremony and ritual decapitation. The decapitation event apparently was performed at the climax of a ritual ball game, seen as a re-enactment of (1) the victory and capture of the defeated king, and (2) the Hero Twins' defeat and decapitation of the lords of Xibalba in Maya mythology.

Other than in the ritual ball court, sacrifices usually took place at the summit of a temple platform or in a courtyard in front of a temple. Human sacrifices were performed in several different ways, as illustrated in painted and sculptured scenes or on ancient graffiti found on abandoned building walls. One famous graffiti at Tikal depicts the ritual of scaffold sacrifice in which the victim was tied to a wooden framework and shot through by a cluster of arrows. In the excavations of Group G at Tikal a graffiti vividly depicts a disemboweled captive, his hands tied to a post behind his back. An example of the self-sacrifice of a young woman by throat cutting is depicted on a famous ceramic vessel excavated at Altar de Sacrificios.

One of the most famous places for sacrificial rituals was the Well of Sacrifice at Chichen Itza, sacred to the gods of rain. When there was drought or famine, the Maya made pilgrimages from all over the lowlands to attend sacrifices to appease the angry rain gods. Human sacrifices were thrown from the rim of this great cenote into the water some 65 feet below. Some victims were used to divine the will of the gods. For example, children were thrown into the Cenote at daybreak; those who survived the plunge were pulled out at midday to be asked by the priests about messages from the gods they might have heard while in the cenote. Offerings of jade, gold, and other precious materials were also hurled into the well by those witnessing the ceremony. At the end of the nineteenth century the cenote was dredged, bringing to the surface about 50 human skulls and numerous human bones. Also found were sacrificial knives made of flint; masks, bells, jewelry, cups, and plates made of gold and copper; and pendants and beads made of jade and shell. The most numerous items were blue-painted cakes of pom incense, many still inside pottery incensarios.

By the time of the Spanish Conquest, the custom of removing the victim's heart (probably acquired from central Mexico) had become prevalent for sacrifices of men, women, and children. The victim was painted blue (the sacrificial color), wore a special peaked headdress, and was led a stone altar. There, after ritual purifications, four chacs or assistant priests (also painted blue) grasped the victim by the arms and legs and held him on his back on the altar. The nacom priest plunged the sacrificial flint knife into the victim's ribs just below the left breast, thrust his hand into the opening, and pulled out the still-beating heart. The heart was handed to the chilan priest, who smeared the blood on the idol to whom the sacrifice was being made. If the sacrificial victim had been a valiant and brave warrior, parts of his body might be prepared and eaten by elite warriors to gain his strength. Later, some of his bones would be worn by his captor as a mark of prowess.

Religious ceremonies provided one of the few occasions for the general population to experience celebration. The **Celebration** Maya did not have leisure time as we know it, so ceremonies provided an important break from the hard work and routine of their lives. The throngs of people who attended and witnessed religious ceremonies undoubtedly believed these events would deeply influence their lives, but they also sought festive celebration. Indeed, the finale of most ceremonies that included dancing, feasting, and drinking was an important release of pent-up emotion. Music and dancing provided a

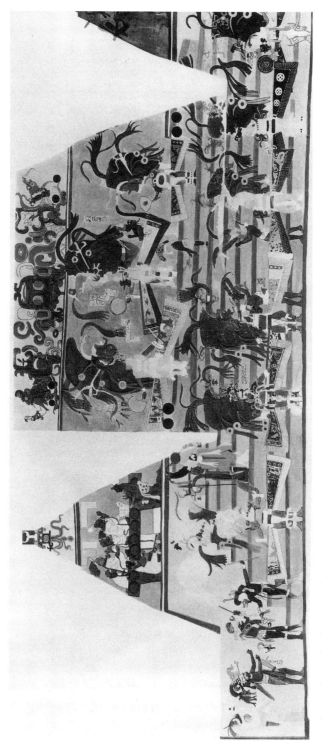

Scene from the Bonampak murals showing elaborately clad dancers accompanying a ceremony performed on a stairway, a festive occasion probably witnessed by a large public assembly. (K. Rupert, J.E.S. Thompson, & T. Proskouriakoff)

physical means of expressing this emotional release. There were separate dances for men and women, and only rarely did they dance together. Various dances required great skill. The dancing and general celebration were enhanced by the many festive foods and fermented beverages that brought most ceremonies to a close.

PRINCIPAL PUBLISHED SOURCES

Benson and Boone 1984; Kelley 1976; Schele and Freidel 1990; Tedlock 1982; Tedlock 1985; Tozzer 1941; Vogt 1969.

11

Recording History: Writing and Calendars

Written records kept by the Maya provide vital historical information, without which our knowledge of Maya civilization would be much less complete. There are many records from the time of the Conquest, accounts written by both Spaniards and the Maya themselves. But the Maya are unique in the Americas because of the amount of pre-Columbian historical records that we can draw on for information. There are inscriptions on stone monuments, buildings, and artifacts, along with three or four surviving Maya books (codices). These records were rendered in a sophisticated writing system and often included references to one or more calendrical systems used by the Maya to place events in time. This chapter examines both pre-Columbian information systems: Maya writing and calendars.

WRITING

Writing allows information to be stored for future use. This greatly increases the accumulation of knowledge and ensures its preservation from generation to generation. Because the Maya believed events were repeated over cycles of time, they kept detailed histories, anchored in time by their calendars, to predict events. Historical records for the Maya were used not only to remember the past but as a means of divination— a way to see into the future.

By keeping records of rainy and dry seasons, the Maya could determine the best times to plant and harvest their crops. By recording movements of the sky deities (sun, moon, planets, and stars), they developed accurate calendars that could be used for prophecy. With long-term records the Maya were able to predict planetary cycles—phases of the moon and Venus, even eclipses. This knowledge was used to determine when the deities would be most favorable for activities such as holding ceremonies, inaugurating kings, starting trading expeditions, or conducting wars.

The Maya writing system was one of the greatest achievements of their civilization. It was the culmination of a long tradition of using notations and symbols originating with the earliest civilizations in Mesoamerica. By the time of Early Maya civilization the basic features of Maya writing were in use by both the southern Maya and the neighboring Mixe-Zoquean peoples. This system made use of standard symbols for several kinds of information, including a means of recording numbers to keep track of both time and economic activities.

Numbers   The Maya, like all Mesoamerican peoples, used a *vigesimal* (base twenty) numbering system, and their numeral expressions reflect this. Mayan languages use new words at the vigesimal multiples (twenty, four hundred, eight thousand, etc.). The first nineteen numerals were similar to our English terms, with unique numerals from one through ten, and the numerals eleven through nineteen produced by combining one through nine with ten.

The symbols used by the Maya to write numbers—bars and dots—were used throughout Mesoamerica. The dot has a value of one, and the bar has a value of five. Very early on, the Maya also began to use a positional numeration system based on the mathematical concept of zero. Scholars believe this is the earliest known example of the concept anywhere in the world. Zero value, or completion, was symbolized by an elliptical shell. Bar and dot symbols were used for the numbers one to nineteen. Numbers above nineteen were indicated by position.

In Maya calculations the values of the positions increase by powers of twenty in rows from bottom to top. The bottom row represents numbers from one to nineteen, the second row the "20's," third row the "400's," and so on. Thus a number such as 999 would be rendered by two dots in the third row ($2 \times 400 = 800$), a bar and four dots in the second row ($9 \times 20 = 180$), and three bars and four dots ($19 \times 1 = 19$) in the bottom row. The number 980 would be rendered in the same way, except a shell (zero) would replace the number nineteen in the bottom row. Maya merchants used this system to record their transactions, and they used counters such as cacao beans to make computations on the ground or any available flat surface. Addition and subtraction was a straightforward process of adding or subtracting counters from the appropriate row.

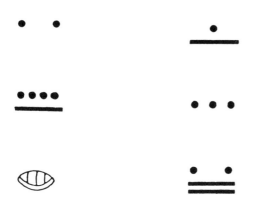

Bar (5) and dot (1) numerals, and the shell (0) were the basis of Maya mathematics; the examples illustrate the Maya positional system: in the left column the number 980 is represented by two dots in the upper row (2 "400's"), a bar and four dots in the middle row (9 "20's"), and a shell in the bottom row (0 "1's"); in the right column the number 2,472 is represented.

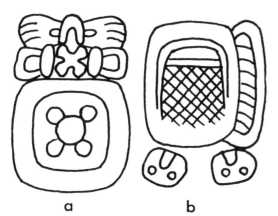

a   b

Example of two Maya glyphs: a) is a logograph meaning pacal (shield) composed of a main sign (below) and prefixes (above); b) is a phonetic spelling of the same word with the main sign pronounced *pa*, the postfix (to the right) pronounced *ca*, and the subfix (below) pronounced *la*, together spelling *pacal(a)*.

Modern studies have shown that more complex functions (multiplication and division) could also be done with this numerical system.

Glyphs

Symbols known as *glyphs* were used to record non-numerical information. The earliest glyphs stood for entire words (logographic symbols). We use some logographs in our modern writing system, as when we write "&" instead of "and." The Maya used logographs—essentially shorthand symbols—for many more words than we do. Another class of glyphs, which probably developed later, stood for the sounds that make up words (phonetic symbols). We use phonetic symbols in our writing system—each of the symbols seen here ("letters") stands for a sound unit in each word. Our phonetic system is alphabetic: there are different symbols for the sounds of each vowel and consonant. The Maya phonetic system was syllabic: there were different symbols for the sounds of each syllable. Because Maya writing used both logographic and phonetic-syllabic symbols, it is an example of a *logosyllabic* script.

Mayan words are generally regular in sound structure. Most syllables consist of two or three sounds, namely a consonant ("C") followed by a vowel ("V"), with or without a final consonant ("C"), producing the shape "CV," as in *k'u* ("divine or sacred entity") or "CVC," as in *k'ul* ("divine or sacred quality"). The prevailing sound system of Mayan languages includes 5 vowels and about 20 consonants (divided into non-glottalized and glottalized, indicated by an apostrophe, as in *ku* versus *k'u*). Thus there are about 100 potential "CV" syllables, so the Maya writing system needed about 100 phonetic symbols to represent all possible syllables. There are a little over 800 known Maya glyphs; about 700 of these are probably logographs. Generally speaking, the most commonly used words were represented by a logograph—a shorthand symbol—whereas all other words had to be "spelled out" by using phonetic symbols for their syllables.

Maya glyphs usually contain several elements that are combined to give individual glyphs an oval appearance. The central and largest glyphic element is the *main sign*. Other elements joined to the main sign are *affixes*. The position of affixes defines *prefixes* (to the left), *postfixes* (to the right), *superfixes* (above), and *subfixes* (below). Elements can also be added inside the main sign *(infixes)*. The reading order of glyphic elements is: prefix, superfix, main sign (infix), subfix, and postfix. Main signs are often logographs; affixes are more often phonetic.

Maya glyphs appear complicated to modern readers. Although some are recognizable as pictures of natural objects, others are unrecognizable even though their meaning was clear to the Maya. But even a glyphic symbol recognizable to us may carry a meaning very different from the object it portrays. For example, a glyph portraying a monkey head is actually a logograph meaning "sacred" or "divine," either as a noun *(k'u)* or an adjective *(k'ul)*.

Maya glyphs for various parts of speech—verbs, nouns, adjectives, and particles—have been identified, as well as glyphs for grammatical prefixes and suffixes. The general pattern of Mayan word order is verb-object-subject in transitive sentences, verb-subject in intransitive sentences. In written examples, glyphs are normally organized into rows and columns. Rows are usually read in pairs from left to right; columns are read from top to bottom, as in the following (numbers represent reading order of a series of individual glyphs):

1	2	7	8
3	4	9	10
5	6	11	12

Many texts from the Early or Middle Maya civilizations are royal accounts of mythical and historical events. Like the records **Texts** of early states in the Old World, ancient Egypt and Mesopotamia, they deal with the histories of cities and the reigns of their rulers, gods, rituals, genealogy, births, marriages, deaths, alliances, wars, and conquests. Like early Old World histories, these accounts must be critically evaluated because they probably contain propaganda intended to boost the prestige of their royal sponsors. There are also more mundane texts, such as those labelling the use and ownership of personal objects (pottery and jewelry). Most texts from the later period of Maya civilization survive in a handful of books or codices (see p. 181). These deal more with astronomy, divination, calendars, and other esoteric matters, although some historical accounts were transcribed into European script after the Conquest.

THE END OF MAYA WRITING

The use of Maya writing was ended by the Spanish Conquest. Church and civil officials considered Maya writing to be "pagan" and did everything in their power to stamp it out. Maya scribes were taught to use European script, and because this offered a more efficient means of record keeping, the ancient knowledge of Maya writing soon disappeared. Fortunately, however, many ancient Maya books were copied in the newly learned European script, so some priceless examples of Maya literature—such as the *Popol Vuh* (see Chapter 10)—have survived. But the Spaniards systematically destroyed the most visible expressions of "paganism," the ancient writings found in Maya books. In Yucatan, Bishop Diego de Landa vividly described this campaign of destruction: "We found a large number of books in these characters and, as they contained nothing in which there were not to be seen superstition and lies of the devil, we burned them all, which they regretted to an amazing degree, and which caused them much affliction" (Tozzer 1941: 78; trans. of Landa's original manuscript of ca. 1566).

Most surviving records in Maya script are carved or painted on durable surfaces, usually stone and pottery. But these are generally brief abstracts; the ancient Maya wrote much more detailed records on perishable materials, such as paper made from the soft inner bark of the amate tree (tropical fig). Most important records were kept in books (or codices) like those destroyed by the Spaniards. These were long sheets of bark paper folded like a screen. Both sides of each page were coated with a smooth white surface made of fine lime plaster. Columns of texts were painted on the surfaces in black and red inks with a fine brush. The text was often illustrated with painted pictures.

But bark paper and codices are not durable; even before the Spanish authorities had a chance to burn Maya books, over time entire libraries of information had decayed in the wet climate of the Maya area. A few decayed fragments have been found by archaeologists in several Classic period tombs, but all had disintegrated and no written information could be recovered.

Up to the time of the Conquest, the Maya kept pace with the forces of natural destruction by recopying their books, much like medieval monks did in Europe. Thus most of the books burned by the Spaniards were relatively recent copies of far older books, containing irreplaceable records extending hundreds or thousands of years into the past. A few codices survived because they were sent back to Europe as mementos by Spanish authorities. Three of these pre-Columbian Maya books are known from the cities where they were rediscovered: the Dresden, Madrid, and Paris codices. A fourth is named after the Grolier Club in New York City, where it was first publicly displayed; it now is held in Mexico City.

The Dresden Codex was purchased in 1739 from a private library in Vienna. Its earlier history is unknown. It suffered water damage after bombing during World War II but has been restored. Today it is held in the Sächsische Landesbibliothek in Dresden, Germany. The Paris Codex was rediscovered in 1859 at the Bibliothèque Nationale in Paris. A fragment of the original book, the lime coating has disintegrated at its margins so that only the text and pictures in the middle of the pages remain. The Madrid Codex was found in Spain in the 1860s in two unequal parts. These were rejoined, and the codex is now held in the Museo Arqueológico in Madrid. How the Grolier Codex was discovered has remained a secret; it is assumed to have been looted or stolen from its place of

Photograph of page 103 of the Madrid Codex with text and drawings dealing with beekeeping and honey. The three seated figures in the middle of the page are representations of the gods Itzamna (left), Chac (middle), and Yum Cimil (right). (Courtesy of the University of Pennsylvania Museum Library)

origin. Tests indicate that the bark paper is pre-Columbian, yet it could be a forgery painted on blank ancient pages.

Although the Grolier's secret origins make its date uncertain, the other three codices date to the last century or two before the Spanish Conquest. All four are concerned with divination and deities more than with historical events. The Dresden Codex is probably the oldest; it is our best record of divination and astronomical calculations, including those for Venus. The Madrid Codex is similar but has fewer astronomical tables. Both were probably used by Maya priests in divination rituals. The fragmentary Paris Codex records a sequence of katuns with their patron deities and ceremonies, and a depiction of sky deities (often referred to as the "Maya zodiac"). The entire Grolier Codex is a simplistic Venus almanac, adding little to the more sophisticated Venus calculations in the Dresden Codex.

DECIPHERING MAYA WRITING

Because the knowledge of Maya writing was lost after the Spanish Conquest, the system had to be deciphered by later scholars. Vital clues for deciphering come from the *Relación de las cosas de Yucatán*, written around 1566 by the Bishop of Yucatan, Diego de Landa. In this history and description of the Yucatec Maya, Landa included information about Maya writing based on interviews with Maya informants. He recorded important accounts of the Maya calendar and a listing of glyphs often called the "Maya alphabet." This was a record of the Maya glyphs that Landa thought corresponded to the letters of the Spanish alphabet. We now know that the Maya scribe who provided these glyphs responded to the Spanish pronunciation of each letter by providing the closest glyph for the sound he heard. Thus, on hearing the Spanish letter "q" (pronounced "cu"), he provided the Maya glyph for the "CV" syllable *cu*.

Decipherment gained momentum following the discovery of an abridged copy of Landa's book in 1863 by a Flemish monk named Brasseur de Bourbourg. A few years later, part of the Madrid Codex was found and Brasseur recognized that its glyphs were so similar to those in Landa's book that he identified the codex as a Maya book. Although most of his attempts to read Maya glyphs were wrong, he did recognize Maya numerals, the *kin* glyph for "sun" or "day," and the glyph for *u*, the Yucatec third-person pronoun. Other early scholars attempted to use Landa's "alphabet" as a phonetic solution to deciphering Maya writing, but they failed because they assumed the Maya used an alphabetical system rather than a syllabic system. By the beginning of the twentieth century the astronomical and calendrical portions of Maya texts were well understood, but there was so little progress in reading other glyphs that attempts at phonetic decipherment were abandoned.

The glyphs recorded in Bishop Landa's *Relacion de las cosas de Yucatan* is given by a Maya scribe for the sounds of the Spanish alphabet. Note that the comb-like symbol for "ca" is equivalent to the second phonetic symbol in the spelling of pacal in the previous example. (A. M. Tozzer)

By the mid-twentieth century, most Maya glyphs had been identified and catalogued. This work was led by Eric Thompson, who established the referencing system still used by Maya scholars for glyphs in both the codices and the inscriptions. But due largely to the work of Thompson and several other scholars, the prevailing view held that the system was logographic, not phonetic. In addition, it was believed that the purpose of Maya writing was to record the abstract passage of time, not the lives of kings or the mundane events of history.

In the late 1950s two major breakthroughs changed these views. The first came from the work of a Russian-born American scholar, Tatiana Proskouriakoff, and a German-born Mexican scholar, Heinrich Berlin. They deciphered the meanings of several key glyphs and thereby proved that many Maya texts were historical in content.

Discovering Texts as History

Proskouriakoff's study was based on a 200-year span of Late Classic monuments from the city of Piedras Negras. The sequence was divided into six groups. Because the individual monuments had dates that could be read, she could see that none of the six groups exceeded a span of 60 years, a normal human lifetime. The earliest monument in each group depicted a male figure seated in an elevated niche, often accompanied by a figure of a woman. Proskouriakoff proposed that a particular glyph and its associated date on these initial monuments referred to the carved scene: the inauguration of the male figure as king, overseen by a woman, probably his mother. By noting a date in the texts that was always earlier than the accession date, Proskouriakoff also identified the glyph for birth. She concluded that each group of monuments recorded the life and reign of a sequence of six Piedras Negras kings.

This revolutionized Maya studies. Prior to Proskouriakoff's work, the figures on Maya stelae were thought to be gods and anonymous priests. Many dates in the texts were thought to be calendrical corrections. Proskouriakoff determined that they were portraits of actual men and women—kings and their mothers—and that the dates were historical events. After her initial discoveries, Proskouriakoff studied the Yaxchilan inscriptions and identified the glyphs for capture, captor, and death.

At about the same time, Berlin noticed a patterned distribution of a glyph that always had the same prefixes but a variable main sign. The specific main sign tended to be unique to a specific site. From this he concluded that the glyphs identified individual sites—either as a place name or as the name of its ruling dynasty—so he referred to them as *emblem glyphs*. The use of one site's emblem glyph at another site was evidence of relationships between Maya cities through alliances, marriages, or wars. This again indicated that Maya texts included historical information and that the prevailing interpretations were wrong.

The breakthroughs made by Proskouriakoff and Berlin did not provide actual *readings* of the Mayan words represented by glyphs. These scholars were able to decipher the meaning of specific glyphs without reading Mayan words from phonetic symbols.

Discovering the Phonetic Code   The second breakthrough involved the discovery of the phonetic code, which enabled scholars to read the actual Mayan words represented by glyphs. It began with the work of the Russian scholar Yurii V. Knorozov. Although his arguments were not as carefully made as Proskouriakoff's, Knorozov used the old Landa "alphabet" as the basis for a system of phonetic signs—not for individual consonants and vowels, but for the "CV" syllables that formed most Maya words. However, under such a system the spelling of common Mayan "cvc" words (those ending in a consonant, not a vowel) presented a problem. Knorozov's solution was to propose that the final consonant was written with a second "CV" sign that agreed with the vowel of the previous syllable, but without pronouncing the final vowel. He called this the rule of *synharmony*. Under such a rule, a Mayan "CVC" word such as *k'ul* would be spelled by two phonetic glyphs: *k'u* and *lu*, yielding *k'ul(u)*.

We can better understand the phonetic system and see how decipherment proceeds by looking at a series of Mayan words that share certain "CV" sounds. We will start with glyphs whose meaning is established, such as *cutz*, or "turkey" (it is often associated with pictures of turkeys).

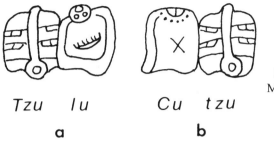

Tzu   lu   Cu   tzu

a   b

Phonetic spellings of two
Mayan words: a) tzul (dog);
b) cutz (turkey), both
illustrating the rule of
synharmony.

The first glyph that should stand for the sound *cu* can be found in Landa's "alphabet," where it represents the sound of the Spanish letter "q" (pronounced "cu"). This works, so now we can propose that the second glyph stands for *tzu*, following the rule of synharmony. We can test our proposal by looking at glyphs for another word that contains the same syllable: *tzul*, or "dog." Sure enough, the glyph associated with pictures of dogs in the codices begins with the same sign as the second glyph in *cutz*. Because the dog glyph must end with the glyph for the syllable *lu*, we can continue testing by looking for examples of this symbol.

Phonetic decipherment proceeds in this way from one proposed reading to another. But the procedure does not lead to the complete reading of all Maya texts, because Maya writing is a complex mixture of phonetic and logographic glyphs. And the phonetic component is not always consistent (any more than our English system of pronunciation is!). As it turns out, not all phonetic spellings follow the rule of synharmony; for example, the word for "vulture" *(kuch)* is spelled *ku-ch(i)*, not *ku-ch(u)*. (We should expect that a writing system used for some 2,000 years would have some antiquated spellings that did not keep up with changes in the language over time.) Some words are spelled phonetically, other words only partially so, and more are purely logographic. Many Maya glyphs were *polyvalent* (they had two or more meanings), and two or more different glyphs may refer to the same word. Despite these difficulties the phonetic breakthrough allows scholars to read well over half of all Maya texts, and more progress is being made with each passing year.

We now know that the constant prefix on emblem glyphs is an antiquated version of the royal title *ahaw*. It is a combined logographic and phonetic element read as *ahpo* (from the ancient title *ahpop*, "lord of the mat"), but it is accompanied by the suffix *wa* as a phonetic complement to indicate the pronunciation *ahaw*. The other constant prefix is the *k'ul* logograph ("holy" or "divine"), so the reading of an emblem glyph would be "divine ruler of . . ." The main sign of the Yaxha emblem glyph reads phonetically *yax ha*, the first proof that an ancient Maya city name has survived to the present day. The glyph for the site of Aguateca reads *Kinich Witz,* or "sun-faced mountain." The *witz* glyph in this case is split, just as the mountain (or escarpment) on which Aguateca sits is split by a deep fissure in the limestone.

Beginning with the emblem glyphs and glyphs for concepts of birth, accession, death, titles, capture, and captor identified by Berlin and Pros-kouriakoff, deciphered glyphs have greatly increased scholars' under-standing of past social and political matters. There are deciphered glyphs for concepts of captive, marriage, and parentage, including forms that read "child of man," "child of woman," and "child of parent." One glyph identifies the founder of many royal lineages, and the *hel* ("change") glyph gives the numerical position for kings in the line of succession. Many personal names and titles have been identified, some of which can be read phonetically. For example, the glyphic name of the Palenque king Pacal combines the logograph for shield *(pacal)* with the phonetic spelling *pa-ca-l(a).*

Numerous objects have painted or carved glyphs, many of which are now being read as "name tags" that accompany the owner's name. For example, the glyphs on a jade ear spool excavated at Altun Ha, Belize, read *u tup,* or "his ear spool." Glyphs on incised bone offerings in Ah Cacau's tomb at Tikal include the phrase *u bak,* or "his bone." Pottery vessels are often tagged with *u lak,* or "his bowl." The function of the tagged object may also be given, as in the glyphs on an Early Classic bowl from Rio Azul labeled as a pot for *kakaw* ("chocolate"). The tomb long proposed to be that of Tikal ruler Yax Kin is verified by a text on a painted vase from the tomb stating it is the "chocolate pot of Yax Kin Kan Chac, 3 katun divine ruler of Tikal." The scene on the vessel shows Yax Kin seated on a cushion accompanied by a small pot decorated with the Naranjo emblem glyph, identifying it as tribute from Naranjo to the Tikal ruler.

Decipherment has increased our understanding of ancient Maya reli-gion. For example, the glyph that reads *way* ("spirit companion" or "co-essence") is fairly common in Classic period texts. It is now clear that some representations once identified as gods or kings are in fact super-natural companions. References to actual gods can now be identified from the glyph *k'u* ("sacred entity" or "deity"). *K'u* is used to refer to the patron gods "owned" by specific Maya kings. The term is also linked to the essence released by the blood sacrifices of kings. This concept of sacredness, seen as well in the adjectival form *(k'ul)* used in the emblem glyph title for kings, designates the divine status claimed by Maya kings that set them apart from the rest of society. Clearly, Maya writing was used for more than recording time; it was also used to reinforce the sacred authority and prestige of kings and their polities.

CALENDARS

The cycles of movements of the sky deities—sun, moon, and planets—were accurately recorded by the Maya through sophisticated arithmetical and writing systems. Of course, they had to rely on observations without benefit of the instruments of modern astronomy. A pair of crossed sticks or similar sighting devices were probably used from heights such as temple summits. With long lines of sight to the horizon, the Maya could fix positions for the rising or setting of sun, moon, or planets to within less than a day's error. When any of these celestial bodies rose or set at the same point a second time, one cycle was completed.

Yet it must be noted that the Maya did not understand these movements as modern astronomy does. The movements were observed and recorded by the Maya to prophesize events the deities were believed to control. Like Babylonian and medieval sky watchers, the Maya used the results of their observations for both mystical and practical purposes. Indeed, they believed that numbers, time, and the entire universe were ruled by supernatural forces. By recording cycles of these forces, they created a series of calendars used to understand events and predict the future. The calendars were matched with the events of history, the reigns of rulers, their conquests and achievements, and the like. Each passing cycle produced the possibility of repeated destiny.

One of the oldest and important calendars was an almanac of 260 days that operated without regard to the celestial cycles. There were several Maya calendars based on the recurring cycles of movements of the sun, moon, and the planets. The first two form the basis of our modern 365-day calendar year and our 30-day (on average) month. The Maya marked the sun's cycle with a solar calendar and the moon's cycle with a lunar calendar, but they also recorded the cyclic movements of the visible planets such as Venus, Mars, and Jupiter. There was also a purely arbitrary count of 819 days associated with each of the four quadrants of the universe, each ruled over by one of the four color and directional aspects of the deity Kawil: red for the east, black for the west, white for the north, and yellow for the south.

Counts of days in these cycles were recorded by the bar and dot and the vigesimal positional notation discussed earlier in this chapter. To record the numbers one to nineteen in calendrical texts, the Maya sometimes used alternative symbols known as *head-variant numerals*. The numbers one to thirteen and zero were represented by a series of unique deity head glyphs. The head-variant glyph for the number ten is a skull. Head-variant numbers from fourteen to nineteen were formed by combining the appropriate head variant (numbers four to nine) with the skeletal lower jaw from the head variant for ten. For example, the number seventeen is the number seven head variant with a skeletal lower jaw.

The most common cyclic counts used by the ancient Maya—the 30-day lunar period, the 260-day almanac, the 365-day solar year, and the Calendar Round cycle of 52 years (discussed below)—were very old concepts shared by all Mesoamerican peoples. It is likely that most of the populace was familiar with these calendars, for they were believed to guide the daily lives and destinies of rich and poor alike. But the more complex calendars, such as those based on planetary cycles and the 819-day count, involved knowledge that must have been guarded by the ruling elite as a source of great power. Having knowledge of the sky deities and being able to predict their movements demonstrated to the common people that the kings and priests were in close communion with the supernatural forces that governed the universe.

The Lunar Cycle The Maya observed the phases of the moon, which they believed helped control human destiny. By recording the length of the lunar cycle—the time span between new moons, for example—they soon realized this period is a little over 29.5 days.

Because Maya arithmetic had no fractions or decimal points, they used another method to keep track of the lunar cycle. It is similar to the way in which we keep our own calendar year in harmony with the true year. Because the actual length of the solar year is between 365 and 366 days, we make a slight overcorrection every four years by adding a day during leap year. This overcorrection is compensated for by a slight undercorrection once every century by skipping one leap year. The system of successive adjustments keeps our calendar in harmony with the sun's annual cycle.

Initially the Maya seem to have alternated lunations (the period between successive new moons) of 29 and 30 days. Although the resulting average lunation is 29.5 days, the exact figure is a little longer. A lunar calendar based on a 29.5-day lunation would gain enough so that the error would reach an entire day every two and two-thirds years. To be more accurate, the Maya figured that 149 lunar cycles was equivalent to 4,400 days. This yields an average lunation of 29.53020 days, extremely close to the modern calculated period.

The Sacred Almanac The basis of prophecy and much of the pattern of daily life for all Maya people was governed by the "count of days," a sacred almanac that repeated itself every 260 days. The origin and significance of the 260-day count are unclear but probably derive from the span of human gestation, which is about the same length of time. In fact, one of the prime uses of the sacred almanac was to determine the destiny of each person's life, which was established by the patron deities of birth dates. Many highland Maya people today continue to use the 260-day almanac for this and other means of divination, even assigning children's names based on the date of their birth.

Each day *(kin)* in the sacred almanac was designated by combining a number from one to thirteen with one of twenty day names. Because the thirteen numbers and twenty days were actually deities, the attributes of each day were determined by the characteristics of the particular combination of number and day. The names of the twenty day deities in Yucatec Mayan are:

Imix	Cimi	Chuen	Cib
Ik	Manik	Eb	Caban
Akbal	Lamat	Ben	Etz'nab
Kan	Muluc	Ix	Cauac
Chicchan	Oc	Men	Ahau

A given day in the sacred almanac would be named 1 Akbal. This would be followed by 2 Kan, 3 Chicchan, 4 Cimi, and so on. After reaching the day 13 Men, the next day would be 1 Cib as the number cycle began again. This would be followed by 2 Caban, and so on. The next time the starting day deity in this example is reached, it would be associated with a new number deity (8 Akbal). One cycle of the sacred almanac cycle is completed when all thirteen numbers have been combined in turn with all twenty day names ($13 \times 20 = 260$).

The calendar based on the solar year of 365 days per year was the *haab*. The solar year was divided into 18 months of 20 days **The** each (the *winal*) with an additional period of 5 days (the *Uayeb*). **Solar** Each division began with a *kin* that was referred to as the "seat- **Year** ing of the month." The first day of the first winal, "the seating of Pop," is usually written as 0 Pop, followed by the day 1 Pop, 2 Pop, and so on until the last day of the winal, 19 Pop, which is followed by "the seating of Uo" (0 Uo). The names of the winals in Yucatec are:

Pop	Xul	Zac	Pax
Uo	Yaxkin	Ceh	Kayab
Zip	Mol	Mac	Cumku
Zotz	Chen	Kankin	(Uayeb)
Tzec	Yax	Muan	

The complete designation of each kin referred to both the position in the sacred almanac and the haab, as in "1 Imix 4 **The** Uayeb," followed the next day by "2 Ik 0 Pop," then by "3 **Calendar** Akbal 1 Pop," and so on. Any given day designation does **Round** not recur for 52 years. The 52-year cycle is the Calendar Round, which was used by most peoples of Mesoamerica even though their names for days and months varied according to their languages.

The Mexica (Aztecs) saw time as an endless succession of 52-year cycles, which they called *xiuhmolpilli* ("year bundles"). But the Maya also conceived and used time periods longer than the Calendar Round.

The   The Maya were unique in Mesoamerica in recording a series
Long   of far longer cycles of time. Of these the Long Count was the
Count   most prominent. It was closely associated with the political sys-
tem based on the rule of kings. Both came into use during the
Late Preclassic period (Early Maya civilization) and disappeared at the end of the Classic period (Middle Maya civilization). In essence, Long Count dates were used by kings as a means to fix the events of their reigns in the great cycles of time. Most kings of Middle Maya civilization dedicated monuments with Long Count dates at each katun ending as part of the important ceremonies marking the occasion (discussed in Chapter 10).

The Long Count recorded Calendar Round dates within a larger cycle of 13 baktuns (1,872,000 days, or some 5,128 years). This anchored any given date within a great cycle of time that began in 3114 B.C. The beginning date probably refers to an important mythical event such as the creation of the current world. It precedes the earliest known use of the Long Count by some 3,000 years. The great cycle will end on December 21, 2012.

Long Count dates record the number of days elapsed from the beginning date. To make this calculation, a modified vigesimal system was used to record (in reverse order) the number of elapsed kins (days), winals (20 kins), tuns (18 winals, or 360 days), katuns (20 tuns, or 7,200 days), and baktuns (20 katuns, or 144,000 days). In a pure vigesimal system, the third order would be 400 (20 × 20 × 1); but the Maya used 18 winals, or 360 (instead of 400) kins, to create a closer approximation to the length of the solar year (365 days). We now express Long Count dates in Arabic numerals—as in 9.15.10.0.0, referring to 9 baktuns (1,296,000 days), 15 katuns (108,000 days), 10 tuns (3,600 days), 0 winals, and 0 kins to reach the Calendar Round date of 3 Ahau 3 Mol (June 30, A.D. 741).

A Long Count date was recorded by a standardized sequence of glyphs that was announced by an oversized introductory glyph. The only variable part of the introductory glyph was the central element, used to depict the patron deity of the haab month of the day being recorded. Following the introductory glyph, five rows of glyphs record the number of baktuns, katuns, tuns, winals, and kins that have elapsed since the beginning date. After this tally of days the first part of the Calendar Round date, the sacred almanac day, was recorded. It was followed by a series of glyphs that recorded the appropriate *Bolontik'u*, or underworld patron of the date, and the lunar cycle—the age of the moon on the date recorded, the length of the lunar month in which the Long

A Long Count date from Stela E, Quirigua, Guatemala. After the Introductory glyph at the top the first three rows of glyphs read 9.14.13.4.17 12 Caban (260-day almanac), followed by a glyphic passage identifying this as the date of Cauac Sky's inauguration as ruler under the authority of the king of Copan. The third coefficient reads "12" but this is an error; it must read 13 to be correct (the crescents in some of the numerals are meaningless space fillers).
(A. P. Maudslay)

Count date fell (29 or 30 days), and other information. The second part of the Calendar Round date, the haab day and month glyphs, closes the standardized Long Count inscription.

Distance Numbers   Long Count dates were precise but cumbersome, requiring more than ten glyphs and a great deal of space in a typical inscription. In many texts the Long Count date is the starting point for recording other dates and events by using a less lengthy formula. These derived dates are known as Distance Numbers because they calculate the distance (in number of days) forward or backward from the Long Count date. Distance Numbers were usually recorded in ascending order (kins, uinals, tuns, etc.). For example, a Long Count date of 9.16.0.0.0 (corresponding to a Calendar Round date of 2 Ahau 13 Tzec) might be followed later in the text by a reference to an event that occurred 11 kins and 8 uinals (171 days) later, on the day 4 Chen 4 Kan (corresponding to a Long Count date of 9.16.0.8.11).

Later Replacements for the Long Count   As Middle Maya civilization began to decline, the Long Count was often replaced by a less bulky count known as period-ending dating. This was used to record the day on which each katun fell—as in Katun 16, 2 Ahau 13 Tzec, equivalent to 9.16.0.0.0. As we saw in Chapter 10, each of the thirteen katuns had its patron deity, its prophecies, and its special ceremonies. Monuments and entire assemblages of buildings (such as Tikal's Twin Pyramid Groups) were erected for ceremonies to celebrate the end of the highly auspicious katun cycle. Once they were dedicated, period-ending notations were used as base dates for recording other dates and events, just like the Long Count.

During Late Maya civilization, historical recording was abbreviated further. Dates were recorded in the *u kahlay katunob,* or "count of the katuns," of Yucatan (also known as the Short Count). This method referred only to the day of a katun ending in the sacred almanac; it did not give the number of the katun or the haab date. The period-ending date mentioned above—Katun 16, 2 Ahau 13 Tzec—would be recorded as Katun 2 Ahau in the *u kahlay katunob.* It was assumed the reader would know the critical information (the katun number) to understand the date.

Because every katun ended on a day Ahau, there were thirteen differently designated katuns in this method of dating (1 Ahau, 2 Ahau, 3 Ahau, etc.). But the number of the day Ahau on each successive katun ending was two less than that of the previous katun, so the sequence was Katun 13 Ahau, Katun 11 Ahau, Katun 9 Ahau, and so on. After Katun 1 Ahau, the next ending date was Katun 12 Ahau, followed by Katun 10 Ahau, and so forth. The same Ahau day repeated every 260 tuns (256 ¼ solar years). One occurrence of the date Katun 13 Ahau ended in A.D. 771, another Katun 2 Ahau ended in 1027, another in 1283, and another in 1539, during the Spanish Conquest. The *u kahlay katunob* was a historical abstract that was useful as long as the sequence remained unbroken. By the time of the Conquest, this record covered 62 katuns from 9.0.0.0.0 (A.D. 435), a span of eleven centuries.

Known to the Maya as *Noh ek* ("Great Star") or *Xux ek* ("Wasp Star"), Venus was Hunahpu, one of the Hero Twins, the most **The** important of the sky wanderers (see Chapter 10). The average **Venus** interval for Venus to make one synodical revolution—the time **Cycle** required to repeat its cyclic movement in the sky—is 583.92 days. These actually run in a cycle of five synodical revolutions of approximately 580, 587, 583, 583, and 587 days each.

The Venus cycle is divided into four parts. (1) For about 240 days Venus is the morning star, (2) then for about 90 days it vanishes (obscured by the sun), (3) then for another 240 days it reappears as the evening star, and (4) then for 14 days it vanishes again before reappearing as the morning star. The Maya used slightly different spans for these four phases, calculating that Venus was (1) the morning star for 236 days, (2) invisible for 90 days, (3) the evening star for 250 days, and (4) invisible a second time for 8 days. The total span of this cycle, 584 days, was too long by 8/100 of a day. To correct the error, the Maya used their knowledge of the variations that ran in cycles of five synodical revolutions. In fact, five synodical revolutions of Venus (2,920 days), which was commemorated as an important ceremonial cycle, is equal to eight solar years ($8 \times 365 = 2{,}920$ days). Their discovery that eight solar years was equivalent to five Venus cycles allowed the Maya to check and correct the Venus calendar.

The Maya observed and recorded the movements of other planets. Mars has a synodical cycle of about 780 days, and cer- **Other** tain tables in the Dresden Codex record multiples of 78 that **Cycles** probably refer to the movements of Mars. The other visible planets—Mercury, Jupiter, and Saturn—were also tracked by the Maya. References to days corresponding to the cycles of both Jupiter and Saturn have been deciphered from several inscriptions of Middle Maya civilization.

CORRELATING MAYA AND EUROPEAN CALENDARS

Because the Long Count system was no longer used when the Spaniards arrived, the Maya Long Count cannot be directly correlated with the European calendar. But there are sixteenth-century references to *u kahlay katunob* dates and their corresponding dates in the European calendar. From this we know that Katun 13 Ahau ended sometime during the year 1539. But because this same date repeated every 256 ¼ years, to correlate this with the older Long Count we have to know which Katun 13 Ahau this date corresponds to in the Long Count.

The accepted solution is called the GMT correlation, named after three scholars (Goodman, Martinez, and Thompson), which equates the end of Katun 13 Ahau in the *u kahlay katunob* with the Long Count katun ending of 11.16.0.0.0 (13 Ahau 8 Xul) on November 12, 1539. This correlation agrees best with the evidence from both archaeology and history. It has also been supported by results of radiocarbon dating of wooden lintels from Tikal that are directly associated with carved Long Count dates. All dates given in this book are based on the GMT correlation.

PRINCIPAL PUBLISHED SOURCES

Bricker 1986; Justeson and Campbell 1984; Kelley 1976; Marcus 1992b; Schele and Freidel 1990; Stuart and Houston 1989; Tozzer 1941.

12

Arts and Crafts

Archaeological remains form the basis for much of what is known about past Maya society. These remains range from monumental buildings and great works of art to the scattered debris of the most mundane objects. But all these remains, great and small, represent the daily lives of the ancient Maya. Therefore it is fitting to look at some of the products of those lives: the arts and crafts made and used by Maya people.

THE ART OF BUILDING

Throughout their long history the Maya were great builders. Their architecture was an art with both practical and religious meanings. Houses and temples both defined the center of the world, one for the family, the other for the state and its gods. Both were constructed on platforms raised above ground level, ranging from low earthen platforms for the simplest houses to terraced masonry-faced "pyramids" for the loftiest temples. The most humble ancient dwellings represent skillful engineering and beautiful craftsmanship applied by individual families to produce practical and well-adapted houses. These were constructed in the same manner as contemporary Maya houses: a pole framework supports a thatched roof with wattle and daub walls made from a lattice of sticks plastered with a thick coating of adobe (mud mixed with straw or other binder). In hotter areas unplastered walls admit cooling breezes. Houses represent the oldest known examples of Maya architecture and the basis for all later elaborations built of stone and plaster.

The grander masonry structures are the best-known examples of Maya architecture. The construction of public buildings, temples, palaces, ball courts, and the like was supervised by architects and other specialists. But the labor was provided by commoners to fulfill their obligations to king and state. The raw material for most masonry construction was limestone. Throughout most of the Maya lowlands and in parts of the highlands, beds of soft limestone lie close to the surface. Quarries provided limestone blocks and plaster (produced by burning the limestone). The plaster was used to pave level plazas and give a smoothed finish to the exterior and interior walls, floors, and roofs of Maya buildings. Masonry architecture was embellished by modeled plaster, sculptured stone, and painting.

Elevated buildings on platforms were reached by one or more staircases. Most platforms supported a single building, but some had more than one. Over time platforms and buildings were expanded and replaced by larger successors, one constructed on top of the other. Thus separate platforms might become welded into a single large multibuilding complex called an "acropolis." Maya masonry buildings usually have relatively little interior space in proportion to their mass, because of the need for thick walls to support corbeled vaulting and roofs. Walls were built of rubble cores faced with masonry blocks and roofed by corbeled vaults. Shaped like an inverted "V," these were constructed of a series of overlapping blocks, each projecting farther inward until a row of capstones could bridge the intervening space between the two walls. Weaker than a true arch, corbeling is a cantilever, each block supported by its overlap with the block below and counterbalanced by the weight of the wall coring that holds it in place.

Even though the limitations of corbeled vaulting made single-storied buildings the norm, two- and three-story masonry buildings were constructed with especially massive walls and narrow vaults. Many Maya buildings had additional vaulted roof decorations, or roof combs, that were backdrops for displays of mosaic or stucco work. Most roof combs rise above the midline of the building, but some are supported by the front wall, giving the building a false, or "flying," facade.

By the time of Middle Maya civilization, several regional architectural styles had developed in the lowlands. The most famous is the central Peten style, epitomized by the lofty and massive temples with single doorways and roof combs found at Tikal (see p. 54). These may have developed from an earlier central lowland tradition of even larger temple platforms that reached its greatest expression at El Mirador (see p. 48). A variation is found along the Usumacinta, as at Yaxchilan, with three doorwayed buildings. Although the style of Palenque's buildings is distinctive, the basic template is related to the Usumacinta region. Temples at Palenque have multi-doorwayed vaulted rooms that are more open

This fine example of a corbeled arch at Labna, Mexico, is part of a Puuc-style palace complex.

Chenes style is defined by elaborate deity masks that frame doorways, as in this example from Chicanna, Mexico.

and bear inward-sloping upper facades that follow the angle of the interior vaulting (see p. 68). In the southeastern lowlands another distinctive style emerged at Copan with elaborate modeled reliefs on building exteriors and large platforms faced with monumental staircases ("reviewing stands").

The elaborate mosaic facade decorations of Copan are prototypes for similar characteristics that developed in the northern lowlands, the setting for the Chenes, Rio Bec, and Puuc styles. Chenes style is defined by elaborately decorated lower facades, especially doorways incorporated into elaborate mosaics that depict deity masks. The Rio Bec style adds false towers, inspired by the temples of the central Peten. The Puuc style is perhaps the most consistent and pleasing variation in Maya architecture: lower facades are usually without decoration, whereas upper facades are decorated with elaborate sculptured mosaics.

Today scholars give labels to Maya structures that suggest their ancient functions: temples, palaces, ball courts, causeways, sweat baths, shrines, and the like. But we are just beginning to appreciate the meanings these buildings had to the Maya themselves. In fact, architecture was a means of realizing the Maya cosmological order. The orientation and location of buildings represented the order of the Maya universe: east represented birth and life; west, death and the underworld; north, the sky and the supernatural realm; south, the earth and the human realm. Temples were sacred places, "mountains" with summit doorways that represented entrances to the abode of the gods. The ball game was played in "courts of creation" that recalled the myth about the origins of Maya society.

STUCCO DECORATIONS

Masonry buildings were often richly decorated with three-dimensional motifs rendered in both stucco (lime plaster) and stone. Decorations of modeled stucco are found on building platforms from the time of Early Maya civilization onward. Stucco was widely used for large deity masks and a variety of other elements. At Copan, excavations tracing the development of Classic period architecture reveal that the earliest buildings in the Acropolis were adorned with masks and panels made from hand-modeled stucco. A shift occurred around A.D. 600, when carved stone elements covered with thin coats of plaster began to appear on buildings. The most famous stucco work is at Palenque; the relief panels there are the finest examples of this art in the Maya area. Stucco work during Late Maya civilization is still visible at Tulum with the famous "diving gods" on recessed panels above several building doorways.

Rio Bec style is defined by palaces with false temple-towers, as in this example from Xpuhil, Mexico.

Decorations in painted stucco were common on many Maya buildings; this example of the "diving god" is from Tulum, Mexico.

SCULPTURE

Carved stone was either attached to architecture or used as free-standing monuments. Single blocks of architectural sculpture were used for lintels, wall panels, door jambs, and steps. Mosaics of carved stone were used for more extensive areas such as facades and roof combs. Interior carved scenes and texts on doors and walls were viewed only by the residents of the buildings, rulers, priests, or other members of the elite class. External architectural sculpture was viewed by the wider populace; this was reflected in propagandistic themes of glorification of the king and state. Often combined with carved texts, similar themes are found on free-standing monuments, including stelae (upright stone shafts), altars (flat rounded or squared stones), and more rarely, boulder sculptures.

Stone Carving   The Maya carved in both stone and wood. Only a few wooden examples have survived, so most of the sculpture that remains today is of stone. Much surviving Maya sculpture is of limestone, the most available resource. Sandstone was used at a few sites, including Quirigua, and a volcanic tuff was used at Copan. Limestone is relatively soft so it is easy to quarry and carve, but it hardens over time with exposure to the air. Quarrying limestone blocks involved cutting along their sides and ends, then prying them loose from the bedrock. They were moved by water (on rafts) and overland (on log rollers) by gangs of laborers. Maya sculptors were specialists and artists. They used tools of harder stone, along with wooden mallets and wedges, to work the stone. Large chisels and hammerstones were used to quarry and roughly dress the stone. Final shaping was done by chisels. For the actual carving, Maya sculptors used small chisels 2–6 inches in length and then finished the stone by abrasion and painting.

Maya sculpture covered all the exposed stone surface, leaving little free space. Carving ranged from low to high relief. Motifs usually combined natural forms (human and animal) and supernatural symbolism. The natural forms are more recognizable to modern eyes, whereas the supernatural elements are less familiar. It is likely, however, that the distinctions we see between natural and supernatural forms did not have the same meaning to the Maya, given what we know about Maya religion.

Indeed, Maya buildings and sculpture were imbued with deep and complex meanings (see Chapter 10 for a discussion of buildings as living entities). Monuments were also imbued with supernatural qualities. The Maya named stelae "stone trees," perhaps because the earliest monuments were carved from trees. Altars were called "throne stones," indicating that the flat stones were not "altars" but the seats used by kings during public ceremonies.

Surviving examples of wood carving are from the interior of buildings. The best-preserved are the carved lintels over doorways in temples at Tikal. These and most other examples were carved from the sapodilla tree, one of the hardest woods **Wood Carving** known. The Tikal lintels were formed of from four to ten beams, with texts and royal scenes carved in low relief. The famous Lintel 3 from Temple I shows the ruler Ah Cacau seated on a throne after his victory over Calakmul. A grander scene is found on Lintel 3 of Temple IV, with the ruler Yax Kin seated on a throne beneath the arched body of the celestial serpent, probably a manifestation of the deity Itzamna. Other carved wooden lintels have survived at Chichen Itza, Uxmal, and a few other sites.

PAINTING

Maya buildings and monuments were originally painted in one or more bright colors. Specialists did this finishing work, and skilled artists created the most intricate painted decorations and murals. Red was the most common color for buildings and carved monuments. Several shades of dark red were made from hematite, an oxide of iron found throughout the Maya area. A brighter red was made from a rarer substance, mercuric sulfide (cinnabar). Yellows could be made from hematite. Blues and greens were also important, usually derived from clays and other minerals. Carbon-based black was used for outlining and other details.

Although the multicolored decorations on monuments and buildings were visible to all, the painted decorations inside most buildings were intended only for the elite residents and were never seen by commoners. The murals at Bonampak are the most spectacular example. Bonampak is significant because it is so unique; most other buildings have long since lost their painted decorations. In most cases only traces of the original paint remain on buildings and some monuments. Painting was also used on portable objects such as ceramics and in illustrating books. The pigments were applied with a variety of brushes. Some were as fine as a single hair; coarser brushes filled in backgrounds and broad spaces.

Wall paintings date from the time of Early Maya civilization. Traces of early frescoes at Tikal and Uaxactun show stylistic similarities to the art of the southern Maya. There is more evidence of interior wall painting during Middle Maya civilization. The best example from the Early Classic was found at Uaxactun: it shows 26 human figures and was painted in black, red, orange, yellow, and gray. A poorly preserved Early Classic fresco panel with hieroglyphs painted in dark red decorated a masonry palace deeply buried beneath Copan's Acropolis. Fragments of designs and hieroglyphs are painted on interior walls of the Late Classic Palenque Palace. The most spectacular and informative murals are those of Bonampak, Chiapas. These Late Classic paintings (ca. A.D. 790) were preserved through a coating of stalactitic limestone deposited by constant water seepage. The scenes show a series of activities recording the historical events surrounding the royal heir designation rituals.

Depictions in the Bonampak murals contrast those carved on most stelae. Sculptured figures were usually shown in static attitudes, but the Bonampak figures express a variety of dynamic poses. Their postures and facial expressions are relaxed in the scenes of preparations, ferocious during the battle, and stern during the judgment and sacrifice. Foreshortening and superposition give an effect of depth. The magnificence of the costumes and headdresses indicates how much has been lost with the disappearance of these perishable materials—featherwork, animal skins, and beautifully woven fabrics (see pp. 140 and 172).

In Yucatan, wall paintings have been found at Chichen Itza, Tancah, Tulum, and several other sites. The best known are frescos from the Temple of the Warriors, the Temple of the Jaguars, and the Monjas at Chichen Itza. These are of a cosmopolitan Mesoamerican style, in keeping with their probable Putun Maya heritage. There are two scenes of human sacrifice and another two of attacks on a village. In contrast, a tranquil coastal village scene from the Temple of the Warriors shows a temple with a feathered serpent rising from its inner chamber. People go about their daily tasks among the thatched houses interspersed with trees; the sea swarms with a variety of marine life, and on its surface are fishermen in canoes.

POTTERY

Because of their durability, objects made of fired clay—pottery vessels, figurines, beads, and other items—are among the most valuable artifacts recovered by archaeologists. Shifts in shape and decoration mark the passage of time. Differences in vessel size and form are clues to their functions, allowing past activities to be reconstructed. Overall, studies of Maya pottery yield information about the origins and development of the early Maya, their trade networks, kinship relationships, social and occupational differences, diet, rituals and religious beliefs, funeral practices, and lives of both elite and commoner.

Most everyday pottery was made in households. Women in many farming families produced vessels for domestic needs; any excess was probably exchanged in markets for other goods. Households that did not make their own pottery exchanged other goods for the vessels needed for cooking, storage, and other uses. In time some households began to specialize in pottery forms or types that were in greater demand; they produced pottery more for external distribution than for local household use. Such specialized production may have occurred in households where pottery making was the primary economic activity, with one or more family members as artisans. In these households farming probably became secondary or ceased. Vessels were produced for artists who decorated them with intricately painted scenes that mark the finest Maya polychromes. A few kinds of pottery were made in more specialized facilities, often using pottery molds and other mass-production methods.

By these means the Maya developed a remarkable ceramic tradition, one of the most varied and diverse in the world. They produced a great variety of pottery types, forms, and decorative techniques over a span of some 3,500 years. Among their outstanding achievements are lustrous, polished monochromes (red, orange, brown, and black); elaborate modeling; mass-produced mold-made vessels, including the only glazed wares in the Americas; and beautiful polychromes, including the famous portrait vases of the Late Classic period.

Polychrome decoration is a hallmark of Middle Maya civilization. The tradition of non-fired polychrome painting (or stuccoed vessels) had its origins almost a thousand years earlier but reached its peak with the multicolored stuccoed vessels of the Early Classic era. The more durable polychrome painting that was fired onto vessels was also developed by this time (these are typically red and black painted designs on an orange or cream base). By the Late Classic era the art of fired polychrome pottery reached its peak, with skillfully and delicately rendered painted scenes. Motifs include both naturalistic and geometric designs, glyphic texts, and portraits of gods, kings, and their entourages. The most famous examples come from the southern lowlands, but other centers for this art were in the northern Maya highlands and along the southeastern periphery. Unfortunately, far more examples of these beautiful vases have been looted and sold to private collections than have been excavated and documented by archaeologists.

Fortunately, one of the most beautiful examples of lowland polychrome pottery, the Altar Vase, was excavated by archaeologists at the site of Altar de Sacrificios. It records the funeral ritual for an elite woman in A.D. 754 that was accompanied by dancing and sacrifice. Some of the figures on the vase are *wayob*, or spirit companions. The vase also depicts the self-sacrifice of a young woman, possibly a member of the dead woman's family. The Altar Vase, together with the knife that presumably killed her, was buried with the young sacrificial victim in a simple grave found near the tomb of the elite woman.

Other finely painted vessels have been excavated from burials and

Close-up of a polychrome pottery vessel from the tomb of Ah Cacau, Tikal,
Guatemala, showing the king seated on his throne. (Courtesy of Tikal Project,
University of Pennsylvania Museum)

tombs at many lowland sites. The tombs of Ah Cacau and other kings
of Tikal contained a variety of polychrome vessels, including ones that
portray the kings receiving tribute, conducting rituals, and participating
in similar royal activities. The scenes on several famous polychrome vessels from the adjacent northern Maya highlands depict elite merchants
rather than kings.

The end of Middle Maya civilization is marked by changes in pottery,
including the appearance of Fine Orange ware (made from fine-grained

This example, also from Tikal, shows the skilled painting style typical of many Late Classic polychrome vessels. (Courtesy of Tikal Project, University of Pennsylvania Museum)

clay). Produced along the western edge of the lowlands, the homeland of the Putun Maya, these vessels have standardized shapes and mold-made decorations reflecting commercial production for export as part of the Putun trading economy. The molded scenes on Fine Orange pottery are often militaristic and may celebrate the conflicts that led to Putun takeovers at several Maya cities, including Seibal and Chichen Itza. The most distinctive new pottery is plumbate, the only glazed ware found in pre-Columbian America. It was produced along the Pacific piedmont in the southern Maya area in specialized facilities. Plumbate pottery was elaborately decorated by molding, or by a combination of modeling and carving, and was traded widely throughout Mesoamerica.

STONE ARTIFACTS

A variety of artifacts were fashioned from stone, ranging from utilitarian tools to beautiful status goods. These were made by two different methods: chipping the stone by percussion or pressure, or shaping the stone by grinding. Flint and obsidian (volcanic glass) were chipped to make sharp cutting and scraping tools, such as blades for household uses and ritual bloodletting. Basalts and other igneous stones were ground to make chisels for cutting stone, axes for felling trees, and bark beaters for softening bark fibers to make the paper used in Maya books. The most common groundstone tools were the manos and metates found in every household and used to grind maize and other seeds into flour.

Eccentrics Although basic stone tools were made within most households, their manufacture required skill and experience. The finest examples of chipped stonework were doubtless created by a few expert artisans. These include skillfully rendered ritual objects—sacrificial knives, scepters, decapitators—that are among the finest examples of chipped stonework ever produced. The most elaborate examples of chipped stone technology are known as eccentrics. These are elaborately shaped sacred objects of flint and obsidian, often found ritually buried under Maya monuments and buildings. The finest were shaped into profile human or god figures, complete with headdresses and other ornaments that were probably emblems of office. Some are undoubtedly from the "manikin scepters" carried by Maya kings. At Copan, when the Early Classic Rosalila temple was about to be buried intact beneath its successor, nine magnificent eccentric flint scepters were carefully wrapped in cloth and placed in the front room of the temple, where they were found by archaeologists excavating beneath the Acropolis.

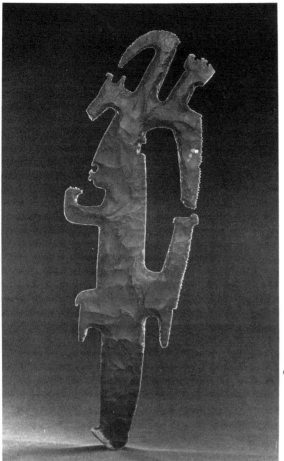

This example of an eccentric flint comes from San Andres, El Salvador, and depicts a lord seated on a throne wearing an elaborate headdress. (Courtesy of Stanley H. Boggs)

The Maya also fashioned ornaments from jade, a very hard semiprecious stone. It was the most precious substance known to the **Jade** Maya, who considered it sacred because its *yax* (blue-green) color symbolized the abodes of the gods: the sky and the watery underworld (*yax* also means "precious" and "first"). Jade accompanied the dead into Xibalba—even the most humble Maya burial often has a simple jade bead placed in the mouth. Jade was obtained from outcrops, boulders, and waterworn pebbles in the streams of the Middle Motagua Valley of Guatemala, and probably other areas as well. Maya jades are usually made from jadeite, which differs in chemical composition from Chinese jade, or nephrite. It is slightly harder and less translucent than nephrite. The colors of jadeite may be mottled, usually dark green to light blue-green, or gray-green. Sometimes jadeite is nearly black or almost white.

Because it is such a hard stone, jade working was a specialized skill. Some jade objects were fashioned from naturally shaped cobbles. Otherwise jade was cut into pieces used for mosaics, pendants, plaques, and similar objects. Cut marks on a waterworn boulder of solid jade, weighing some 200 pounds, show that many pieces were sawed from it before it was ceremonially cached under a platform at Kaminaljuyu, where it was found by archaeologists. To cut jade, tough cords were drawn back and forth over it embedded with fine stone abrasives and continuously rinsed with water. Jade was perforated with drills of bone or hardwood, again using abrasives and water as the cutting agents. After the shaping and drilling was complete (probably done by an apprentice), a master artisan carved the delicate portraits and other scenes found on the finest examples. The Maya also carved other, softer green stones not easily distinguished from jadeite.

There are many notable examples of Maya jade work, although far too many have been found by looters rather than archaeologists. Perhaps the most famous is the Leyden Plaque, incised with the portrait of a Maya king from Tikal and a text dated to A.D. 320. A carved jade head found at Chichen Itza was originally from Piedras Negras, because the historical date it presents (equivalent to A.D. 674) pertains to the royal succession of that Usumacinta city. The largest Maya jadeite sculpture was discovered in a tomb at Altun Ha, Belize. It is carved in the round and portrays the Maya sun god, Kinich Ahau.

Mosaics   The Maya fashioned masks, mirrors, and similar objects from mosaics of jade, obsidian, pyrite, turquoise, and shell. These represent the efforts of highly skilled artisans, made for the exclusive use of kings and their elite kin. Mirrors were sacred symbols of high status worn by rulers from Olmec times onward. The Maya had mirrors of fitted mosaics of pyrites attached to backs of wood or stone. These were probably made by artisans in the highlands, but they have been found at both highland and lowland sites. Several mosaic disks of turquoise, a semiprecious stone imported from central Mexico, have been found in caches at Chichen Itza. Maya kings were often buried with jade mosaic masks fitted over their faces. One such mask has been reconstructed from the jade pieces found in the tomb of Pacal at Palenque. A spectacular mask of jade, shell, and pyrite was excavated from a royal tomb at Tikal, and another was found at Calakmul. The finest examples of Maya jade mosaics are two cylindrical vessels from Tikal, discovered in fragments but now reconstructed. Both come from Late Classic royal tombs: one from that of Ah Cacau, the other of Yax Kin. In each case, the covers are adorned with mosaic portraits of the king (see p. 66).

This life-sized mosaic mask of jade and other materials was excavated from a royal tomb at Tikal, Guatemala. (Courtesy of Tikal Project, University of Pennsylvania Museum)

METALWORK

The Maya used several metals, more for their sacred symbolic qualities than for practical applications (such as tool making). Mercury, a liquid metal, apparently had powerful symbolic meaning for the Maya. As mercuric sulfide (cinnabar) it is a brilliant red, symbolizing the life essence, or blood. In rituals involving fire the Maya priests would burn cinnabar, transforming it into metallic mercury with mysterious qualities. Both forms of mercury, and traces of the transforming fires, have been found in ritual deposits by archaeologists.

The Maya used solid metals—copper, silver, and gold—for adornments and ritual objects. These metals came into use at the very end of Middle Maya civilization, largely through trade with the metal-using societies in lower Central America. Parts of a small hollow figurine made of a gold-copper alloy from lower Central America was found at Copan cached under Stela H, dedicated in A.D. 782. Copper bells and ornaments found at Quirigua date from the final period of occupation of the site.

Metal objects from Late Maya civilization are more common. The largest assemblage came from the nineteenth-century dredging of the Cenote of Sacrifice at Chichen Itza. Many may have been imported from Central America; others may have been traded from central Mexico. They include disks, necklaces, bracelets, mask elements, pendants, rings, earplugs, bells, and beads. Small copper bells were the most common objects. A few imported objects from the cenote at Chichen Itza were probably reworked by Maya craftsmen. These were thin, cast-gold disks on which local artisans impressed scenes of battle. The warriors in these designs resemble those in the reliefs and frescoes at Chichen Itza.

TEXTILES

The Maya cultivated cotton and wove beautifully decorated textiles for clothing and other uses. But only a few specimens of ancient Maya weaving have survived. Small pieces of carbonized cloth were recovered from the Cenote of Sacrifice at Chichen Itza. These date from Late Maya civilization and bear complicated designs. Moreover, impressions of woven materials are often found in caches or tombs. Occasionally fragments of woven material do survive, as in the wrapping around eccentric flints found in the termination cache inside Rosalila temple at Copan.

The best evidence for this well-developed craft are the representations of textiles in Maya art. Clothing depicted on sculptures indicates that the cotton fabrics of the period were of complicated weaves that were elaborately embroidered. The Bonampak murals portray a variety of beautiful fabrics used for capes and clothing (see p. 124). Woven cotton textiles *(patis)* of fixed size were used as articles of trade in ancient times, and after the Conquest they became the principal form of tribute exacted by the Spaniards.

Women of the Maya highlands today continue the rich tradition of weaving. Cotton is spun into thread with a pointed stick weighted by a disk of pottery as a spindle. These disks, or spindle whorls, are often found in archaeological deposits. Weaving is still done on a belt loom. A stick is fastened to each end of the warp to keep the cloth stretched to the desired width. One end is tied to a tree or post, and the other to a thick cord around the weaver's belt, allowing her to tighten the warp by leaning backward. Dyed threads are passed back and forth to create intricate patterns. The traditional patterns and color symbolism used in highland textile designs derives from ancient times. Black represents weapons because it is the color of obsidian; yellow symbolizes food because it is the color of corn; red represents blood; blue represents sacrifice. Green remains the royal color because it is the color of quetzal feathers, once reserved for the headdresses of Maya kings.

Today, most traditional organic and mineral colors are being replaced by commercial dyes. The most highly prized traditional dye was a deep purple obtained from a Pacific mollusk *(Purpura patula).* Modern Maya women still decorate hand-woven clothing with cross-stitch embroidery, known in Yucatec Mayan as *xoc bil chui* ("threads that are counted"). But traditional woven fabrics are being replaced by machine-made clothing.

BASKETS AND MATS

Baskets and mats were important to the ancient Maya for both practical and symbolic uses. The natural fibers from which they were made are found throughout the area. Baskets and mats represent ancient crafts now known mostly by depictions in carved or painted art. A variety of decorated baskets are represented on painted Maya vases. Elaborately woven baskets appear in Maya sculpture, as on Yaxchilan Lintel 24. This example has a twilled pattern in its upper half, a design of stepped frets and small squares around its middle, and a base decorated with featherwork (see p. 169). Maya baskets made today are less elaborate. Those used to carry corn and other rough tasks are woven from thin, tough vines. Smaller and more carefully woven baskets made of split cane are for household uses.

A related craft was the weaving of mats, which are still used in many Maya households for sleeping. Mats played an important practical and symbolic role in ancient Maya life. Sitting on a mat was a mark of authority, as indicated by the royal title *ahpop,* "lord of the mat," used by

Maya kings. Depictions of Maya rulers often show the king seated on a mat. The hieroglyph for the first month of the Maya solar year, Pop, was a piece of matting combined with the sun symbol, also associated with royalty. Few pieces of ancient matting have survived, but impressions have been found on pottery and plaster. At Copan several burials have been excavated with impressions of matting still in place. In one case the body was placed in a seated position on a mat, indicating his high status. In another, the corpse of a sacrificed warrior was wrapped in a mat before burial. The weaves of these mats are identical to those made and used in the Copan area today.

FEATHERWORK

This ancient craft is now all but completely lost, for the traditions of Maya featherwork—especially those marking royal status—did not survive the Conquest. A few examples of Mexica (Aztec) featherwork have been preserved, most notably a headdress given by Moctezuma to Cortés, but no ancient Maya examples have survived. Impressions occasionally found in tombs, and representations from Maya art, show that featherwork was a highly developed craft. The best examples can be found in the Bonampak murals, and almost every sculptured portrait of a Maya king includes a feathered headdress.

Feathers were used in making panaches, crests, capes, and shields and in decorating canopies, fans, personal ornaments, and pendants for spears and scepters. Featherwork was also used in embroideries and fringes for cotton fabrics and baskets. Feathers were taken from birds trapped in forests of both the highlands and lowlands; the magnificent scarlet macaw was a common source. The feathers used by kings came from the sacred quetzal of the northern highlands of Guatemala. Spanish writers relate that the highland Quiche Maya had aviaries where birds were bred for their plumage. The throne of the Quiche Maya ruler was described as having multiple canopies made of rich and multicolored plumes.

Today, all these ancient symbols of Maya royal power have disappeared. But the sacred quetzal bird still can be found in remote highland cloud forests. The Maya believe the quetzal can only live in the wild and will die in captivity. Like the Maya people, these sacred birds will thrive only if they are allowed to live free in their own lands.

PRINCIPAL PUBLISHED SOURCES

Andrews 1975; Kowalski 1987; Kubler 1962; Miller 1986b; Osborne 1965; Proskouriakoff 1963; Sharer 1994.

13

The Meaning of Maya Civilization

It is often remarked that those who do not learn from the past are likely to repeat the problems and tragedies suffered by our forebears. But the past can teach us both to avoid the failures and to adopt the successes experienced by people of long ago. Maya civilization is no exception. Provided we heed the lessons of the past, it offers a number of ways to better our lives today and in the future.

LEARNING FROM SUCCESSES IN THE MAYA PAST

Over the long course of their history, the Maya learned much about their environment that improved their lives and contributed to the success of their civilization. From the Maya come many plants and foods that have benefited people all over the world. Along with their neighbors in Mesoamerica, the Maya spent thousands of years of effort to domesticate and improve maize. Today, by most measures, the many varieties of maize grown worldwide produce the largest yields of any single food crop. The Maya have also given us chocolate, one of the greatest pleasure foods. The list also includes several varieties of beans, squashes, pumpkins, papayas, pineapples, manioc, chili peppers, and vanilla.

An even greater benefit for agriculture and the environment may be realized if we learn a valuable lesson from the Maya before it is too late. We are all aware of the tragic loss of tropical forests throughout the world. The habitat for the greatest biological diversity on our planet is being destroyed for short-term profits by a few timber and cattle interests. Once the great trees are cut and the soils are exhausted by over-grazing, this fundamental resource will be lost. The Maya succeeded in utilizing the tropical forest within their area so that it could yield a tremendous harvest without destroying it. They made the lowland lakes and swamps into renewable agricultural breadbaskets by building canals and raised fields. They culled the nonproductive trees and plants in the forest, allowing productive ones to prosper and yield huge harvests of fruits, nuts, and other products. In a few places, modern farmers are being taught the ancient techniques learned from the Maya and other native Americans in Central and South America. If they succeed—more to the point, if they are *allowed* to succeed in the face of the threat posed by timber and cattle exploiters—society will benefit from a new and renewable source of food that preserves rather than destroys most of the natural environment of the world's tropical forests.

Finally, the Maya have taught us the value of tradition and family life. They preserved their languages and culture in the face of oppression and violence over a span of thousands of years. When their own kings failed them, the Maya people left the devastated southern lowlands to find peace and prosperity in new areas. When the Spaniards conquered their land and established 500 years of economic and social exploitation, the Maya people took refuge in the strengths of their family life and ensured that their traditions were preserved from generation to generation. For the most part, their resistance to exploitation and persecution has been passive. In some cases they have been forced to meet the violence directed against them with violence for self-preservation. But they have usually responded to direct attacks by moving away from the forces of oppression. Of course, the doctrine of nonviolence has had other proven successes: Mohandas Gandhi in India and Martin Luther King Jr. in the United States both urged their people toward freedom by this philosophy. Perhaps the Maya people will yet succeed in finding their freedom by their traditional path of nonviolence.

LEARNING FROM FAILURES IN THE MAYA PAST

The Maya also made mistakes, and at times their very successes brought about failures. They were so successful in producing food from raised fields and forests that in time they created two problems that are familiar today: environmental destruction and overpopulation. Their success in harvesting great quantities of food allowed their population to grow unchecked until the environment reached its limit to support people. Ultimately the demands of overpopulation damaged the environment, created severe malnutrition among the population, and—as the failures mounted—fostered disillusionment with the leaders of society.

Most Maya people survived by moving away from the centers of disaster to continue their lives in new settings. But the lessons for today's world should be clear. What happened to the Maya is a relatively small-scale example of what is occurring on a larger scale today. If society does not solve the problems of environmental destruction and overpopulation, the disaster that awaits us will be profound and will affect the entire planet. The Maya were able to move from the lowland disaster areas to adjacent undamaged regions. Where will we be able to find such undamaged refuges in today's world?

PRINCIPAL PUBLISHED SOURCES

Farriss 1984; Harrison and Turner 1978; Jones 1989; Sabloff 1994; Sullivan 1989; Turner and Harrison 1983.

Bibliography

Adams, R.E.W., ed. 1977. *The Origins of Maya Civilization*. Albuquerque: University of New Mexico Press.

Andrews, G. F. 1975. *Maya Cities: Placemaking and Urbanization*. Norman: University of Oklahoma Press.

Ashmore, W. A., and R. J. Sharer. 1996. *Discovering Our Past*. Mountain View, CA: Mayfield Publishing.

Aveni, A. F. 1975. *Archaeoastronomy in Precolumbian America*. Austin: University of Texas Press.

Benson, E. P., and E. H. Boone, eds. 1984. *Ritual Human Sacrifice in Mesoamerica*. Washington, DC: Dumbarton Oaks.

Bove, F. J., ed. 1989. *New Frontiers in the Archaeology of the Pacific Coast of Southern Mesoamerica*. Tempe: Arizona State University Anthropological Research Papers.

Bricker, V. R. 1986. *A Grammer of Mayan Hieroglyphs*. New Orleans: Middle American Research Institute, Tulane University.

Chase, A. F., and D. Z. Chase, eds. 1992. *Mesoamerican Elites: An Archaeological Assessment*. Norman: University of Oklahoma Press.

Chase, A. F., and P. M. Rice, eds. 1985. *The Lowland Maya Postclassic*. Austin: University of Texas Press.

Chiappelli, Fredi, ed. 1976. *First Images of America*. Berkeley: University of California Press.

Culbert, T. P., ed. 1973. *The Classic Maya Collapse*. Albuquerque: University of New Mexico Press.

———, ed. 1991. *Classic Maya Political History*. Cambridge: Cambridge University Press.

Díaz del Castillo, B. 1956. *The Discovery and Conquest of Mexico, 1517–1521*. Translation by A. P. Maudslay (original published 1632). New York: Grove Press.

Diehl, R. A., and J. C. Berlo, eds. 1989. *Mesoamerica after the Decline of Teotihuacan AD 700–900*. Washington, DC: Dumbarton Oaks.

Drennan, R. D., and C. A. Uribe, eds. 1987. *Chiefdoms in the Americas*. Lanham: University Press of America.

Edmonson, M. S., ed. & trans. 1982. *The Ancient Future of the Itza: The Book of Chilam Balam of Tizimin*. Austin: University of Texas Press.

————, trans., 1986. *Heaven Born Merida and Its Destiny: The Book of Chilam Balam of Chumayel*. Austin: University of Texas Press.

Farriss, N. M. 1984. *Maya Society under Colonial Rule: The Collective Enterprise of Survival*. Princeton: Princeton University Press.

Fash, W. L. 1991. *Scribes, Warriors, and Kings: The City of Copan and the Ancient Maya*. New York: Thames & Hudson.

Flannery, K. V., ed. 1976. *The Early Mesoamerican Village*. New York: Academic Press.

————, ed. 1982. *Maya Subsistence: Studies in Memory of Dennis E. Puleston*. New York: Academic Press.

Fox, J. W. 1978. *Quiche Conquest*. Albuquerque: University of New Mexico Press.

Freidel, D. A., and J. A. Sabloff. 1984. *Cozumel: Late Maya Settlement Patterns*. New York: Academic Press.

Grove, D. C. 1984. *Chalcatzingo*. New York: Thames & Hudson.

Harrison, P. D., and B. L. Turner, eds. 1978. *Pre-Hispanic Maya Agriculture*. Austin: University of Texas Press.

Helms, M. W. 1975. *Middle America: A Cultural History of Heartland and Frontiers*. Englewood Cliffs, NJ: Prentice-Hall.

Hirth, K. G., ed. 1984. *Trade and Exchange in Early Mesoamerica*. Albuquerque: University of New Mexico Press.

Houston, S. D. 1992. *Hieroglyphs and History at Dos Pilas: Dynastic Politics of the Classic Maya*. Austin: University of Texas Press.

Jones, G. D., ed. 1977. *Anthropology and History in Yucatan*. Austin: University of Texas Press.

————. 1989. *Maya Resistance to Spanish Rule: Time and History on a Colonial Frontier*. Albuquerque: University of New Mexico Press.

Justeson, J. S., and L. Campbell, eds. 1984. *Phoneticism in Mayan Hieroglyphic Writing*. Albany: Institute of Mesoamerican Studies, State University of New York.

Kelley, D. H. 1976. *Deciphering the Maya Script*. Austin: University of Texas Press.

Kowalski, J. K. 1987. *The House of the Governor: A Maya Palace of Uxmal, Yucatan, Mexico*. Norman: University of Oklahoma Press.

Kubler, G. 1962. *The Art and Architecture of Ancient America: The Mexican, Maya, and Andean Peoples*. Baltimore: Pelican History of Art.

Lowe, J. G. W. 1985. *The Dynamics of Apocalypse: A Systems Simulation of the Classic Maya Collapse*. Albuquerque: University of New Mexico Press.

Marcus, J. 1992a. "Dynamic Cycles of Mesoamerican States." *National Geographic Research & Exploration* 8: 392–411.

————. 1992b. *Mesoamerican Writing Systems: Propaganda, Myth, and History in Four Ancient Civilizations*. Princeton: Princeton University Press.

Meyer, K. E. 1977. *The Plundered Past*. New York: Atheneum.

Miller, M. E. 1986a. *The Murals of Bonampak*. Princeton: Princeton University Press.

———. 1986b. *The Art of Mesoamerica from Olmec to Aztec*. New York: Thames & Hudson.

Osborne, L. de Jongh. 1965. *Indian Crafts of Guatemala and El Salvador*. Norman: University of Oklahoma Press.

Proskouriakoff, T. 1963. *An Album of Maya Architecture*. Norman: University of Oklahoma Press.

Sabloff, J. A. 1994. *The New Archaeology and the Ancient Maya*, 2nd ed. New York: W. H. Freeman and Co.

Sabloff, J. A., and E. W. Andrews V, eds. 1986. *Late Lowland Maya Civilization: Classic to Postclassic*. Albuquerque: University of New Mexico Press.

Sabloff, J. A., and J. S. Henderson, eds. 1993. *Lowland Maya Civilization in the Eighth Century A.D.* Washington, DC: Dumbarton Oaks.

Sanders, W. L., and B. Price. 1968. *Mesoamerica: The Evolution of a Civilization*. New York: Random House.

Schele, L., and D. A. Freidel. 1990. *A Forest of Kings*. New York: W. Morrow & Co.

Sharer, R. J. 1990. *Quirigua: A Classic Maya Center and Its Sculptures*. Durham, NC: Carolina Academic Press.

———. 1994. *The Ancient Maya*, 5th ed. Stanford: Stanford University Press.

Sharer, R. J., and D. C. Grove, eds. 1989. *Regional Perspectives on the Olmec*. Cambridge: Cambridge University Press.

Sheets, P. D., ed. 1983. *Archaeology and Volcanism in Central America: The Zapotitlan Valley of El Salvador*. Austin: University of Texas Press.

Stephens, J. L. 1841. *Incidents of Travel in Central America, Chiapas, and Yucatan*. 2 vols. New York: Harper. Reprinted by Dover, 1962.

———. 1843. *Incidents of Travel in Yucatan*. 2 vols. New York: Harper. Reprinted by Dover, 1963.

Stuart, D., and S. D. Houston. 1989. "Maya Writing." *Scientific American* 261(2): 82–89.

Sullivan, P. 1989. *Unfinished Conversations: Mayas and Foreigners between Two Wars*. New York: Alfred A. Knopf.

Tate, C. 1992. *Yaxchilan: The Design of a Maya Ceremonial City*. Austin: University of Texas Press.

Tedlock, B. 1982. *Time and the Highland Maya*. Albuquerque: University of New Mexico Press.

Tedlock, D. 1985. *Popol Vuh: The Mayan Book of the Dawn of Life*. New York: Simon and Schuster.

Tozzer, A. M. 1941. *Landa's Relación de las cosas de Yucatán*. Cambridge, MA: Peabody Museum, Harvard University.

Turner, B. L., and P. D. Harrison, eds. 1983. *Pulltrouser Swamp: Ancient Maya Habitat, Agriculture, and Settlement in Northern Belize*. Austin: University of Texas Press.

Urban, P. A., and E. M. Schortman, eds. 1986. *The Southeast Maya Periphery*. Austin: University of Texas Press.

Vogt, E. Z. 1969. *Zinacantan: A Maya Community in the Highlands of Chiapas.* Cambridge, MA: Harvard University Press.

Wilk, R. R., and W. Ashmore, eds. 1988. *Household and Community in the Mesoamerican Past.* Albuquerque: University of New Mexico Press.

Willey, G. R. 1987. *Essays in Maya Archaeology.* Albuquerque: University of New Mexico Press.

Wolf, E. R., ed. 1959. *Sons of the Shaking Earth.* Chicago: University of Chicago Press.

ILLUSTRATION CREDITS

Graham, Ian, and Eric von Euw. 1979. *Corpus of Maya Hieroglyphic Inscriptions.* Vol. 3, pt. 1. Cambridge: Peabody Museum, Harvard University. Reprinted by permission of the President and Fellows of Harvard College.

Maudslay, A. P. 1902. *Biologia Centrali Americana: Archaeology.* London: R. K. Porter, and Dulau and Co.

Ruppert, K., J. E. S. Thompson, and T. Proskouriakoff. 1955. *Bonampak, Chiapas, Mexico.* (Publication 602) Washington, DC: Carnegie Institution of Washington. Based on an original painting by Antonio Tejada, reprinted by permission of the Peabody Museum of Archaeology and Ethnology, Harvard University.

Tozzer, Alfred M., ed. 1941. *Landa's Relación de las Cosas de Yucatan: A Translation.* Papers of the Peabody Museum of American Archaeology and Ethnology, Harvard University, vol. 18, 1941. Reprinted courtesy of the Peabody Museum, Harvard University.

Turner, B. L., and P. Harrison. 1981. "Prehistoric Ridged-Field Agriculture in the Maya Lowlands." *Science* 213 (4506): 399–405. Copyright 1981 American Association for the Advancement of Science. Reprinted by permission.

Index

About the Author

ROBERT J. SHARER is Shoemaker Professor in Anthropology at the University of Pennsylvania and Curator of the American Section at the University of Pennsylvania Museum. He has lived and worked in Central America for over thirty years, directing five major research projects in El Salvador, Guatemala, and Honduras for the University of Pennsylvania Museum. He is currently investigating the architectural history of the Copan Acropolis in Honduras. He has written and/or edited more than twenty books and over sixty articles and book chapters.